Secrets of the
STONE of DESTINY

Secrets of the
STONE of
DESTINY

Legend, History, and Prophecy

Adrian Gilbert

4th Dimension Press   •   Virginia Beach   •   Virginia

4th Dimension Press
215 67th Street
Virginia Beach, VA 23451–2061

ISBN 13: 978–0–87604–548–0

Image of the Coronation Chair of King Edward I © Dean and Chapter of Westminster.

Image of the Stone of Destiny © Crown Copyright Reproduced Courtesy of Historic Scotland; www.historicscotlandimages.gov.uk.

Image of Miletus, the amphitheater; Downtown Miletus; Temple with Ionic capitals © Michael Ives.

Pictures and diagrams © Adrian Gilbert.

Cover design by Christine Fulcher

To His Royal Highness Prince Charles, Prince of Wales,
Duke of Cornwall and Lord of the Isles.

May your seed sit forever on Jacob's Pillow,
in fulfillment of Prophecy and Destiny.

Contents

Acknowledgments

Thank you to the staff, ecclesiastical and lay, at Westminster Abbey. Visiting this great church is always a pleasure, and they do a wonderful job of looking after King Edward's Coronation Chair: a priceless artifact even without the Stone of Destiny. Thanks, too, to Edinburgh Castle, the current home of the Stone, which after seven hundred years has itchy feet and needs careful handling. My hearty appreciation to the National Museum of Scotland (in Edinburgh), Perth Museum and Art Gallery, and the Abbey of Iona where I was able to take many pictures of other extremely interesting stones.

Heartfelt thanks to my friends Mike and Emma Ives who kindly allowed me to reproduce pictures they had taken of the ruins at Miletus. One can only imagine what a wonderful city this must once have been.

A big thank you to the staff of the A.R.E. Publications and most especially to Cassie McQuagge and John Van Auken. Your stalwart support for my work is most appreciated.

Finally thanks, as always, to my wife Dee without whose constant support and encouragement this book could not have been written.

1

The Stone and the Spear

Unless the fates be faulty grown
And prophet's voice be vain
Where'er is found this sacred stone
The Scottish race shall reign.
(Sir Walter Scott's translation of a verse
once attached to the Stone of Destiny.)

On November 30, 1996, to the accompaniment of bag-
pipes, a strange ceremony unfolded in Edinburgh Castle. The venerable
walls of this imposing edifice have, over the centuries, witnessed the
comings and goings of many kings and princes. It was, for example, the
home of Mary, Queen of Scots and the birthplace of her son James VI of
Scotland who was later to become James I of England. Yet, even for this
castle, the ceremony about to be enacted was historic. For what was

being celebrated was the return from England of a symbol of kingship against which all other tokens of royalty pale in comparison—the **Stone of Destiny**.

About ten thousand people watched in carnival mood as a Land Rover bearing this curious relic slowly inched its way up the Royal Mile. Half way along, at St. Giles' Cathedral, it was received by the Reverend John McIndoe, the moderator of the Church of Scotland. Greeting the stone on behalf of the Church, he said it would "strengthen the proud distinctiveness of the people of Scotland."[1] Once inside the Great Hall of the castle it was carefully placed on a low oaken table. There was no sword poking out of it for a would-be "King Arthur" to pull free, but all the same Michael Forsyth, the secretary of state for Scotland, received it with thanks from Prince Andrew, the Queen's representative. This strange, almost Masonic ritual completed, a twenty-one gun salute was fired from the Half-Moon Battery on the castle walls to be answered by another from HMS Newcastle lying at anchor in the Firth of Forth.

The handover of the stone had gone smoothly enough, yet not everybody was happy with the situation. Back in London the Dean and Chapter of Westminster Abbey were deeply upset at losing such a prized relic. Some two weeks earlier, on November 13, they had had to stand by in impotent silence as workmen prized the stone out from its long-time resting place in the coronation throne. To these clergymen, if not to the largely oblivious public, the return of the stone to Scotland was a mistake of grand proportions. At the very least it was portentous of bad luck. Worse still, separating it from the coronation seat seemed like a harbinger of further change—the unleashing of forces that threatened not just the survival of the monarchy but the sovereignty of the United Kingdom itself.

A block of sandstone with two rusted handles protruding from its ends, the Stone of Destiny is quite unspectacular. Yet, much older than the Crown Jewels, it is of enormous cultural and symbolic significance. Known variously as "Jacob's Pillow," "*Lia-fail,*" and the "Stone of Scone," it had been brought to London from Scotland in 1296 by Edward I (1239–1307), who was himself of partly Scottish descent. It was he who gave it pride of place in Westminster Abbey and there—apart from a brief interlude of a few months in 1950, when it was stolen and taken back to Scotland by a group of students—it had rested ever since. Housed in its purpose-made throne, it has witnessed the coronations of nearly all of England's subsequent monarchs and from 1603, following the uniting of the two thrones under James VI and I, those of Scotland, too.

Sending the stone back to Scotland on the seven hundredth anniversary of its removal was the idea of Michael Forsyth, then MP [Member of Parliament] for Stirling and secretary of state for Scotland. He had seen cabinet papers dating from 1950 (the last time the stone had been in the news) in which it was promised that it would eventually be transferred back to Scotland. Under the fifty-year rule these papers would soon be released and, he believed, cause embarrassment to Scottish MPs of the Conservative Government. He warned Prime Minister John Major that Alex Salmond (the leader of the Scottish National Party or "SNP") could be relied upon to harness any feelings of grievance over the issue in his campaign for an independent Scotland.

Though the secretary of state had maybe exaggerated the case, as a committed unionist he had good reason to be concerned. The release in the previous year of Mel Gibson's film *Braveheart* had already fanned the flames of Scottish nationalism to unexpected heights, and the unity of the kingdom was indeed being questioned. Major knew he needed to do something to counterbalance the view that the English Conservative establishment was out of touch with Scottish opinion. Returning the Stone of Destiny to Scotland would be a gesture well worth making if it garnered a few more votes and helped to maintain the union between Scotland and the rest of Great Britain. Accordingly, acting in the name of the Queen, he instructed that the stone be returned to Scotland forthwith. He agreed with Michael Forsyth that it should arrive there in time for the St. Andrew's Day celebrations of 1996 (November 30)—seven hundred years almost to the day since its removal from Scone.

If Major had expected gratitude for his magnanimity, he was to be sorely disappointed. As Sir David Steel (former leader of the Liberal Party and now Lord Steel of Aikwood) remarked, "The majority of the people of Scotland . . . want not just the symbol but the substance, the substance of the return of democratic control over our internal affairs in Scotland." [2] This view was put more bluntly by John Maxton, then Labour MP for Glasgow Cathcart: "Those of us who believe in the establishment of a Scottish Parliament . . . do not believe that the return of a feudal medieval symbol of tyranny is any more than a total irrelevance." [3]

In the event Major's gesture proved pointless, for in the landslide election of 1997 the Conservatives went on to lose their last few parliamentary seats in Scotland. Almost immediately, the "New Labour" Government of Tony Blair set about answering the growing demand for

Scottish independence with a radical solution of its own—a new Scottish Parliament that was subordinate to Westminster but with control over internal affairs such as health and education.

This Parliament was duly set up in 1999. At first it met in the General Assembly Hall of the Church of Scotland, but since 2004 it has been sitting in a new modernistic building in the Holyrood area of Edinburgh. Meanwhile the Stone of Destiny, the ancient symbol of Scottish sovereignty, has remained in Edinburgh Castle on permanent display alongside other symbols of royalty such as the crown once worn by Mary, Queen of Scots.

Regarded as irrelevant by the new establishment, the stone's very authenticity was called into question in 2008 by none other than the SNP leader Alex Salmond himself, who was by then First Minister of the Scottish Parliament.[4] In June of that year he went on record as saying that he believed the stone now residing in Edinburgh Castle to be at best a medieval fake that was palmed off on Edward I by the wily Abbott of Scone.[5] He was not the only person to cast doubt on the stone's authenticity. Other commentators, while agreeing with Salmond that it must be a fake, were of the opinion that it was made much more recently than this, that the students who took the stone from Westminster Abbey in 1950 had made copies of their own, and that it was one of these that was subsequently returned in time for the Queen's coronation in 1953. The real Stone of Destiny, or so they claimed, had remained in Scotland and was hidden there still. Such rumors notwithstanding, most experts are of the opinion that the stone which Edward took back to Westminster was considered genuine at the time (1296) and that it was the self same stone that was transferred from London to Edinburgh in 1996.

For reasons that will become clear later and having long had a personal interest in the stone, I followed these events closely. I had first seen it in 1973—shortly after returning to England from Israel. There, after a short stint working on a kibbutz in Upper Galilee, I'd spent several months working in a youth hostel in Tel Aviv. It was while working there and not in my native London that I had first heard mention of it.

The hostel was a busy place, and while there I met many people. Most were young backpackers, either on their way to or from a kibbutz. A few (and I would count myself in this group) were more serious travelers—pilgrims you might say—ever hopeful that they might find clues to their own destinies while walking among the ruins of this once Holy Land. These people, many of them older than the grapefruit pickers, were recognizably different. Quieter than the others, they would often sit for hours in the corner of the canteen, either reading books or scribbling notes. Often the book that so occupied their attention was the Bible, but this was not always so. Such people tended to have a wide taste when it came to literature, and American imports like *The Tibetan Book of the Dead* and *Remember, Be Here Now*[6] (which could be purchased in "The Third Eye"—then Israel's only alternative bookshop) were also on their reading lists. There would be debates that went on long into the night as they discussed the pros and cons of a belief in reincarnation versus the allure of living for the moment. Are we, as westerners are wont to believe, endowed by God with our own free will, or are we, as the Tibetan Buddhists teach, bound to the wheel of *karma* and therefore doomed to an inevitable suffering? There seemed no immediate answers to these questions, but that was no bar to their being discussed. The core concept that united both views was destiny about which, at the time, I had only a hazy understanding.

The subject of destiny is linked with the concept of prophecy, and this, as it lay at the core of two books that were much discussed at the time, was another subject then very much on my mind. Both books were in their own ways concerned with destiny, and both were major best sellers. The first (later to be turned into a movie narrated by Orson Welles) was *The Late Great Planet Earth* by Hal Lindsey. Probably the only fundamentalist Christian book ever to have made it onto the New York Times bestseller lists, it presented a scary hypothesis that certain biblical prophecies—notably those contained in the Books of Daniel and Ezekiel—were being fulfilled in our own times. Using the date for the refounding of the modern state of Israel (May 14, 1948) as a marker in time on which to hang his predictions, Lindsey interpreted biblical prophecies for the "end-of-days" as referring to the 1970s and '80s. He predicted that a coalition of nations would soon attempt to crush the state of Israel. These forces, he said, would include armies from a reintegrated Roman Empire (by which he meant the countries that now comprise the European Union) but be under the leadership of "Gog from the land of Magog"—a reference, he believed, to the USSR. However, the invasion would prove to be unsuccessful when, through divine intervention, the massive army sent by Gog was destroyed by angels in the great battle of Armageddon. In the immediate aftermath of this apocalyptic battle, Jesus would return to the Temple Mount in Jerusalem. He would lift true believers to safety in the sky (the rapture), and then while sitting on the throne of David and Solomon, he would set about judging the nations.

Thankfully, Lindsey's predictions have so far not come to pass, and with the breakup of the Soviet Union, they are now unlikely to in quite the way he envisaged. However, reading this book in Israel, where evidence of an earlier holocaust was still painfully visible, was itself a sobering experience. While working on the kibbutz, I had met several survivors of Hitler's death camps: people with tattooed numbers on their arms. These people, who bore the involuntary marks of the beast that was Nazism, were a constant reminder to all who saw them of the fragility of modern civilization. Few in number, even by 1972, and now almost extinct, they were regarded as heroes in more than one way: for not only had they survived the Holocaust, but it was also through their labors that the modern state of Israel had become a reality. Indeed, with my own eyes I had seen how they had transformed the region of Upper Galilee from a malarial swamp into something a little short of paradise.

The sudden rebirth of Israel after two thousand years certainly did seem predestined, yet there was still something about this that troubled me. The determination of those first settlers (not to mention the fighting spirit of their sons and daughters who had so recently in the Six-Day War of 1967 routed the combined armies of Egypt, Syria, and Jordan) contrasted strangely with the fate of all those others who had been rounded up like sheep and gassed by the Nazis. I wondered how this could have been allowed to happen if the Jews really were God's chosen people. Yet, in a perverse way, I could see that the contribution of those who had died in the camps was even more important to the genesis of the modern state of Israel than that of the survivors. For had they not made the ultimate sacrifice—and in such numbers—then the conscience of the world would not have been so pricked as to allow the survivors to emigrate to Palestine. At some deeper level I understood it had been their fate, destiny, call it what you will, to be taken as sacrificial lambs; it was their blood that had paid for the land now inhabited by their kin. Strange as this seemed, this also explained the Israelis' gritty determination in the face of all adversity. For the land having been bought with blood, they felt they had an obligation to defend it to the last, even when for them personally life would have been easier in New York, London, or even now Berlin. With such an attitude they were more than a match for their many enemies and, as far as I could see, didn't need God to protect them.

This was one way—the secular—of looking at recent history, but there was another. Among the people who passed through the hostel, there was one man who stood out from the rest. Canadian, I suspected, his face hardened by time, he was very different from the fresh-faced grapefruit pickers. For hours he would sit reading his Bible, its margins heavily annotated with scribbled notes. Perhaps because he seemed so busy with this work, few people spoke to him. However, I was curious to discover what he found so absorbing in his Bible and accordingly engaged him in conversation.[7]

"What" I asked him, "do you think of *The Late Great Planet Earth*? Has Hal Lindsey got it right that the rebirth of Israel means we are now living in the end of days?"

"Not exactly," he replied. "The Bible prophesies that not just the Jews will return but all of Israel. Read it for yourself. It's all in there: how the original state of Israel broke up into two separate kingdoms. After the split, the northern kingdom, which consisted of ten tribes, continued to be called Israel. The southern one, known as Judah—the original kingdom of the Jews—consisted of only two tribes. So when you talk about the rebirth of Israel, it's not happened yet. So far only some of the Jews have returned. The descendants of the northern kingdom of Israel—the ten tribes led by Ephraim—have not come back. When they do, the two kingdoms must be reunited. Only then will Jesus return to sit on the throne of David in Jerusalem."

"What you mean an actual king's throne? Like a chair? The Israelis don't have one, do they? It's a republic."

"Maybe it is for now, but the Kingdom of Heaven on Earth is not a metaphor. You do know about Jacob's Pillow Stone, don't you, young man?" I shook my head. "Well, you should. Your own Queen sat on it for her coronation, and you can see it in Westminster Abbey in London. That's the throne of David, and it will be returned to Jerusalem in time for Jesus to be crowned as King of Kings. Don't take Lindsey's word. Read about it for yourself in the Bible."

Taking his words to heart, I did as he suggested and the next time I was in Jerusalem I bought a Revised King James Bible of my own.[8] Sure enough it told the story of an earlier northern Israel, one separate from Judah. This kingdom, which had its capital at a place called Samaria, came to a sticky end in 722 BC when the Assyrians invaded the Holy

Land. The people of this Israel were forced out of their homes and taken away, some being settled in northern Mesopotamia but most in Media on the southern banks of the Caspian Sea. In a switch of populations they were replaced by tribes of Medes: the ancestors of the much-reviled "Samaritans" of New Testament times.[9]

Meanwhile the southern kingdom of Judah, with its capital at Jerusalem, survived the Assyrian onslaught. It was not until 586 BC that Jerusalem was sacked,[10] and its people were taken away as slaves to Babylon. In 539 BC the great city of Babylon fell to the Medo-Persians. The Jews, as the descendants of the people of the southern kingdom were now called, were set free and allowed to return home to Jerusalem. Later still in Roman times, the descendants of these returnees were again expelled from the Holy Land. Since the modern-day Israeli-Jews claim to be descended from these exiles rather than from those who were taken captive by the Assyrians half a century earlier, it seemed the Bible scholar was right when he said that "Israel" (i.e. the descendants of the ten northern tribes) had not yet returned. As for Jacob's Pillow Stone, the only biblical references I could find to this curious relic were a few lines in the book of Genesis. Nevertheless, intrigued by what I had heard and read, I decided that when I returned home, I would investigate the matter further to see if there was any truth in what he said about the Queen being crowned while sitting on it.

The second book then doing the rounds in the youth hostel was *The Spear of Destiny* by Trevor Ravenscroft. A former British commando, he had spent most of the war in Germany as a prisoner of war after a failed attempt at assassinating Rommel in 1941. If anything were even more controversial than *The Late Great Planet Earth*, *The Spear of Destiny* was not, as the title might seem to suggest, about its author's daring attempt to kill the head of the Afrika Corps with a javelin; rather it told the story of Adolf Hitler's curious fascination with another holy relic: *Die Heilige Lance* (Holy Lance)—the "Spear of Destiny" of the title.

Also known as the Lance of St. Maurice, this object (actually only the head of a spear but also containing a nail said to have been used in the crucifixion of Jesus) had once belonged to Charlemagne. For a thousand years thereafter it had been a sacred totem of the Holy Roman Emperors of Germany. For in addition to the nail—itself an important relic—it derived sanctity from legends identifying it as the very spear used by a Roman centurion, Gaius Cassius Longinus, to pierce the side of the crucified Christ. This seemingly random act of violence against an already

dead man was apparently done to save Jesus from having his legs broken. Had he been found to be alive at sunset, the Romans would have
broken his legs to hasten his death. As a consequence, Longinus' act led
to the fulfillment of a certain prophecies that "not a bone of his [the
messiah's] body would be broken" and "they would look upon him
who they had pierced."[11] This gave the spear a totemic significance as an
agent not so much of death as of merciful deliverance through death.
During the Middle Ages it attained an importance analogous to the
Holy Grail in which, according to legend, some blood from Christ's
wounds was collected. Because of its importance as a holy relic and
agent of destiny, the spear was carried in procession at the coronation
ceremonies of Holy Roman Emperors. Their possession of the spear was
thought to confirm that they ruled over their vast empire—in reality
neither "Holy" nor "Roman"—with the blessing of God himself. In other
words the emperor was God's agent, and his role was to fulfill the destiny allotted to him.

Ravenscroft's primary source for his book was Walter Johannes Stein,
a Viennese-born doctor of philosophy who during the War had acted
as an advisor to Winston Churchill on matters pertaining to Nazi oc-
cultism. According to Stein, Adolf Hitler himself, during the days when
he was a struggling artist living in Vienna, had also researched the mythology of the spear. On first seeing it, he had apparently gone into
some sort of reverie and from that day onwards he had harbored a
longing to wield its power.

"Once again his immediate experience was one of complete baffle-
ment. He could feel something strange and powerful emanating from
the iron Spearhead which he could not readily identify. He stood there
for a long while perplexed by its inscrutable riddle: 'Studying minutely
every physical detail of its shape, colour and substance, yet trying to
remain open to its message.'

I slowly became aware of a mighty presence around it—the same
awesome presence which I had experienced inwardly on those rare occasions in my life when I had sensed that a great destiny awaited me.

And now he began to understand the significance of the spear and
the source of its legend, for he sensed intuitively that it was a vehicle of
revelation—'a bridge between the world of sense and the world of spirit
(Geistliche Welt).'

Adolf Hitler later claimed that it was on this occasion while he was
standing before the Spear that: 'a window in the future was opened up

to me through which I saw in a single flash of illumination a future event by which I knew beyond contradiction that the blood in my veins would one day become the vessel of the Folk–Spirit of my people.'"[12]

It is tempting to dismiss such reportage as mere speculation, but Walter Stein knew Hitler better than most people in his student days and visited the spear with him on at least one occasion. There he saw how Hitler went into a trance–like state in its presence while he himself also experienced a sense of mystical exaltation of a quite opposite kind as he contemplated its role in the death of Jesus Christ.

Such experiences, though irrational from a scientific point of view, are more common than we generally suppose and frequently are triggered by ancient relics of one sort or another. In a famous incident, Napoleon experienced something similar during a visit to the Great Pyramid of Giza. In 1798 his French army had just won a great victory over the Marmelukes, who had ruled over Egypt for centuries. After the battle, Napoleon went into the pyramid, insisting that he be left alone in the King's Chamber. When he emerged, about an hour later, he was ashen faced but refused all entreaties to say what had happened in there; he took the secret with him to the grave. It has been speculated, however, that he had had some sort of vision concerning the destiny of the world and his own place in history.

Although, like Hitler's, Napoleon's career was to end in failure, he was not to know this at the time. As far as he was concerned, in conquering Egypt he was following in the footsteps of two of history's greatest generals: Alexander the Great and Julius Caesar. Alexander, who was to go on and conquer almost the entire known world, had a mystical experience of his own while visiting the shrine of Amun at the Oasis of Siwa. In this shrine was a meteorite sacred to the god. History does not record whether Alexander went into a reverie before the meteorite, but the priests told him that Amun, not Philip of Macedon, was his true father. As a demigod, it would be his destiny to conquer the Persian Empire and thereby inaugurate a new, Hellenic, age. Just a little under three hundred years later, Julius Caesar visited Egypt. While there he visited the tomb of Alexander, in tears over the fact that he was already a man in his fifties, unlike the conqueror of Persia who was just thirty–three when he died.

Alexander and Julius Caesar were undoubtedly the greatest generals of their respective ages, perhaps of all time. However what make them even more important from a historical point of view is not just their conquests but the fact that they irrevocably changed the world in ac-cordance with the biblical prophecies of the Book of Daniel. Daniel lived during the period of the Babylonian captivity of the Jews and rose to prominence as interpreter of King Nebuchadnezzar's dreams. During one of these, the king saw a statue with a head of gold, breast and arms of silver, belly and thighs of bronze, legs of iron and feet partly of iron and partly of clay. Daniel told the king that this statue represented a sequence of kingdoms. The head symbolized the Babylonian Empire while the others were to come after the king's death.

The first of these, symbolized by silver, represented the Medo–Per-sian Empire, which conquered Babylon in 539 BC and went on to seize Egypt in 525 BC. It was Alexander who brought to an end the Persian Empire, inaugurating the next phase of Nebuchadnezzar's dream: the belly and thighs of bronze, symbolic of the Hellenic Empire. Following Alexander's death, this Empire was split among his generals. Neverthe-less Greek rule, under the Ptolemies, continued in Egypt up until the Roman takeover. As consort of Cleopatra, the last Queen of Egypt, Julius Caesar was the first Roman ruler to set foot in that land. Although Egypt was not fully integrated into the Roman Empire until the time of his grandnephew Augustus, Caesar inaugurated the transition from the "belly and thighs" empire of the Greeks to the start of "legs of iron" or the Roman Empire.

These facts of history were well known to Napoleon who consciously styled himself on Alexander even to the point of having himself por-trayed on horseback in a pose made famous from statues of the former king. He also organized the French army on Roman lines, issuing eagle standards of a very similar type to the Roman. It is, therefore, not un-reasonable to suppose that what he saw in the pyramid was somehow connected with the idea that his destiny was to bring change to the world, inaugurating some sort of new age.

Napoleon was an inspiration for Adolf Hitler in much the same way as Caesar and Alexander had been for him. Hitler saw how close he had come to realizing his dream of establishing a French Empire over the whole of Europe. Napoleon, however, had been thwarted in his attempt at getting hold of the Spear of Destiny; it had been transferred from Nuremburg to Vienna before he could steal it. Hitler was determined that he would not be cheated in the same way. On March 12, 1938, it was announced that forthwith Austria was annexed to Germany: an event termed the *anschluss*. The following day Hitler, now the *führer* of what was, in effect, a reborn "Holy Roman Empire," came once more to the Hofburg Museum. This time it was not to look at but rather to claim the totemic symbol of his destiny: the Holy Spear of Longinus.

Stein attributed Hitler's undoubted charisma and hypnotic powers to the spear's ability to act as a channel for unseen forces. There was, he said, a *zeitgeist* or "spirit of the times" associated with the spear. Though itself neither good nor bad, it provided Hitler with the power to make his dreams come true. The fact that this had such terrible consequences for the world was because of Hitler's own dark character. In the hands of a better man, such as Charlemagne, the same power might have produced a good result.

Ravenscroft's book, sensationalist in tone and clearly in part fictional, caused quite a stir at the time it was published. However, what made it so interesting was not just the story of Hitler's obsession with an old spearhead with royal connections—not so surprising given the Nazis' kleptomania—but its occult significance. For according to Stein (and hence Ravenscroft), Hitler saw his destiny as paralleling, in some way, that of the hero in Wagner's opera *Parzifal*. But whereas Wagner could only fantasize on a tiny stage about the possibility of a hero wielding a magic spear, Hitler had the will and means to turn fantasy into reality. Moreover, if taking possession of the spear in 1938 had coincided with one of his greatest moments: the annexation of his homeland of Austria to the greater *Reich* that he was creating, its loss was also deeply symbolic. For, unknown to Hitler, at just the time he was contemplating suicide in his Berlin bunker, it passed into the custody of the American army. The Spear, with its occult power, was still in American hands when Germany surrendered and shortly afterwards when the first atomic bombs were dropped on Japan. It was eventually returned to the Hofburg Museum, where today it once more lies on its velvet cushion—in the very same spot where Hitler had first seen it in 1912—on January 6, 1946.

Whatever the truth about the legendary spear, there is no disputing that after Hitler claimed it, he went through some sort of transformation. For seven years he wielded immense power, spreading his despotic rule throughout nearly all of Europe to parts of Africa and deep into Asia. However, according to Ravenscroft's other major source, (the private records of Eliza von Moltke, widow of General Helmuth von Moltke (1848–1916)) it had been prophesied long before the time of the *anscluss* that Hitler would fail in his ultimate goal of world domination.[13] As early as 1916 Eliza von Moltke named Adolf Hitler, then an unknown corporal, as a false messiah who would ultimately bring Germany to ruin.

I found *The Spear of Destiny* deeply shocking, but I had to admit that viewed in this light, much about the Nazis that otherwise seems inexplicable to us from the point of view of twenty-first century rationalism makes perfect sense. In a deeply twisted way, Hitler and his close circle of associates: Herman Goering, Joseph Goebbels, Adolf Eichmann, Martin Bormann, and others saw themselves as fulfilling a German destiny proclaimed by such "prophets" as Nietzsche and Schopenhauer that their country, the ancestral home of the Aryan races of Europe, would bring into being a new age of man. They were anti-Christian in the literal sense of the word, and the Nazi millennium that they tried but failed to inaugurate was intended to be the complete opposite of that forecast in Chapter 20 of St. John's Revelation. There it is promised that following the overthrow of the "beast" and "false-prophet," the earth will enjoy a period of peace under the benevolent rule of Jesus Christ himself; the souls of martyrs will rise from the dead: " . . . those that were beheaded for the witness of Jesus, and for the word of God, and which had not worshipped the beast, neither his image, neither had received his mark upon their foreheads, or in their hands;" (Rev. 20:4)

The Nazis despised what they regarded as Christian sentimentality, and Hitler himself had almost as much loathing for Christians as for Jews. In his opinion they were "men [who] betrayed their pure Aryan blood to the dirty superstitions of the Jew Jesus—superstitions as loathsome and ludicrous as the Yiddish rites of circumcision."[14] Yet for all of Hitler's bluster, his reign of terror did not usher in an Aryan millennium. Instead it brought only death; firstly and on an unprecedented scale to the Jews and then, in a "Twilight of the Gods" beyond the imagination of even Richard Wagner of the cream of the German nation.

The awful reality of these events is even today hard to comprehend. Still harder (because it smacks of irrationalism) is the idea that the Hofburg Spear—or any other object for that matter—could have associated with it the sort of occult power that Ravenscroft claimed. To even entertain such thoughts must, for many people, smack of empty superstition tantamount to idolatry. However I had been brought up as a Roman Catholic and early in my life had been exposed to the idea that holy relics can be channels for occult power. I attended Catholic schools and can well remember the day when a priest brought a crucifix to school that contained, we were told, a fragment of the One True Cross. We little boys, aged only six or seven at the time, knelt to receive a blessing from this—on the face of it gruesome—relic of the crucifixion. Though it was for us an unfathomable mystery, we believed in the power of the relic as a link between worlds, just as the wafer at the Mass—the transubstantiation of which was as big a mystery to our teachers as ourselves—could act as a bridge that linked our material world with one that we could not see. Through mediation of such relics, our prayers could cross the void and to enter the ear of God himself.

This fragment of wood (supposedly of the True Cross but in my opinion just as likely to have been a fake) was but the first of many such relics with which I have since become acquainted. In Istanbul's Topkapi Museum I have seen "the arm of John the Baptist," considered especially holy as it was with this limb and its attached hand that he baptized Jesus in the river Jordan. At Drogheda, a city whose name is infamous to this day as the scene of Cromwell's worst atrocity in Ireland, there are relics of more recent saints, such as the head of Oliver Plunkett.[15] I have seen how this and other bony relics are daily prayed to by earnest supplicants in the hope that the particular saint would intercede on their behalf.

It is easy to dismiss the veneration of such relics as mere superstition. Yet on at least one occasion I have witnessed the result of a saint's bone being used in the performance of what appeared to be a miracle. As a teenager, I was sent as a boarder to my father's *alma mater*: St. Edmund's College: the oldest post-Reformation Catholic school in England. The original college had been founded at Douai (in Northern France) in 1568, with the purpose of training English priests to serve the country's remaining Catholics.[16] A preparatory school was later founded in England itself, moving to its present location at Old Hall Green, near Ware in Hertfordshire in 1769. With the closure of Douai in 1793 (on account of the French Revolution) the remaining priests and teachers moved to Old Hall. Its patron was St. Edmund of Abingdon, archbishop of Canterbury, who died in exile in France on November 16, 1240. The doors of the senior school were opened on his Feast Day.

In 1853 St. Edmund's left fibula was presented to the school by Cardinal Wiseman—the first archbishop of Westminster following the restoration of English Catholicism in 1850. "The bone," as we boys called it, was kept in a transparent, ruby glass tube above the altar of a purpose-built shrine chapel. It was therefore plainly visible for all to see.[17] By the

1960s reverence for this somewhat ghoulish relic was deeply ingrained in school tradition, and each year on St. Edmund's Day (November 16) it was carried in procession around the college grounds. The highlight of this procession was when we came up, one by one, to kiss the ruby glass tube and have it pressed to our foreheads.

Fortunately, for the sake of hygiene, the tube was wiped clean between kisses, and there was no question of actual contact between lips and bone. However, I always found "kissing the bone" an unsettling experience: one vaguely reminiscent of voodoo practices in the jungles of South America or Africa rather than a school in modern Britain. The ritual also seemed curiously at odds with what I was learning about chemistry and physics—then taught to a very high standard at St. Edmund's—that bones, even saintly ones, are nothing more than crystalline growths of calcium phosphate. Nevertheless, for all the irrationality of venerating such a relic, the bone, or rather St. Edmund, it seemed to have healing powers as he was credited with the performance of many miracles.

An example of this power in action occurred in my first year. As at most public schools, the winter sport was rugby rather than soccer, and given the small size of the school (about two-hundred and fifty at most), the first fifteen of 1962-3 year were of surprisingly high caliber. The key to this success was in the hands of a rather small boy who, as "fly half," had the unenviable task of fending off opposing forwards twice his size. This, however, was not his only responsibility. As far and away the best kicker in the team, it also fell to him to convert tries into goals. In this he was usually successful—so much so that for a short time the school was near the top of its league. It was then that tragedy struck. Whether he was "nobbled" or it was a simple accident, we will never know for sure, but the result was just the same. Halfway through an important match he was kicked in the head and rendered unconscious. Taken to hospital, he lay for a week in a coma, the prognosis being that he was likely to die.

It was in these difficult circumstances that the bone of St. Edmund came to the rescue; for understanding that conventional medicine had nothing further to offer, a posse of priests took the relic to the boy. As he lay comatose in his hospital bed, they laid it (still in its glass tube) on his forehead and uttered the appropriate prayers to St. Edmund. What the doctors and nurses must have made of this strange ritual, one can only imagine; however, strange as it seems, it worked. From that time onwards the boy began to recover, and by the following term he was back at school studying for his "A" levels and playing rugby.

I tell this story, which I remember vividly and can be confirmed by anyone else who was attending St. Edmund's at the time, because there can be no suggestion here that it was the boy's faith that brought about the healing. Unconscious throughout the proceedings, he could not have known what was going on. That means that mind–over–matter, auto–suggestion, or the placebo effect cannot have been responsible for what happened. It could be argued that the boy's cure was a case of spontaneous remission but then that can be said of any healing. It should also be noted that as far as the bone's reputation was concerned, the stakes could not have been higher. For had the boy died (as expected), the relic itself would have been devalued. After all why go to all the trouble of parading and kissing a seven–hundred–year–old leg bone if when he is most needed, the saint is unable to deliver the goods?

So how, then, was this relic able to heal a boy when conventional medicine had all but given up hope? The answer to this—at least from a Catholic point of view—is very simple: it was not the bone or even St. Edmund that did the healing but God. Seen from this perspective, it was but a means of communicating with the dead. The bone—tangible, physical, and very much of this world—still carries the saint's vibrations. It can, therefore, act as a link between our world of matter and the heavenly world of spirit wherein dwells the soul of St. Edmund. Once alerted, it was down to him to intercede with God himself on behalf of the boy.

If venerating saintly relics was a rarity in Britain in the 1960s—and it is probably even rarer now—in earlier centuries this was certainly not the case. Prior to the Reformation there were thousands of relics of saints, many credited with healing powers throughout the length and breadth of Europe. Christians venerated these relics not just because of what they were in themselves but for the ones to whom they were connected. Conversely, the church often went out of its way to destroy all physical traces of those it condemned as heretics. This is one reason why they were burnt at the stake: not just because this was visibly a horrendously painful death and therefore a warning to others, but to destroy any bones that might service as relics. In the case of Jan Huss further strict precautions were taken.[18] Not only was he burnt at the stake but to deny his followers any relics, the ashes from the fire and even the earth beneath it were taken and scattered into the Rhine.

Such indeed was the perceived power of bones whether these belonged to saints or heretics. But, as we have seen, in the Middle Ages
not all relics were body parts. Besides fragments of the One True Cross,
the Holy Grail, and the Spear of Destiny, there were also memorial stones
that, if not credited with healing powers, were certainly totems of authority. Thus a number of Saxon kings were crowned at Kingston–upon–
Thames while seated upon a particular stone (still to be seen in the
market place to this day) that gave the town its name. Similarly, King
Arthur is said to have drawn his first sword from a stone in a churchyard in London. History doesn't record which church or what happened
to this stone but his crown—or what was claimed to be his crown—was
also a cherished relic. In 1284 it was given to Edward I at the tourna-
ment of Nevyn that followed his conquest of North Wales. Other relics
of his—inherited, given, or captured in conquest—were the Sword of
Constantine, the crown and scepter of Edward the Confessor and, of
course, the Stone of Destiny.

This, as I was discovering, is perhaps the most important relic in the
whole of the British Isles. On June 2, 1953, just as the old man in Tel
Aviv had said, it had been witness to the most regal event to take place
in my lifetime. It had rained that day but that did not damper the ardor
of the four million people lining the streets of London or the twenty
million watching on TV. For this very special day—the coronation of
Queen Elizabeth II—Westminster Abbey was crammed full with dignitaries from around the world in addition to almost the entire peerage[19]
and all the senior clergy of the Church of England. Prior to the Queen's
arrival and in preparation for the ceremony to come, the most important items of the Crown Jewels were carried up to the altar. Leading the
procession was the Marquis of Salisbury, KG. As Leader of the House of
Lord he had the honor of carrying the Sword of State. This is the largest
of four swords in the Crown Jewels collection and the one always born
before the sovereign at the state opening of Parliament. To his right,
carrying a cushion bearing a crown, was the High Constable of England, Lord Viscount Alanbrooke, KG, GCB, DM, GCVO, DSO and Bar.
During the Second World War he had been Chief of the Imperial General Staff and as such, Winston Churchill's most trusted confidant.

On Salisbury's left was Bernard Marmaduke Fitzalan-Howard, six-
teenth Duke of Norfolk, KG, GCVO, GBE, TD, PC, carrying a cushion
bearing one of the scepters. As hereditary Earl Marshal the entire organization of the coronation was his responsibility: as had been that of

the Queen's father, George VI, in 1937. There is a delicious irony in this
that would probably only be tolerated in England; for the Dukes of
Norfolk are not only holders of the oldest and therefore most senior
peerage in Britain, but by tradition and belief their family is also Roman
Catholic. Given that possibly the most important part of the coronation
ceremony is the monarch's oath and that this requires that he or she
will swear to remain true to the Protestant faith and not marry a Roman
Catholic, the Duke must have been aware that there was a curious contradiction in his role. If so, he didn't show it, performing his duties with
the utmost propriety. Behind this first row of three dignitaries (and their
pages), followed a second. At the center of this group was the Lord High
Steward, Admiral of the Fleet, Viscount Cunningham of Hyndhope, KT,
GCB, OM, DSO and two bars. To him was given the honor of carrying
the St. Edward's Crown—the centerpiece of the coronation ceremony.
On his right side carrying the orb was Earl Alexander of Tunis, KG, GCB,
OM, GCMG, CSI, DSO, MC, PC, who as Commander of Allied Ground
Forces had overseen the invasion of Sicily and Italy in the Second World
War. On the other side of Viscount Cunningham was the Duke of Rich-
mond and Gordon who carried the dove scepter on a cushion.

All these eminent men made their way up to the High Altar where
the props required for the high drama that is a British coronation were
carefully laid out. Soon the Queen herself arrived,[20] as radiant as any
bride on her wedding day. Seated on the Chair of Estate, placed to the
side of the dais leading to the main throne, she followed the lead of Dr.
Fisher, the archbishop of Canterbury, as she took the coronation oath:

> Archbishop: Will you solemnly promise and swear to gov-
> ern the Peoples of the United Kingdom of Great Britain
> and Northern Ireland, Canada, Australia, New Zealand, the
> Union of South Africa, Pakistan, and Ceylon and of your
> Possessions and other Territories to any of them belong-
> ing or pertaining, according to their respective laws and
> customs?"
> Queen: "I solemnly promise so to do."
> Archbishop: "Will you to your power cause Law and Jus-
> tice, in Mercy, to be executed in all your judgments?"
> Queen: "I will."
> Archbishop: "Will you to the utmost of your power main-
> tain the Laws of God and the true profession of the

Gospel? Will you to the utmost of your power maintain in the United Kingdom the Protestant Reformed Religion established by law? Will you maintain and preserve inviolable by the Settlement of the Church of England, and the doctrine, worship, and discipline, and government thereof, as by law established in England? And will you preserve unto the Bishops and Clergy of England, and to the Churches there committed to their charge, all such rights and privileges, as by law do or shall appertain to them or any of them?"

Queen: "All this I promise to do. The things which I have here before promised, I will perform, and keep. So help me God."[21]

Having taken these oaths she was then presented with a copy of a complete King James Bible by the Moderator of the General Assembly of the Church of Scotland with the words: "Here is Wisdom; this is the Royal Law; these are the lively Oracles of God."

After this a full Communion service commenced, interrupted for the actual coronation service. For this, the Queen first removed her outer robes: the crimson surcoat and the Robe of State of crimson velvet. Dressed only in a simple, white anointing gown she was then led up to King Edward's Chair in which was lodged the Stone of Destiny. There, screened from public gaze (and the cameras) by a canopy held aloft by four Knights of the Garter, she underwent the anointing: the most religious part of the coronation ceremony. For this the archbishop of Canterbury used the anointing spoon.[22] Using oil poured into the spoon from an eagle–shaped ampulla, he anointed her on hands, chest, and head.

Following this, the Queen was re-robed, this time with first the *Colobium sindonis* or "shrouded tunic." This is a simple, white undergarment of fine linen edged with lace. Over this was placed the heavy *Supertunica*: a long coat of gold silk with large, wide sleeves. Trimmed with gold lace and lined with rose–colored silk, it is a garment whose design derives from the full dress uniform of a late Roman consul. Over this was placed the Royal Robe or *Pallium Regale* and the Stole Royal or *Armilla*, again made from spun golden silk.

Thus robed in all these heavy garments, the Queen was ready to receive the symbols of her authority. Still seated in King Edward's Chair, she received first the orb and cross, symbolic of Christ's authority over the world. Then, after removing the orb and putting it back on the altar, the Archbishop replaced it with the crossed scepter. This contains the Cullinan I: the largest cut diamond in the world and is symbolic of her authority as a Christian monarch. Into her left hand he placed the dove scepter, symbolic of the importance for a monarch to temper justice with mercy. Finally he placed on her head the exquisite St. Edward's Crown, its jewels flashing in lights of the Abbey. This was the moment all had been waiting for, and as the gathered nobles placed their own coronets on their heads, a spontaneous roar of "God save the Queen!" rang out, to be answered by canon fire from the Tower of London.

All this, as a three-year-old, I had witnessed on television. Nobody then or indeed later had ever mentioned to me the importance in all of this ritual of the Stone of Destiny. Indeed, as can be seen in the film of the event, even the BBC commentator, who comments in meticulous detail on the various garments and regalia in use for the coronation, doesn't mention the stone even though it is clearly visible under King Edward's Chair.[23] However, the conversation I had had with the Bible-reading stranger in Tel Aviv must have pricked some deep memory of all of this for I was determined to see the stone for myself on my return to England.

2

Throne of Kings

I returned to London richer in spirit but financially broke. Already planning my next trip (a long journey through the US), I set about finding work. This task turned out not to be as hard as I had expected, for within a week or two of my return I found myself working at an office in Victoria Street. As this was just down the road from Westminster Abbey, I decided to pay the coronation seat and Stone of Destiny a visit to see them for myself.

How the stone came to be in Westminster Abbey in the first place is itself the stuff of legend. Edward I (1239–1307), grandson of the feckless King John of Robin Hood fame, looked upon himself as a latter-day King Arthur. He believed it was his duty to unite all of Britain under one crown: his own. Thus it was that in 1296, having already subjugated Wales,[1] he invaded Scotland. During the campaign he captured the royal castle of Stirling and sent his men to Scone to take possession of the

21

Scottish Crown Jewels. Besides the crown and scepter, these regalia in-cluded the Stone of Destiny. Plain as it was, this stone was of great cultural importance. Edward, who was partly Scottish himself, knew this. He took the Stone because he wanted to make it clear, north as well as south of the border, that he was paramount king of the Scots as well as of the English and Welsh; thus although he later returned the crown and scepter—on the face of it much more valuable items—he hung onto the Stone of Destiny.

Norman, Saxon and Scottish ancestry of Edward I

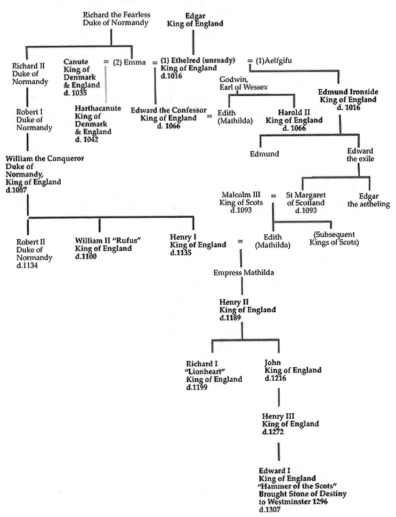

Then, as now, Westminster Abbey lay at the center of England's cult of royalty. The reasons for its eminence are many but in the main stem from the presence there of the shrine-tomb of Edward I's patron and namesake: Edward the Confessor. This Edward had been king of England from 1042–66 and was very largely responsible for the transformation of the small abbey church of St. Peter's Westminster into England's richest and most prestigious religious institution. Edward the Confessor was by no means an able king, and during his reign the powerful earls of Wessex (Godwin and his son Harold Godwinson) effectively ran the country. He did, however, have a reputation for sanctity. This was enhanced by the legend that he refused to sleep with his wife Edith, Godwin's daughter, and that it was for this reason she remained childless. This may have been true for she does not seem to have repulsed him: by all accounts she was a very beautiful as well as a learned lady. He seems to have chosen celibacy as a result of a perceived higher calling. Whatever is the truth of the matter, Edith nursed Edward during his final illness, and when she herself died in 1075, she was buried next to him.

Edward the Confessor's death without progeny was the catalyst for the most traumatic event in all of English history: the Norman invasion. Almost before the body was cold, Edith's brother, Earl Harold Godwinson, was crowned as King Harold II. This was a blow to the ambitions of Edward's maternal nephew, Duke William of Normandy, who in 1054 had been named by Edward as his heir. William was furious; he assembled a fleet and on October 14, 1066, defeated and killed Harold at the Battle of Hastings. Then, to reinforce his claim to the throne, he had himself crowned in front of Edward's tomb. In William's eyes at least, God's will had been done and the legal succession restored.

In actuality, although Edward the Confessor was William's uncle and himself strongly pro-Norman, when it came to the throne of England, the latter had no direct blood claim of his own. Neither, it has to be said, had he been elected as king by the *Witan* or council of Anglo-Saxon elders. Indeed most of them had been slaughtered at the Battle of Hastings. William's legitimacy (and that of his whole dynasty) therefore rested solely on Edward's 1054 promise or "confession" that he should be succeeded by William. It was undoubtedly for this reason that William arranged for his coronation to take place in front of the tomb and therefore, as his Christian subjects would have understood it, in the presence of Edward's soul. This set a precedent; thenceforth coronation before the tomb of Edward the Confessor became the norm for kings of England and remains so up to the present day.

After his death the Confessor's stature grew substantially. Even while alive he was known as a healer: his "royal touch" being especially effective in curing skin complaints. Very soon posthumous miracles of healing were being attributed to his intervention. William, who had everything to gain from Edward's popularity, had a new gold and jewel-encrusted tomb built for his predecessor. In 1102 this was opened by the abbot in the presence of Henry I, the youngest and most well liked of William's sons. Inside, Edward's body was found to be uncorrupted—a sure sign of his saintliness. Indeed the corpse was in such good condition that the bishop of Rochester could not pull out so much as a single hair from the dead king's yellow beard and the Confessor's joints were also found to be as flexible as if he were simply sleeping.

After all the turbulence of William's conquest and the oppressive rule of his eldest son, William II, the reign of Henry I was a breath of fresh air. He did much to win the affection of his English subjects by making a popular marriage. His wife (another Edith but more commonly known as Maud), was a daughter of Malcolm III, King of the Scots. Her mother, the Princess Margaret (later canonized as St. Margaret of Scotland), was Edward the Confessor's great-niece. She had been a girl at the time of the Norman Conquest of England and had fled to Scotland, bringing with her another piece of the One True Cross. This relic had previously been kept at Walsingham Abbey in Norfolk and a new abbey was built at Dunfermline to house it.[2] Margaret and her brother Edward, "the aetheling," were grandchildren of King Edmund "Ironside"—Edward the Confessor's older, half-brother. As such they had a much more legitimate claim to the throne of England than William the Conqueror. By reason of Henry's marriage to Maud this claim now transferred to his children. As importantly, it brought together the royal houses of Scotland and England, forging a blood alliance with consequences for the future.

In 1163 Edward the Confessor's body was transferred to a new shrine in Westminster Abbey: one with recesses beneath it for sick pilgrims to spend the night. He had by now been canonized and was regarded as a great healer of the sick, so much so that his shrine was busy round the clock. The body was moved again (and an even more elaborate shrine constructed to house it) by Henry III, the father of Edward I.[3] In 1540, following the Reformation, the shrine was robbed of its gold and jewels and the Confessor's body buried elsewhere in the Abbey. The shrine was restored by Mary I but again, at the time of Oliver Cromwell's puritans, robbed of its gold and jewels. The shrine itself, however, was not destroyed, and it is this, the only surviving, medieval, saint's shrine in all of England, that visitors see today.

Entering the abbey for the first time through the north entrance or "Solomon's Porch," I found myself facing the center of the church. To the west (my right) lay the nave: the more public area of the church. Immediately ahead was the sanctuary leading to the high altar and to the east of this was the area reserved for royalty. It was in here, not far from the Shrine of Edward the Confessor, where I found the coronation chair. It was much more worn than I had expected, an impression made worse because it was defaced by centuries of graffiti; it also looked rather uncomfortable to sit on. Yet despite its Spartan qualities and tatty appearance, there was still something regal about it. The handiwork of "Master Walter," it had once been covered all over with gold leaf. I could imagine how wonderful this must have looked when it was intact. For although most of it has been worn away with time, here and there traces remained, giving a tantalizing glimpse of late thirteenth century royal splendor.

The design of the chair was also well thought-out, and I could see that it had clearly been intended to symbolize "Solomon's Seat"—the throne on which this wisest of Old Testament kings had sat while dispensing justice to the people of ancient Israel. The back of the chair rose up to a triangle which, fringed with carved flames, was clearly emblematic of the Holy Trinity. On either side of this "Trinity" and aligned with the rear corners were two wooden pillars. There had originally been four of these—one from each corner of the chair and rising much higher to terminate in crocheted finials. I assumed that, although there was no trace of it today, these had once supported some sort of canopy. Below these pillars stretched out the armrests or at least what would have been armrests had they been accessible for further joinery (including curved "balustrades") made them unusable to an occupant of the chair. This meant that while waiting to be crowned, the seated occupant had nowhere to put his or her hands except on the lap.

Supporting the feet of the chair were four small lions and slotted into a shelf above these I could just make out the Stone of Destiny. Not much of the Stone was visible, but it seemed strange nonetheless that this simple, unadorned block was possibly the most valuable item in the entire abbey. For strip away the artistic merit of the numerous tomb effigies and the more obvious value of the church's gold and silver, this could be said to be the very foundation stone of Britain. As a symbol of royal authority it was priceless.

I had with me a guidebook to the abbey which, after reiterating the story of how Edward I had taken the stone from Scotland, confirmed the story told to me by the old man in Tel Aviv that it was Jacob's Pillow but also furnished further details as to how it came to be in Britain:

> "Tradition identifies this stone with the one upon which Jacob rested his head at Bethel—'And Jacob rose up early in the morning and took the stone that he had for his pillow, and set it up for a pillar, and poured oil upon the top of it.' (Gen. 38: 18) Jacob's sons carried it to Egypt and from thence it passed to Spain with King Gathelus, son of Cecrops, the builder of Athens. About 700 BC it appears in Ireland, whither it was carried by the Spanish king's son Simon Brec on his invasion of that island. There it was placed upon the sacred hill of Tara and called Lia-Fail, the "fatal" stone, or "stone of destiny," for when the Irish kings were seated upon it at coronations, the stone groaned aloud if the claimant was of royal race, but remained silent if he was a pretender. Fergus II (d. 501), the founder of the Scottish monarchy, and one of the Blood Royal of Ireland, received it in Scotland, and King Kenneth (d. 860) finally deposited it in the monastery of Scone (846). Setting aside the earlier myths it is certain that it had been for centuries an object of veneration to the Scots, who fancied that 'while it remained in the country, the State would be unshaken.' Upon this stone their kings, down to John Balliol, were crowned, and it is said that the following distich had been engraved upon it by Kenneth:
>
> *Ni fallat fatum, Scoti quocunque locatum*
> *Invenient lapidum regnare tenentur ibidem.*[4]

A prophecy which was fulfilled at the accession of James VI of

Scotland and I of England [1603]."[5]

This seemed to confirm much of what the old man had told me about our present Queen Elizabeth II being crowned while sitting on Jacob's Pillow Stone, assuming, that is, that the legend was true. The story of Gathelus, whoever he might have been and the epic journey of the stone from Egypt, via Spain, to Ireland and then to Scotland were all news to me. How, when, or why such a difficult journey could have been undertaken seemed to lie outside of accepted recorded history. Accordingly, I could see why the authors of the *Official Guide* had found it necessary to "set aside the earlier myths,"[6] for even if medieval deans and monarchs had been willing to believe such legends, in the skeptical 70s this was no longer an option, because without archaeological evidence to support these legends, to admit to believing them would excite only derision from the intelligentsia. Nevertheless, perhaps because they really did believe this was Jacob's Pillow Stone, the Dean and Chapter had recorded the legends in the abbey guide. For this I felt grateful.

There were two further footnotes in the guide that were also of interest. The first concerned the stone's physical dimensions and weight. It said that it was 26¾" x 16¾" x 10¾" and that it weighed 458 lb.[7] That meant it was a truly hefty piece of rock, weighing in at over four hundred weight. This explained the iron carrying rings attached to its sides. Since the rock was too heavy to lift in the normal way, it made sense that several men would lift it together. This would most easily be accomplished by passing a strong pole through these rings and using it to lift the stone. The only snag with this theory was that it made nonsense of the Jacob's Pillow legend, for if he existed at all, he would have lived in the Bronze Age. At that time iron was extremely rare, the only available source being meteorites. The Egyptians used a small amount of this naturally occurring iron for the manufacture of certain special implements they used in religious rituals, but a shepherd such as Jacob would not have had access to such material; even if he had, he would not have wasted it on making carrying rings for a large lump of stone. The conclusion was that they must have been inserted much later than this—perhaps even on the orders of Edward I himself.

It was not until 2001, several years after the Stone of Destiny had been sent back to Scotland, that I went back to Westminster Abbey, this time to visit the library. First, though, I was curious to see how the coronation seat looked now that it no longer fulfilled its primary func-

tion of providing a storage space in which to keep the stone. Entering
once more through the north doorway, I discovered it had been moved
and found the chair in a roped-off area, immediately behind the tomb
of King Henry V. Though it had pride of place close to what was once
the apex of the old church, it looked quite out of place.[8] Without the
stone in its base, the throne seemed dead. I saw how today it resembles
a discarded stage prop rather than arguably the most important piece
of furniture in the kingdom. In the abbey, too, there was a sense of loss.
It was a feeling that was difficult for me describe but could be likened
to visiting a friend's house after one of his parent's has died. Similarly, I
had the sense that the removal of the stone had affected the abbey staff
in a quite profound way although they were not going to admit to
strangers how upset they were. Placing the empty throne in such a
prominent position was a soundless cry from the heart: it was both a
celebration of what was left (the chair) but also testimony to the act of
political vandalism which had taken place (the removal of the stone).

Leaving the chair to the swarming tourists, I moved on to the library.
At one time every abbey had a library but as a result of the Reformation
nearly all of these have been either destroyed or dispersed. Fortunately,
because of its royal connections, this library has been preserved. Entry
was through a doorway off the cloister and up some narrow stairs. Entering the library itself was like passing through a time warp into the
seventeenth century; it looked virtually untouched since the days Sir
Christopher Wren was put in charge of the abbey's restoration by King
Charles II. I could see rows of leather bound volumes, many of them
extremely valuable, gathering dust on antique shelves in the high-
ceilinged room. At the far end of the main room was a rickety staircase
leading into an attic which looked as though it hadn't changed one iota
since the time when bombs were raining down on London in the blitz
of 1940. Having made an appointment by phone, I was expected and a
selection of books referring to the Stone of Destiny had already been
set aside for me. These were now brought in for my inspection by a
middle-aged lady who, in keeping with her surroundings, was straight
out of an Agatha Christie novel.

I took my place at the end of one of two tables and began examining
the pile of books before me, but I quickly discovered that only two were
really relevant. The first, published in 1996 by Historic Scotland, was
entitled *The Stone of Destiny: Symbol of Nationhood*. It gave the dimensions
of the stone in millimeters as 670 x 420 x 265, which in Imperial mea-

sures translates as 26⅜" x 16½" x 10⅜": in other words slightly different from those published in the *Official Guide* of 1973. At 152 kg (336 lb.), the listed weight was considerably less than the earlier figure of 458 lb. Since 336 lb. is exactly three hundred–weight (one hundred–weight is 112 lb.), this seemed a surprisingly exact figure for such a rough stone, chipped and pitted with age. So reluctantly I concluded that this was a guesstimate; in reality nobody had actually weighed the stone.

The other book, entitled *The Coronation Stone*, was a small, hardback volume that was published in Edinburgh in 1869. Its author, William F. Skene, was quite famous in his day as a researcher (and for much of the time debunker) of ancient myths. I had come across him before while writing *The Holy Kingdom*.[9] Skene brought together the evidence of earlier historians as he sought to trace the legend of the Stone of Destiny to its roots. His primary sources were John of Fordun's (died 1384) *Chronicle of the Scottish Nation*, an edition of which Skene had himself edited and published in 1872; William Rishanger's *Opus Chronicum* (written c. 1327); and Hector Boece's *History of the Scottish People* (published 1527).

I was interested to see that, quoting from Rishanger, he presented the account of the crowning of John Balliol on the Stone (1292), which was mentioned in the Westminster guide book and that this included the legend that the stone was the same as was used by Jacob as his pillow:

> "John de Balliol, on the following feast of St Andrew's, placed upon the regal stone, which Jacob placed under his head when he went from Bersabee to Haran, was solemnly crowned in the church of the canons regular at Scone."[10]

John Balliol was the last Scottish king to be crowned on the stone at Scone prior to its removal by Edward I. Since William Rishanger was writing about this in 1327, this was proof positive that the story of the stone being Jacob's Pillow went back to at least this time. I suspected, however, that the legend was probably much older than this.

Looking further on in Skene's book I found he also made several references to the legend of Gathelus having come from Egypt to Spain, apparently bringing with him a mysterious chair.

> "Neolus, a Greek, has a son called Gaythelus, who goes to Egypt, marries Scota, daughter of Pharaoh, king of

Egypt and leads the remnant of the people who were not drowned in the Red Sea (viz. while pursuing Moses and the Israelites during the Exodus of the Israelites) through Africa to Spain. One of his descendants, a king of Spain, has several sons, and sends one of them, Simon Brec, to Ireland, to whom he gave 'Marmoren Cathedra,' the marble chair, diligently and carefully sculpted by ancient art, on which the kings of Spain, of Scottish race, were wont to sit . . . He adds that of the origin of the stone there were two accounts: one that Gaythelus brought it from Egypt; the other, that Simon Brec having cast anchor on the shore of Ireland, and again weighed anchor in consequence of a storm, raised with his anchor a stone of marble, cut in the shape of a chair."[11]

Skene explains the strange story (which he derives from Fordun) of Simon Brec dredging up the coronation seat from the seabed off Ireland by referring to another document, the *Chronicon Rhythmicum*: "The 'Chronicon Rhythmicum,' which may be classed with Fordun as an authority, gives the same account, stating, however, that Gaythelus brought the stone, which it calls 'Lapis Pharaonis,' or Pharaoh's Stone from Egypt, and applies to it the epithet of 'anchora viti' (anchor of life), probably the origin of Fordun's second account that it was raised with an anchor."[12]

There are quite a number of versions of John of Fordun's *Chronicle of the Scottish Nation* with small variations between them. Although not all mention the "Pharaoh's stone," they do, consistently, carry the story of a migration from Egypt. An earlier source for this migration story is the *Historia Brittonum* of Nennius, which was compiled in its present form in the tenth century though parts of it were clearly written as early as the sixth. It contains the following:

"According to the most learned among the Scots, if any one desires to learn what I am now going to state, Ireland was a desert, and uninhabited, when the children of Israel crossed the Red Sea, in which, as we read in the Book of the Law, the Egyptians who followed them were drowned. At that period, there lived among this people, with a numerous family a Scythian of noble birth, who

had been banished from his country, and did not go to
pursue the people of God. The Egyptians who were left,
seeing the destruction of the great men of their nation,
and fearing lest he should possess himself of their territory, took counsel together, and expelled him. Thus reduced, he wandered forty-two years in Africa, and arrived
with his family at the altars of the Philistines, by the Lake
of Osiers. Then passing between Rusicada and the hilly
country of Syria, they travelled by the River Malva through
Mauritania as far as the Pillars of Hercules; and crossing
the Tyrrhene Sea, landed in Spain, where they continued
many years, having greatly increased and multiplied
Thence, a thousand and two years after the Egyptians
were lost in the Red Sea, they passed into Ireland, and
the district of Dalrieta. At that period, Brutus, who first ex-
ercised the consular office, reigned over the Romans; and
the state, which before was governed by regal power,
was afterwards ruled, during four hundred and forty-seven
years, by consuls, tribunes of the people, and dictators."[13]

According to Roman historians, Brutus, the first consul of Rome (after
the expulsion of Rome's last king, Tarquinius Superbus) became consul
around 509 BC, so if Nennius is to be believed, the Scots arrived in
Ireland around this time.

This story of a Scottish migration from the Mediterranean area was
evidently well known in the medieval period, so much so that when in
1320 the nobility of Scotland wrote their famous letter to the pope, the
"Declaration of Arbroath," they included this legend as part of their argument that their country should not be subject to the crown of England:

"We know, Most Holy Father and Lord, and from the
chronicles and books of the ancients, that among other
illustrious nations, ours, to wit the nation of the Scots, has
been distinguished by many honours; which passing from
greater Scythia through the Mediterranean Sea and Pillars
of Hercules, and sojourning in Spain among the most sav-
age tribes through a long course of time, could nowhere
be subjugated by any people however barbarous; and

coming thence one thousand two hundred years after the
outgoing of the people of Israel, they, by many victories
and infinite toil, acquired for themselves the possessions
of the West (viz. Scotland) which they now hold."[14]

The same basic story of this migration is also repeated in the Irish
Annals of Clonmacnoise. Here the wandering Scythians are referred to as
"sons of Miletus": Miledh or Miletus being an alternative name for
Gathelus ("Gallo"):

"The most part of our Irish Chronicles agree that the sons
of Miletus came to this land in the beginning of the destruction of Troy, and that Hermon and Heber sons of the
said Miletus reigned together jointly when Agamemnon
with his Gretians came to that destruction. The occasion
of their coming is as follows. In the year after the flood (of
Noah) 1245 being about the 12th year of the reign of David
king of Israel and Judah, Gallo the son of Billus king of
Scythia after surnamed Miletus of Spain for his many and
great exploits, hearing of the great wars which the Egyptians held then with their neighbouring countries, being
before in some displeasure at home for the strife that grew
between him and his kinsmen for the kingdom of Scythia
and being also himself much given to war, ambitious of
honour and desirous to increase his name (as the manner
of his country was) passed out of Scythia with a number
of his friends, kinsmen and followers into Egypt, where
he was no sooner arrived than well entertained by the
Egyptians, and in short time after did so well acquit himself in their service, that he was made general of their
armies and with all married the daughter of Symedes then
the greatest prince in Egypt or Pharao as they did then
commonly call their monarch, his other daughter was
married to Solomon, King of Jerusalem. This Symedes or
Symenides by other authors is called also Silagh and became so great and mighty, that he had in his army 1200
chariots, 60,000 horses, and 400,000 footmen.

After the death of king Solomon and also after the departure of Gallo out of Egypt he (viz. Symedes) entered

with the same (*viz.* his army) into the city of Jerusalem, ransacked the city spoiled the Jews, and carried away all their treasure and jewels with him into Egypt."[15]

The *Annals of Clonmacnoise* have quite a bit to say about the Stone of Destiny too, although they attribute its manufacture to the craftsmanship of an earlier race in Ireland, the "Twathy de Danann" (or *Tuatha de Danaan*), who it says were vanquished by the sons of Miletus:

"This people Twathy de Danann were most notable Magicians and would work wonderful things thereby; when they pleased, they would trouble both sea and land, darken both sun and moon at their pleasure. They did frame a great broad stone which they called Lya Fail, or the stone of Ireland, by their art and placed the same at Tarragh, which by Enchantment had this property: when anyone was born to whom to be King of Ireland was predestinated, as soon as the party so born stood upon this stone forthwith the stone would give such a shouting noise that it was heard from sea to sea, throughout the whole kingdom, which presently would satisfy the party standing on the stone, and all the rest of his future fortune to the right of the crown. This stone remained a long time in the King of Ireland's palace of Taragh, whereon many kings and queens were crowned until it was sent over into Scotland by the King of Ireland with his son Fergus, who was created the first King of Scotland on that stone and for a long time after all the Kings of Scotland received their crowns thereon until the time of King Edward the first, who took the same as a monument from thence into England in the wars between him and Scotchmen & placed it in Westminster Abbey, where many a King of England have been likewise crowned thereupon and is to be seen there amongst other monuments this day."[16]

There are other Irish chronicles, too, that mention the arrival of the Milesians and the founding of the palace of Tara, notably *The Annals of the Four Masters*:

M3500.1

The fleet of the sone of Milidh came to Ireland at the end
of this year, to take it from the Tuatha De Dananns; and
they fought the battle of Sliabh Mis with them on the third
day after landing. In this battle fell Scota, the daughter of
Pharaoh, wife of Milidh (Miletus or Gathelus); and the grave
of Scota is *to be seen* between Sliabh Mis and the sea . . .

M3502.2

Tea, daughter of Lughaidh, son of Ith, whom Eremhon
(Milidh's son Heremon) married in Spain, to the repudia-
tion of Odhbha, was the Tea who requested of Eremhon a
choice hill, as her dower, in whatever place she should
select it, that she might be interred therein, and that her
mound and her gravestone might be thereon raised, and
where every prince ever to be born of her race should
dwell. The guarantees who undertook to execute this for
her were Amhergin Gluingeal and Emhear Finn. The hill
she selected was Druim Caein, i.e. Teamhair. It is from
her it was called, and in it was she interred. [17]

The Irish version of Nennius' *Historia Brittonum* confirms the presence
of the Lia–fail at "Teamhar" or Tara: " . . . These are the three wonders of
Teamhar, . . . the Lia Fail, i.e. the stone which shouted under every king
whom it recognised in the sovereignty of Teamhar."[18]

Now I have been around medieval chronicles long enough to know
that they are often anything but an accurate reportage of history. Firstly
the chronicler himself is often not in full possession of the facts that he
is writing about and is liable to fill in any lacunae with events of his
own imagination. Add into this a bias of interest and personal prejudice
or that of his patron(s), and it is clear that it would be foolhardy to take
these reports at face value; however, so too, in my opinion, is the reverse approach (adopted by all too many historians) of dismissing all
such material as "mythical." To do that is to lose the baby with the bath
water and in so doing deny ourselves what is often the only way of
gaining access to the truth. Of one thing I am clear and this is that
whatever the truth in the legends concerning the Stone's origins and
the migrations of the Scots, it is a major relic of the past and what
happens to it matters.

Given these facts, then it seems to me to be eminently sensible to use the ancient texts as raw material in our search for truth concerning the origins, purpose, and history of the Stone of Destiny. It is, therefore, worth listing the salient points of the legend in its various renditions:

1) The stone is to be equated with Jacob's Pillow/Pillar stone: the one which he is said to have rested his head while dreaming of a ladder reaching to heaven (Gen. 28).[19]

2) The Stone was taken from Egypt and brought to Ireland via Spain by the family of a Scythian–Greek mercenary called either Gathelus or Miledh (Miletus), who had married a pharaoh's daughter called Scota. Alternatively, the Stone was made by the Tuatha de Danaan, an earlier group of immigrants who arrived in Ireland a century or more before the Milesians, and was simple taken over by the latter. In either event, the Stone was kept at Tara: a royal palace built for a Princess Tea (Tamar), who married Eremon (Heremon): a King of Ireland who was also the son of Miletus and Scota.

3) When the Scots emigrated from Ireland to Britain in the sixth century, they took the stone with them. It was deposited at Iona Abbey, the royal religious foundation of St. Columba. The first independent King of the Dalriada Scots, Aidan mac Gabran, was crowned by St. Columba while sitting on the Stone.

4) The Stone was moved by Kenneth MacAlpin either directly from Iona or via Dunstaffnage Castle (on the mainland and not far from Iona) to Scone. He became the first king of both Scots and Picts and was also crowned while sitting on the stone.

5) This stone was captured by King Edward I of England and taken back to Westminster Abbey in 1296.

Reflecting on these elements of the myth, I decided I would take a journey to Scotland and metaphorically back in time. My first port of call would be Edinburgh (where the stone is now), then Scone, and finally Iona. I already had many ideas concerning the origins of the stone, but before putting these on paper and publishing them for the world to see, I first wanted to look at the Scottish connection. It would turn out to be well worth the trouble.

3

Isles of the Sea and Legends of Migration

John Major's decision to send the Stone of Destiny back to Scotland reminded me of its existence. Having only recently co-authored *The Orion Mystery*,[1] I was intrigued by the legend of the stone's Egyptian/Israelite origins, and it was not long before I found geometric evidence (which will be presented in a later chapter) indicating that this might be so. Nevertheless it had been over thirty years since I had last seen it, so in 2009 I decided to put this right. Since it was no longer in Westminster, this meant a trip to Scotland. To make such a journey more worthwhile I decided that I would visit Scone and Iona as well as Edinburgh, which is where the stone currently resides. I chose these locations not for their scenic beauty—for which they are justly famous—but rather because the legends say they were staging posts in the stone's long journey from Egypt to London.

No one would disagree that the history of the Stone of Destiny is

intricately woven with that of Scotland itself. Indeed, we cannot properly understand the former without first getting a grip on the latter.
Unfortunately, this is not quite as straight forward as most people think,
for Scotland (like England and Wales) has two divergent histories. The
first history, which we may call the orthodox, is rather minimalist in
scope. Heavily dependent upon archaeology and references made to
northern Britain in the works of a few accepted authorities, it leaves out
much of the detail to be found in the medieval chronicles. The second,
which is more romantic, relies heavily on traditions that, because they
are less tangible than the bric-a-brac of archaeology, are somewhat suspect. Nevertheless we should not ignore them, for if we want to truly
understand the stone's significance, they, too, need to be assessed.

The orthodox history of Scotland begins in earnest with the writings
of the Roman historian Tacitus. He tells us of the Caledonians who in
his eyes were a barbarian people and on account of their predilection
for tattooing their bodies, the Romans called "Picts."[2] In AD 83, southern
Britain having been more or less pacified, the Roman governor of Britain, Gnaeus Julius Agricola (Tacitus' father-in-law), led his legions deep
into the Caledonian heartland. A great battle was fought at *Mons
Graupius*, a location thought to be somewhat north of Perth in the region of what are today called the Grampian Mountains. Although the
Romans won this battle, they made little attempt to follow up their
victory. In any case, Agricola was recalled to Rome by the Emperor
Domitian, who was jealous of the fame his exploits won for him. He
was forced to accept early retirement, leaving the campaign against the
Caledonians incomplete. Thereafter the Romans, who had little interest
in settling the barren mountains of northern Scotland themselves, pur-
sued a policy of containment rather than wholesale conquest. To facili-
tate this, in AD 121 the Emperor Hadrian ordered the building of a
seventy-mile long wall that still runs from just north of Newcastle-on-
Tyne on the east coast of Britain to the Solway Firth on the west. It
effectively divided the island of Britain into two parts: a Romanized
south and an independent, barbarian north.

For some twenty years Hadrian's Wall formed the northern frontier
of Roman Britain. During this time the region of lowland Scotland immediately to the north of the wall (but south of the Forth and Clyde
Rivers) formed a sort of buffer state that insulated Roman Britain from
the Caledonians proper. Within the buffer state, the tribes were semi-
Romanized: enjoying the benefits of trade without too much political

MAP 1: ROMANS IN SCOTLAND

interference. However, after Hadrian's death (AD 138) his successor, Antoninus Pius, decided to solidify Rome's influence in this buffer zone by building a new, much shorter wall further north. This one, really more a turf rampart than a wall, ran between the western extremity of the Firth of Forth to the eastern extremity of the Clyde Estuary. Thirty-nine miles long and with fortresses every few miles, it more or less linked what are now the cities of Edinburgh and Glasgow. This meant that "Pictavia," the Roman name for the region north of this wall, was now fully separated from the region between the two walls.

This situation did not go uncontested, and there were frequent invasions of Roman Britain by the Picts beyond the Antonine Wall, often aided by their compatriots living south of it. Sometimes these invaders even penetrated south of Hadrian's Wall, threatening the Roman colonial city of York. To put an end to such uprisings, in AD 208 the Emperor Septimius Severus took a large army to Britain with the intention of utterly exterminating the Picts. Fortunately for them, he died (at York) in AD 211 before he could fully achieve his war aims.[3] Severus was succeeded by his evil son Bassianus ("Caracalla"), who had little interest in conquering Pictavia and immediately returned to Rome to press his claims as Emperor. Though bad for Rome this gave the Picts a breathing space and allowed them to recover their strength.

After the visit of Severus, Roman Britain enjoyed relative peace for over a century. Then, as Roman power weakened in the mid-fourth century, the Picts began once more to raid the wealthy but relatively weak province to their south. To deal with this latest threat, in AD 367 Emperor Valentinian sent over Theodosius, his most trusted general. As part of a long-term strategy, Theodosius renamed the region between the walls Valentia, while at the same time reorganizing the command structure of the army guarding it. Peace, however, proved to be short-lived. By now the Roman Empire was starting to fracture, and in Britain, in particular, there was a tendency for the local governor to take on the role of a regional "emperor." In AD 385 Magnus Maximus, *de facto* emperor of Britain, took the bulk of his army to Gaul as he made a bid to usurp the entire Roman Empire of the West. The attempt failed and in AD 389 he was executed. However, because the men he took with him never returned to Britain, the garrison manning the walls was much reduced. In AD 406 the already weakened Roman province of Britain was made weaker still when another British emperor with ambitions, Constantine, further depleted it of its fighting men by sending a second army to Gaul—this time to drive out the Vandals. Though they were successful in saving Gaul, the Vandals were channeled into Spain instead, and Constantine's army didn't return to Britain either. The final nail in the coffin came in AD 410 when the Romans withdrew from Britain altogether. Thenceforward the island, now seriously short of fighting men, was wide open and having to deal with invasions from all directions.

The Anglo-Saxon conquest of what was to become England need not concern us here. However, what is important to note is that the Angles, who founded the successor kingdom of Northumbria in northeast England, also settled in large numbers in the southeastern part of Scotland—what we now call Lothian. The western part of "Valentia," (south of the Clyde and including Dumfries and Galloway) was for a long time retained by the Welsh-speaking Romano-Britons. Meanwhile the northwest—the coastal region and islands that had previously been the western part of Pictavia—was invaded from northern Ireland by the Scots. They renamed their new land Dalriada.

At the center of our story and an essential connecting link to everything else stands the remarkable personage of Columba or "Columkille" as he is more generally known in Ireland.[4] Because he is such a key personage, I decided to start my search by making him a special subject

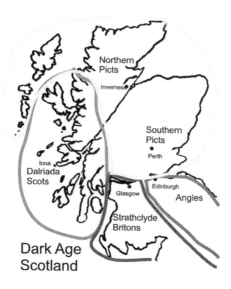

MAP 2: DARK AGE SCOTLAND

of investigation culminating with a personal pilgrimage (which I shall describe in a later chapter) to the monastery that he founded on the Hebridean island of Iona. Scotland, however, is not where he began life: that honor belongs to Glen Columkille in Donegal, a county in the far northwest of Ireland. Curiously enough, by one of those strange coincidences that shapes our lives, this little village lies just few miles from Carrick: a not much larger village where my mother-in-law was born and where my wife still has many relatives. Consequently, without realizing that it would have any importance on my later work, I have visited Glen Columkille on several occasions in the past. I can attest that, even now, it is a special place and in some ways gives a clearer view of the Irish soul than the bars of Dublin or the rolling downlands of Tipperary.

Donegal, and especially its Atlantic coastline, is a place humbled by the sea. Here, with agriculturally poor soils, a landscape bereft of trees and an economy dependent of sheep and fish, people have for thousands of years had to huddle together for their very survival. They still cut peat for their fires, round up sheep, go fishing, sing in the pubs, and play musical instruments: mainly guitars, violins, and flutes but sometimes, as of old, harps and bagpipes. On Saturdays the men watch football or, just as likely, hurling.[5] Meanwhile, the women of Donegal have always been exceptionally busy. Even today they weave cloth and knit jumpers using styles that are probably not much different from how they were in the time of St. Columba. These Donegal women are often strikingly beautiful, with raven dark hair, blue eyes, and exceptionally pale skin that freckles or burns easily in the sun.[6]

Glencolumkille itself is a microcosm of Donegal as a whole but with the added difference that much of the village is today a museum. Down near the seashore but afforded some shelter from crosswinds by steep cliffs on either side are some of the oldest cottages in Ireland. It is hard to say just how old these are—three hundred, five hundred, a thousand years old? And it doesn't really matter. In form—rectangular in shape, with thick walls of stone, small windows, and thatched roofs—they are exactly the same as those that would have been common in the area at the time of St. Columba. Because of the frequent storms that blow up without warning from the Atlantic, the thatch is tied down with ropes anchored to pegs driven into the walls. Inside each house is a turf or peat fire that burns throughout nearly all the year. The fire provided heat enough for the wives of fishermen to weave cloth or knit jumpers: skills which though still highly prized in the area are today under threat from foreign imports. This, then, is Glencolumkille today: a window into Irish life as it might have been lived in the time of Columba himself, yet as different as can be imagined from my own home town in the suburbs of London or, indeed, anywhere else in southeast England. Though it might be different from England, the desolate yet beautiful county of Donegal is very like parts of Scotland and not just because of similarities in climate.

If there are similarities now between this northwest extremity of Ireland and the Hebridean islands of Scotland, then they were probably even more marked in the sixth century—a time when the Scotland was in turmoil. Scots–Irish and born in 521, Columba was of royal blood. He was taught by St. Finian of Clonard (470-552), who was educated in Wales and is one of the early saints of Ireland; indeed as an Irish saint, he is perhaps second only to St. Patrick in importance. In ca. 520 Finian founded Clonard Abbey in County Meath, which until its destruction at the hands of the Vikings was a major center of learning. Here Columba had a falling out with his mentor over the ownership of a psalter he himself had decorated. As a result of this dispute, war broke out and in 561 many men—perhaps as many as three thousand—were killed at the

Battle of Dreimhne. Columba was filled with remorse at this senseless loss of life and vowed to make amends for the Christians who had died in the battle by converting pagans to Christianity.

By this time his own people, the Gaels or Scots-Irish, were busy establishing colonies on the islands and peninsulas of northwest Britain (Argyll). Ordered into exile from his native land of Ireland, it was only natural for him to join them. Thus it was that in 563 he and twelve disciples established a small monastery on the remote island of Iona, which is situated off the southwest coast of the larger inner Hebridean island of Mull. Thenceforth this would be his base while he went about the major task of his life—the conversion of the Picts.

Sources vary as to exactly what happened next, but shortly after he is said to have had a meeting with a Pictish king called Bridei at the latter's fortress near Inverness. The king is said to have been so impressed by Columba's miracle working (which according to some accounts included scaring away the Loch Ness Monster) that he immediately converted to Christianity. Other accounts are not so clear-cut and say that Bridei himself remained a pagan. Either way there is no doubting that Columba's mission was successful and that huge numbers of the Picts converted to Christianity around this time.

Columba's great friend and patron was Aidan MacGabran, who in 574 succeeded his kinsman Connall as king of the Dalriada Scots. Aidan was crowned (by Columba) on Iona, thereby confirming the island's importance and setting a precedent for the future kings of Dalriada. In 575 Columba returned with Aidan to Ireland in order to establish the latter's overlordship with respect to the Scots of Ireland. Their mission seems to have been successful, for from then on the Dalriada Scots, previously only a colony of the Irish Scots became the dominant partner.

Thus it was that in the Dark Ages what would later become the Kingdom of Scotland was inhabited by four distinct national groups, all of whom were Christians of one church or another. Argyll and the Hebridean islands closest to Ireland were the home of the Dalriada Scots; north of the Antonine Wall and north and east of Dalriada was the kingdom of the Picts; south of the Firth of Forth and north of Hadrian's Wall was inhabited by Anglo-Saxons (who most of the time were part of the Kingdom of Northumbria), while west of them and south of the Dalriada Scots were the Strathclyde Britons. These four nations were often at war with one another and power shifted between them. How they came to be a united kingdom with a single king who was crowned on the Stone of Destiny tends to be glossed over in modern history books. However, after studying the matter in some detail, I am sure that it had at least something to do with the stone's supposed supernatural power to assert a hidden destiny. The next stage of my own journey was to make a pilgrimage of my own to once more see the stone up close and this meant going to Edinburgh.

The Castle Built on Rock

Edinburgh, today the capital of Scotland, is arguably the most attractive city in all of Britain. With its historic center situated a few miles south of the Firth of Forth, it is sometimes referred to as the Athens of the North. In part this is due to its strong philosophical tradition that grew up in the eighteenth century. Men such as Adam Smith, David Hume, John Millar, and Thomas Brown laid the bedrock of a new philosophy of economics that in the nineteenth century was to provide the theoretical basis for what we now refer to as capitalism. During the eighteenth and nineteenth centuries Edinburgh prospered as never before. The Act of Union between Scotland and England (1707) opened up both a much larger domestic market and also provided possibilities for Scots to be involved in the burgeoning British Empire in America. This brought wealth to the city, some of which is still visible today in the form of architecture, much of it in the classical style of Vitruvius.[7] Mercifully spared from the pounding that London took in the Second World War and also the architectural vandalism that disfigured so many British cities in the "swinging" sixties, Edinburgh—or at least its center—has retained its streets of Georgian town houses. In addition, many public buildings—such as libraries, museums, banks, and even some shops—are fronted by Parthenon-styled colonnaded porticos. This amplifies the classical feel to the city, further adding to the sense that Edinburgh is a reincarnation of ancient Athens.

Rising above the city are several extinct volcanoes. Long since eroded by time, weather, and ice, all that remains of these are the basalt plugs that once lay in the center of their cones. These plugs rise to several hundred feet.[8] They dominate the skyline, brooding over the city that has grown up at their feet. It is little wonder, therefore, that from time immemorial one of these rocky mounds has been used as the principle fortress in the area. The Romans, who occupied this area of Scotland on and off for three hundred years, built a *castra* [military camp] on top of the rock but long before their arrival it was occupied by a *caer* or Iron Age hill fort. After the Romans departed Britain's shores, the city and surrounding area of Lothian fell first to the southern Picts (about whom we will be saying much more later). Then, in 617 or thereabouts, the city, along with its castle, was captured by Edwin, King of the Angles of Northumbria, and he renamed it *Edwinesburgh* (now Edinburgh) after himself.

Today the rock is crowned by Edinburgh Castle, which seems well nigh impregnable when looked at from the back. However this bastion has been successfully stormed on a number of occasions since Edwin's time. Off and on for some four hundred years, Lothian continued to be considered as part of Northumbria. Then in 1018 Malcolm II, king of the Picts and Scots, decisively defeated the Northumbrians at the Battle of Carham. Lothian was ceded by England shortly afterwards, and thereafter Edinburgh became a Scottish city. The castle was sieged several more times after that, the last being the "long siege" of 1571-3 at the time when civil war raged between forces loyal to Mary, Queen of Scots and her son James VI. Still a royal castle, today it is, like the Tower of London, a mecca for tourists from all over the world.

It was with all this history buzzing in my brain that I made my way to the foot of the castle. The main objective of my visit was to examine the Stone of Destiny, but I was also keen to see the "Honours of Scotland" as the Scottish Crown Jewels are known. A signpost told me that I would find all of these items displayed together in the main castle complex at the very top of the hill. On my way up there I stopped by St. Margaret's Chapel, which I found strangely moving. As we have mentioned, in 1070 Margaret, a niece of Edward the Confessor, married Malcolm III, king of the Scots. This chapel, said to be the oldest building in Edinburgh, was built for her own private use. I could imagine her, who history tells us was in manner more like a nun than a queen, praying on the very spot on which I was standing taking pictures of the stained glass windows. One of these was of her, the royal arms of Edward the Confessor above her head, while another was of St. Columba, whom she evidently held in very high esteem.

Margaret's husband Malcolm was directly descended from Kenneth MacAlpin through a line of kings whose names are known to history. They include his father Duncan I, who in Shakespeare's "Scottish play" was murdered by Macbeth. The link between the royal houses of Scotland and England continued when Matilda, one of Margaret's daughters and therefore a great–great niece of Edward the Confessor, married Henry I of England, the youngest son of William the Conqueror. This marriage, which imported blood from the old Anglo–Saxon royal family into the Norman line, added a measure of legitimacy to the dynasty of William the Conqueror. It also meant that all future kings and queens of England would be partly Scottish.

All this seemed clear enough but what of the stone? The official history has little to say about it other than to note that it had probably always resided at Scone, the implication being that it was once the coronation seat of the Picts. Yet William Forbes Skene (1809–92), the most revered Scottish historian of his age, could not find any reference in any of the ancient annals that he consulted, Irish or Scottish, making mention of any Pictish kings (prior to Kenneth MacAlpin) ever having been crowned on the stone. In fact the earliest mention of the stone being used for a coronation is the *Scotichronicon* or "Chronicle of the Scots" which was compiled by the historian John of Fordun between 1381 and 1389. Drawing on earlier sources, he describes the coronation at Scone of Alexander III who, in 1249 and at the age of eight, was evidently inaugurated on a throne containing the Stone of Destiny:

> "And it was done that the same Earl Walter Comyn, and whole clergy, the Earls Malcolm Earl of Fife and Malise Earl of Stratherne, and the other nobles uniting with them, they immediately led the future King Alexander to the cross, which stands in the cimitarium or church-yard at the east end of the church and, having there placed him in the regal chair decked with silk cloths embroidered with gold, the Bishop of St Andrews, the others assisting him, consecrated him king, the king himself sitting, as was proper, upon the royal chair—that is the stone—and the earls and other nobles placing vestments under his feet, with bent knees before the stone. This stone is reverently preserved in that monastery (Scone) for the consecration of kings of Scotland; nor were any of the kings in wont to reign anywhere in Scotland, unless they had on receiving the name of king, first sat upon the royal stone in Scone, which was constituted by ancient kings the 'sedes superior' or principal seat, that is to say of Albania."[9]

Alexander III died in 1285, an event that was to plunge Scotland into crisis. His only surviving heir was his granddaughter, Margaret, better known as the "Maid of Norway." In 1290, though only six years old, she was betrothed to Edward's son, later to become Edward II of England. It was a bold move which would have united the two crowns of England and Scotland some three hundred years before James VI of Scotland took the throne of England. Unfortunately for both countries, she died the following year, before the marriage could take place. This plunged Scotland into turmoil as there were a number of claimants to the throne, all more distant relatives of Alexander's. As king of England, Edward was invited to resolve the issue, and he accordingly called for a conference to be held at Berwick-on-Tweed.[10] Eventually the field was narrowed down to two candidates: John of Balliol and Robert the Bruce. Edward decided in favor of Balliol, and he was duly crowned in 1292.

The coronation of Alexander III was only forty seven years before the stone was taken by Edward, yet the evidence of the stone itself—it suffers severely from wear and tear—is that it must have already been pretty ancient. After all for seven hundred years, from 1296 to 1996, it was safely tucked away under the coronation chair in Westminster Abbey. This means that any wear and tear must have occurred before it was taken to England. Not only that, if we assume that Kenneth MacAlpin (of whom more will be said later) really did sit on the stone for his coronation in 844, this still does not properly explain the wear and tear. We know that from 1259 to 1296 it was kept in Scone Abbey and looked after by the monks there. There is no reason to think that it would have been looked after any less carefully before 1259. The inference is that it is much older than historians are prepared to admit and that prior to its being moved to Scone it was the property of the Dalriada Scots.

At first sight the geology of the Stone does not appear to support this view, the following being taken from a recent book published by Historical Scotland:

> "It (the Stone of Destiny) is formed from a coarse-grained, pinkish-buff sandstone very similar to sandstones of the Lower Red Sandstone age. This stone is found in Perthshire and Angus, indeed within a few miles of Scone. It would be entirely possible therefore for the stone to have been quarried near to Scone and for it not to have

> been brought from elsewhere. Deposits of this type of
> rock are found elsewhere in Scotland but not in sufficiently
> large deposits to allow the quarrying of such a substantial
> block. It has been suggested that the stone is a cut-down
> Roman altar but it bears no evidence to support this."[11]

This would appear to be quite damning of the idea that the stone could have been brought to Scotland from Ireland let alone from the Middle East. Yet when I looked at it myself, it didn't look at all like a slab of red sandstone. I am not a geologist, but if anything, it seemed rather bluish in color. Not only that but red sandstone is found in many places around the world besides Scotland, including Egypt and Israel. Had anyone checked for matches with rock samples from these areas, I wondered. If they had, then the results have not been widely published.

The following day I took a train from Edinburgh to Perth. As the local bus service was erratic and would anyway drop me off a long way from my destination, I decided to walk from the station to Scone Palace—a distance of about three miles. On my way I stopped at the Perth Museum, which turned out to be a curiously old-fashioned institution with the collections all jumbled up together. Nevertheless, among the assorted stuffed animals, old shotguns, and portraits of long-dead local worthies, I did find a few interesting stones. There were a couple of inscribed Roman stones that proved the legions had at one time been busy in this area in a rather more permanent way than history records. In addition there was a strange pre-Christian stone head that looked very similar to pictures of some Celtic stone heads that had been sent to me from France a couple of years earlier. Stranger still was a stone with four heads sculpted into it as though they were struggling to break free: to emerge from the stone like spirits forming in ectoplasm. One looked remarkably like the TV cartoon character Homer Simpson, proving there is nothing new under the sun. Clearly even the experts were baffled by this stone because all that the caption said was: "Boulder with four carved heads, probably connected with Celtic religion. The stone was found reused in a dry stone wall at Glenfort Abernathy." We know from ancient sources that the Druids believed in reincarnation so I suspected that the stone was meant to symbolize the "Well of Souls"—the place or level of existence where according to Gnostic teachings the spirits of the dead merge between lives.

A third stone was covered in "cup-marks"—a form of decoration that is quite common with ancient stones from France as well as Britain and Ireland. The accompanying message was: "Stone with cup-markings and cross. This stone from Shenvail bears Bronze Age cup-marks on one side and an early Christian cross on the other. The cup-marked stone appears to have been deliberately Christianized, perhaps for use as a marker stone for the monastic community at Dull." I couldn't find Shenvail on my map, but Dull is not very far from Perth. Abernathy, where the "Homer" stone was found, is even closer—just a few miles from Scone on the other side of the river.

Outside the gallery in the main lobby of the museum were two larger memorial stones. The first of these was found at Collace in Perthshire in 1948. The farmer who discovered it didn't appreciate just how important it was, for until 1962 he had been using it as a paving slab and barrow ramp. It, too, was very clearly pre–Christian as it features typically Pictish designs of a mirror and a duck–billed beast that is probably meant to represent a bottle-nosed dolphin. Only the front of the other stone was visible, but a caption card informed me that the design on the back was of three hooded riders. This stone, which may have originally been pagan, had a large Irish-style cross sculpted on the front. Surrounding this and clearly dominated by it were more Pictish beasts.

The "Homer" stone and the "Celtic" head seemed silent testament to the idea that the Picts belonged to the same cultural group that inhabited Gaul in the era before the Roman invasions changed everything. These other stones, however, showed that not only did the pre-Christian Picts have an enigmatic religion of their own, but even after they became Christian, they still found ways of working traditional motifs into their art. This made rather nonsense of the idea, floated by modern historians, that it was local Picts who had carved the Stone of Destiny. Given the evidence of these stones, it seems reasonable to assume that had they done so, they would have made it much more ornate than it is. Carving out a block of sandstone and then leaving it undecorated without so much as a geometric squiggle does not fit the pattern of what we see of their art. It was not only that, but in another section of the museum they had on display a block of the local red sandstone: the type of material that geologists say the Stone of Destiny was cut from. This block was, as the name would suggest, decidedly red in color; it also had a very different texture from the Stone of Destiny. This did not seem to me to support the geologists' report that the Stone of Destiny was quarried in the local area.

Leaving the museum I walked over the bridge that spans the River Tay. With a warm October sun on my back and a cold wind blowing on my front, I walked with a spring in my step. Soon I found myself at the gateway leading into the park of Scone Palace. As the road through the park was itself the best part of a mile long, it took me a further half-hour to reach the palace itself, which looked like something out of a Jane Austen novel. This in itself was not so surprising, as the present building, which took the place of an earlier one, was only erected in 1808—around the time she was writing. With rolling meadows all around and hills in the distance, its location was picture-postcard perfect. The overall impression, however, was enhanced further by clever landscaping and the collection of trees—some of them quite rare—that were dotted throughout the park. These took away from the severity of what might have otherwise appeared a rather austere building: a square looking mansion built from the local red sandstone. My primary interest, though, was not the house but rather the "Moot" or meeting place where tradition relates that the kings of Scotland were for centuries crowned. Back in Edinburgh Castle, which I had visited the day before going to Perth, the coronation ceremony on the Moot was represented on an ornamental frieze. It depicted, in graphic form, a Dark Age king sitting on the Stone of Destiny and receiving the acclamation of the assembled nobility. The place where this was supposed to have taken place was the very spot where I was now standing and in front of me was a replica of the Stone of Destiny.

The Moot itself was a flat-topped hillock. Clearly man-made, an information sign spiked into it said that the soil used in its construction had been carried there by the nobles themselves, using their own boots to transport it. Even by the standards of medieval mythmaking, this story sounded extremely unlikely. I could only think it had come about because of the similarity between the words "moot" and "boot." What seems to me much more likely is that the Moot started life as a Bronze Age tumulus or burial mound that was erected over some very important personage or even king. Coronation on top of such a tumulus would then signify the invocation of this personage as a witness to the royal succession in just the same way as the coronation of William the Conqueror in front of the tomb of Edward the Confessor conferred authority on his dynasty.

We don't know when the custom of crowning kings at Scone started but, as we have seen, John of Fordun relates in his chronicle how in

1249 the elders of Scotland gathered on the Moot to witness the coronation of King Alexander III. This is the earliest eyewitness record we have of the Stone of Destiny being used as a throne stone, but according to tradition he was only the latest in a long line of kings to be similarly acclaimed at Scone. Back in Edinburgh opposite the frieze, depicted on a mural on either side of the entrance way leading to the Crown Jewels, there is a wall painting featuring all the kings of the Scots from Kenneth MacAlpin to Robert the Bruce.[12] While there I examined this painting thoroughly and made a careful note of their names and dates, which going backwards are as follows:

Robert the Bruce (1306–29)
John I Baliol (1292–96)
Margaret "Maid of Norway" (1286–90)
Alexander III (1249–86)
Alexander II (1214–49)
William I "the Lion" (1165–1214)
Malcolm IV (1153–65)
David I (1124–1153)
Alexander I "the Strong" (1107–24)
Edgar (1097–1107)
Donald III Ban (1094–1097)
Duncan II (1094)
Donald III Ban (1093–4)
Malcolm III "Canmore" (1058–93)
Lulach (1057–58)
Macbeth (1040–57)
Duncan I (1034–40)
Malcolm II (1005–34)
Kenneth III (997–1005)
Constantine III (995–7)
Kenneth II (971–95)
Culen "the Whelp" (966–71)
Dubh "the Black" (962–6)
Indulf (954–62)
Malcolm I (943–54)
Constantine II (900–43)
Donald II (889–900)
Eochaid/Gini (878–889)

Aed (877–8)
Constantine I (862–77)
Donald I (858–62)
Kenneth MacAlpin (843–58)

The progression of these kings was not always father to son: some of them were brothers, cousins, or even more distant relatives of the previous king. It was, however, a consistent dynasty, and it begins with Kenneth MacAlpin, who legend says brought the Stone of Destiny to Scone following a Scottish takeover of the lands of the Picts. How King Kenneth found himself in the position to unite the two kingdoms of Picts and Scots is in itself an interesting story. As I was now to discover, it has much to do with religion.

The Birth of the Kingdom of Scotland

It is important to remember that for most of the period from the termination of the Roman Empire (fifth century) to Kenneth's unification of Dalriada and Pictavia, most of Scotland was not known by this name. It was, as we have seen, populated by four distinctly different nations: the Picts and Dalriada Scots in the north, the Angles in Lothian, and the Brito-Welsh in Galloway and Strathclyde. These nations were not only different in language and customs but also in times of conversion to Christianity and church affiliation. The first group to be converted were the Britons of Strathclyde who are said to have adopted (or more likely readopted) Christianity as a result of the missionary efforts of St. Ninian. As he is said to have heard of the death of St. Martin of Tours while construction was underway of his missionary church at Whitherne, the center of the Ninian mission, we know he was active in ca. 397. According to the Chronicles of Scotland at the time of the fall of the Western Roman Empire, while the rest of Britain was Christian, the Picts were pagan. This, however, is not entirely true. St. Ninian had already set up missionary churches among the southern Picts: those who lived just to the north of what had been the old Antonine Wall.

Ninian himself is said to have been born in Galloway[13] and to have studied at Rome. However, as a native Briton, he was a member of the British church which, following the withdrawal of the Roman legions, had its center in Wales. Thus the doctrines, practices, and outlook of St. Ninian's church would almost certainly have been much the same as those adhered to by such Welsh saints as Teilo, Dyfrig, Samson, and David, who all lived in the fifth and sixth centuries. British churches were typically collegiate in nature. Emulating the methodology of Jesus himself, they usually featured a teacher or "saint" around whom would be gathered a circle of disciples—again usually twelve in number. These college churches were more or less self-sufficient. They were run more or less independently of the local bishops, and proud of their own apostolic foundation (through the first century missionary work of Joseph of Arimathea) paid scant regard to any central authority in Rome.

This independence of spirit meant that provided they had the means, impressive and charismatic individuals, such as Ninian, were more or less free to do as they pleased. They could build churches, proselytize among the local population, and establish missionary outposts among pagan communities that had not yet received the word of God. One such community was, of course, the Picts.

A century after the building of Ninian's church at Whitherne or the "White House," the Scots began settling in Argyll and the Isles. They, too, were already Christians, belonging to the church set up in Ireland by St. Patrick and continued after his death by his Irish and Scots-Irish disciples. Like Ninian's church Patrick's was Welsh in origin, he having come from South Wales.[14]

The Scottish invasion of northernmost Britain was checked for a while by a Pictish king called "Bruide son of Maelcon, king of the Cruitne (Picts)." In 560 he successfully drove the Scots back into the narrow coastal strip of Argyll and its neighboring islands. It is this event more than anything else that seems to have provoked the next major mission to convert the Picts—that of St. Columba. As he is a central figure in the legend of the Stone of Destiny, we will be looking more closely at his career later on. For now it is enough to mention that unlike Ninian's, his missionary efforts were mainly directed towards the northern Picts: those whose capital was on the shore of Loch Ness near to the modern day town of Inverness.[15] Meanwhile further south in 625, King Edwin of Northumbria (after whom Edinburgh is named) was converted to Christianity by Paulinus—a disciple of St. Augustine.

This is an important distinction as Augustine's church was Roman, not Brito-Welsh or Irish in origin. In 597 he arrived in Canterbury, the capital city of Kent, the oldest of the Anglo-Saxon kingdoms, with instructions from the pope that he should convert their king, Ethelbert, to the Roman branch of Christianity. As it happened, Ethelbert's wife (a

French princess) was already a Christian. No fool, Ethelbert could see the advantages of adopting her faith, too, as this would provide him with powerful allies on the continent. Thus it was that St. Augustine became the first archbishop of Canterbury: a rank that as far as Rome was concerned gave him primacy over all the Christian churches throughout Britain. In reality, however, outside of Kent his authority was rather more symbolic than actual. Most of England was still pagan while the Welsh bishops did not accept the primacy of Canterbury. They were of the opinion that their own church, which they claimed had been founded centuries earlier by Joseph of Arimathea, and the apostle Paul had primacy over this new church in Kent.

In 603 Aethelferth, the pagan king of Northumbria, won a decisive battle against Aidan, the king of the Dalriada Scots. However, in 617 Aethelferth was himself killed in battle by Raedwald, the king of East Anglia. As a consequence, Aethelferth's sons Eanfrith, Oswald, and Oswy were driven out of Northumbria. Edwin, from a rival dynasty, took over as king of Northumbria.[16] In 623 he received Paulinus, a disciple of Augustine, and was baptized by him. As a result of Edwin's conversion, Northumbria and Lothian were attached to the Augustinian church and hence to Rome. This was not to last, for in 633 Edwin and his son Osfrith were themselves killed in battle, and the sons of Aethelferth, who had been living in exile on the island of Iona, regained the kingdom of Northumbria. During their period of exile they'd been exposed to the Columban form of Christianity and consequently looked towards Iona rather than Canterbury as their spiritual home. Thus it was that St. Aidan, a disciple of Columba's, was invited to found an equivalent community to that of Iona on the Northumbrian island of Lindisfarne. In 641 Oswald was killed in battle and his brother Oswy became king of Northumbria. He went on to conquer Pictavia, or at least the southern part of it, but as all parts of his kingdom at that time championed the church of Columba, this made little difference from a religious point of view. However, this was soon to change.

In 664 with Oswy still king, a church council was held at Whitby: a monastery on the coast of Northumbria. The supposed reason for the council was to debate differences between the ways the Roman and Columban churches tonsured monks and computed Easter. However, as always, the real issue was one of power: which church was going to hold sway in Britain. In the event St. Wilfrid, a follower of the Augustine tradition, won the argument and the King Oswy decided to take his kingdom back into communication with the Augustinian church. This represented a major defeat for the Columban church, which was effectively driven out of not just Northumbria proper but also those places north of Hadrian's Wall that were under Northumbrian rule.

In 685 the Northumbrians were defeated by the Picts with major losses, including the life of their king, Ecgfrith. The Picts were now once more the major power in north Britain and at first this favored the Columban church. Soon, however, the Picts also changed sides, abandoning the Irish church in favor of the Roman. In 710 their king, Nectan, was sent to Jarrow (near Newcastle) requesting instruction in the Roman way of calculating Easter. Henceforth St. Peter, not St. Columba, was to be the patron saint of the Picts and, as in Northumbria, the Columban clergy were expelled from their monasteries and sent back to Dalriada. This was a disaster for Iona and for the Irish school of Columba which had, after all, been responsible for converting the northern Picts in the first place. Things, however, were about to get a whole lot worse. In 728 Nectan abdicated from the throne to enter a monastery. This led to fierce infighting, but by 729 Angus MacFergus had established himself as king of the Picts. In 732 he invaded Dalriada, captured the stronghold of Dunadd[17] and affirmed his position as the Scots' overlord. Further campaigns against the Britons of Strathclyde were less successful, for though in 756 he succeeded in capturing the old Brito-Welsh fortress town of Dunbarton, his army was wiped out ten days later. In the interim, however, he imported a new saint to be the patron of the Picts: St. Peter's brother, Andrew. A new church was built on the east coast at St. Andrews and what were believed to be the saint's relics were transferred there. St. Andrew very quickly became the most popular saint in all of Alba (the old name for Scotland), displacing both St. Peter and St. Columba.

All this had dire consequences for the followers of Columba, now pretty much confined to the Island of Iona. With Dalriada subjugated to the kingdom of the Picts they could only dream of one day reversing the situation. All this is well summarized by William Skene:

> "It is hardly possible to suppose that the Columban Church thus ejected from the Pictish kingdom, and her clergy deprived of their ecclesiastical establishments in that part of the country, should have quietly acquiesced in their defeat, or given up the desire and hope one day to recover

their footing among the people whom their founder had converted; and we may well believe that the whole of the Irish Church, of which they were but an offshoot, shared in the feeling. It is hardly possible, therefore, to doubt that, among the causes which led to the revolution which placed a Scottish dynasty on the Pictish throne, not the least influential must have been an effort on the part of the Columban clergy to recover possession of their old establishments."[18]

The Columban church wasn't going to accept its eclipse without fighting back, but what happened next took everyone by surprise. Towards the end of the eighth century a new military power, the Vikings, began their invasions of Britain, seriously affecting the balance of power among all the island's inhabitants. At first the Vikings contented themselves with raiding coastal settlements, stealing what they could and returning home to Scandinavia. Since abbeys and churches were repositories for quite large quantities of silver plate, gold, and jewel-encrusted books, they made very tempting targets. The Anglo-Saxon Chronicle, which was prepared for the kings of Wessex in southwest England, makes its first mention of these raiders in its entry for the year 787:

"Brihtric (a king of Wessex) took Offa's (King of Mercia, in the west Midlands) daughter Eadburg for his wife. In his days came the first three ships of the Northmen from Hõrthaland (Hardanger in Norway). The reve (sheriff) rode there, and meant to force them to the king's dwelling, because he did not know what they were; and then he was killed. Those were the first ships of Danish men (actually Norwegians) to seek out the land of the English."[19]

These may have been the first Vikings to land in southern England, but they were not to be the last. In 793 the Anglo-Saxon chronicler writes of ominous signs in the sky that seemed to be a warning from God of what was coming: "In this year fierce, foreboding omens came over the land of Northumbria, and wretchedly terrified the people. There were excessive whirlwinds, lightning storms, and fiery dragons were seen flying in the sky. These signs were followed by great famine, and shortly after in the same year, on January 8th, the ravaging of heathen men [Vikings] destroyed God's church at Lindisfarne through brutal robbery and slaughter; . . . "[20]

In 794 having already plundered Lindisfarne, Iona's daughter church in the east, the Vikings turned their attention to Jarrow.[21] The following year, in 795, they sacked Iona itself, returning again in 802, 806, and 825. The impact of these raids was devastating for the Columban Church. In 802 the wooden church built by Columba himself was burnt to the ground; in 806 sixty-eight monks were martyred and in 825 those who had replaced them, including the Abbot St. Blathmac, were also put to the sword. After this last massacre Iona was effectively abandoned, its treasures—those which had not already fallen into the hands of the raiders—were moved either to the mainland of Scotland or to Ireland.

Meanwhile Pictavia, the closest point in Britain to Norway, was also under attack. As a result of these attacks, the Picts were greatly weakened and this left the way open for a Scottish takeover. Exactly how this happened is a matter of dispute; however there is no disagreement that in 843 Kenneth MacAlpin became king of both the Picts and the Scots, or that the two nations needed to unite to face the common menace of the Vikings. It would appear that he was acceptable to both peoples because while his father Alpin was a Scot, his mother was a Pict and for them royal succession passed through the female line. In terms of religion, he seems to have favored the Columban church over that of St. Andrew's. Hence his conquest of Pictavia, if that is how he gained power, involved the return of the Columban priesthood as well as the transfer of the holy relics of St. Columba himself. To properly house these, a new church was built at Dunkeld: a town on the River Tay that is some miles upstream from Perth. Tradition suggests that the Stone of Destiny was also moved at this time, having already made the journey from Iona to a safer repository on the mainland: either Dunedd, the former capital of the Dalriada Scots or Dunstaffnage Castle.[22] So that he could be crowned in the tradition manner of a Scottish king, Kenneth MacAlpin is said to have taken the stone with him to Scone, and it was to remain there until its removal by Edward I of England in 1296. As it was King Kenneth who united the Picts and Scots into one nation, it seems not unreasonable to assume (as the Chroniclers do) that it was he who brought the Stone of Destiny to Scone, placing it on the Moot which was probably already the coronation place of the kings of Pictavia. In this way he may have been able to justify what many Picts would have seen as a usurpation of their throne by virtue of the immense authority of the ancient stone.

This is what tradition tells us—at least as recorded in some of the later chronicles of the Picts and Scots—but might we not suspect that in actuality the stone was removed at some time before Kenneth became king of the Picts and Scots? Given that the Picts were native to the north of Britain from long before the Roman invasions, they can only have regarded the Dalriada Scots as interlopers. Having finally conquered Dalriada in 735 and taken possession of Dunadd, it would be quite natural for them to appropriate the stone and take it back with them to Scone as a trophy. If this was so, then it points to a different conclusion entirely. Walter Scott's translation of the legendary inscription tells us that wherever the "sacred" stone is found, there the Scottish race shall reign. Columba's bringing it to Argyll ensured the viability of the tiny Scottish kingdom of Dalriada. If the Picts now moved it to Scone, then they were setting up the conditions for their own kingdom to be taken over by the Scottish monarchy. This, of course, happened again and in a much more significant way when Edward took the stone back to London. A little over three hundred years later James VI of Scotland became also James I of England. In other words the Scottish monarchy had, through peaceful means, taken over the much more powerful kingdom of England.

On the face of it, it seems ludicrous, even superstitious, to attribute such a takeover to the influence of the Stone of Destiny. However, if we see it as not just a lump of rock but rather as the physical embodiment of something more numinous, then this begins to make sense. Like the Spear of Destiny, it would seem that what happens to the Stone can signify changes in "higher worlds" that can have an impact on world history. With this in mind, it seems worthwhile to look further back at the legendary history of the stone to see if we can discern its true origins and what this might mean for us in our own times.

4

The Migration Legends of Ireland

*I*n the last chapter we looked at the history of Scotland in some detail, but this is not the beginning of the story. The legend of the Stone of Destiny is that the Scots brought it with them to Britain from Ireland at some time during the seventh century AD. Discovering how it may have come to be in Ireland in the first place involves unraveling Irish legends of migration to the British Isles. These are contained in the Irish Annals which speak of several waves of settlers coming to Ireland (mostly from the region of the Eastern Mediterranean) during the Neolithic, Bronze, and Early Iron Ages. Though the recorded number varies from text to text and there is some overlap or repetition, in general five distinct waves can be recognized. These are:

1) The people of Ceasir.
2) The people of Bartholeme (also called Parthalon).
3) The Fir Bolg.

4) The Tuartha de Danaan.

5) The Milesians.

How the first two waves of these migrants fit into the pattern of
known archaeology of the Neolithic and Bronze Ages is a matter of
conjecture. Fortunately, as they have no bearing on the origins of the
Stone of Destiny, any debate about their identity goes outside of the
remit of the present work. The only waves that need to concern us are 3,
4, and 5—especially the last two.

The origin of the name *Fir Bolg*, the people who make up the third
wave, is a matter of keen debate. The Irish word *Fir* comes from the
same roots as the Latin word *vir*, or Welsh *gwyr (gwr)*, meaning "man."
Bolg is thought by some to be derived from the Irish for either "bag" or
"trousers." So the *Fir Bolg* would be either the "men of the bag" or "men
with trousers (pants)." This latter makes some sense, for the Roman recorded that one of the distinguishing characteristics of ancient British
dress was that, unlike themselves, they wore trousers rather than a tunic or kilt. We can only conjecture, but it seems likely the *Fir Bolg* of
Ireland did the same. Whatever the etymology, *Fir Bolg* seems to have
the same roots as *Belgae*: the name given by the Romans to certain Celtic
tribes living in what is now the eastern part of northern France and
southern England as well as Belgium itself. Thus it would seem that the
Fir Bolg, the "men with trousers" of Irish legend should be recognized as
close relatives of the ancient Britons.

What makes this association more interesting is that according to the
Welsh Annals, the pre–Roman Britons were in the main descended from
the ancient Trojans: the people who once lived in the city of Troy. As is
well known, the legendary history of Rome begins with the story of
Aeneas: a Trojan prince who escaped the destruction of Troy and found
his way to Italy. Here he is said to have met and married the daughter of
the King of Latium and eventually founded the city that was destined to
become Rome. The Romans of Caesar's day were immensely proud of
their Trojan ancestry, but what is less well known is that the Britons had
an equivalent legend. In their version of the Aeneas legend, he has a
great–grandson called Brutus (*Brwth* in Welsh). Banished from Italy for
the crime of killing his father in a hunting accident, he journeys to
Epirus in northwest Greece. Here he discovers a remnant of the Trojans,
who are being held as slaves by Pandarus, the local king. Outraged, he
instigates an uprising, overthrows Pandarus, and seizes both the latter's
daughter (whom he marries) and his fleet. The now-free Trojans sail

first to the nearby island of "Leogetia," which is identifiable today as a small island just to the north of Corfu called Leuca. While on the island, which is deserted, Brutus sleeps in a ruined temple of Diana and has a dream. In this he meets the goddess herself. She tells him that to be safe from Greek reprisals he must take his people and sail through the Pillars of Hercules where, beyond Gaul, they will find a large, verdant island.

Migration of the Fir Bolg

MAP 3: MIGRATION OF THE FIR BOLG

The island is, of course, Britain, and here the Trojans quickly subjugate a race of giants—remnants, it is said, of an earlier migration from Syria to Britain. In honor of Brutus, their first king, they rename the island Britain and call themselves Britons.[1]

The common identity of the Irish *Fir Bolg* and the ancient Britons is confirmed by an equivalent Irish legend that they, too, were enslaved by the Greeks before escaping on ships and going to Ireland. They are said to have arrived in three groups, the *Fir Bolg, Fir Domnann,* and the *Gaileanga.*[2] Interestingly, the ancient Greeks themselves referred to the inhabitants of both Britain and Ireland as "Prydain," which the Romans Latinized as *Britanni.* The commonality of origins of the "Trojan" Britons and the *Fir Bolg* as belonging to the same wave of migration is further confirmed by the similarity of archaeological finds of the period—broaches, swords, shields, etc.—from each country. Thus, while the details of these legends may have been elaborated upon over the centuries, there can be little doubt that both populations belong to the same wave of migration that occurred during the late Bronze Age. As we will discover in the next chapter, the Late Bronze Age (ca. 800 BC) is almost certainly the real period during which the city of Troy was destroyed by the Greeks.

Whatever the truth concerning their origins, from the Irish point of view, the most important legacy of the *Fir Bolg* was that they divided Ireland into five provinces: Ulster, North Leinster, South Leinster, Munster, and Connacht. These divisions are still relevant today; for while Ulster is a part of the United Kingdom and therefore separate from the four other provinces, they make up the country of Eire today.

MAP 4: ANCIENT IRELAND

The fourth wave of immigrants to enter Ireland was the *Tuatha de Danaan*. According to the *Annals of Clonmacnoise*[3] they were kinfolk of the *Fir Bolg* and like them came from Greece. The *Tuatha de Danaan* are said to have arrived as little as thirty-seven years after the *Fir Bolg*, which is only a generation. The *Annals* say that a great battle was fought between the two groups at Mag Tuired, near Lough Arrow in County Sligo. Defeated, the *Fir Bolg* were driven out of the most fertile parts of Ireland but allowed to retain the western province of Connacht along with its neighboring islands such as Inishmore.

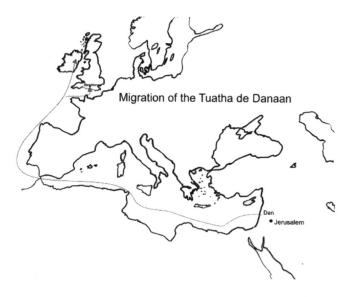

Migration of the Tuatha de Danaan

Dan
• Jerusalem

MAP 5: MIGRATION OF THE TUATHA DA DANAAN

In the legendary history of Ireland, the *Tuatha de Danaan* are credited with occult knowledge and are, therefore, associated with sorcery. This, however, has to be understood in context. Such a reputation probably means they were literate and understood at least some mathematics and the related science of engineering. Armed with this knowledge, they would have been able to achieve feats that, to those who didn't understand the science behind what they were doing, appeared like magic. But this doesn't answer the question as to who they were or what their name, *Tuatha de Danaan*, actually means. The academic consensus is that *tuatha* means something like "people" or "tribe" while *de* translates as "goddess" and *Danaan* derives from the proper name of an old Irish goddess called "Danu." Mythological evidence used in support of this assumption is that in later periods, after the Irish were Christianized, the names of some of the supposed leaders of the *Tuatha de Danaan* were remembered as otherworldly beings. Confirmation of this attribution is derived from the story that following their subsequent defeat at the hands of the Milesians, the *Tuatha de Danaan* were given rulership of the underworld. In effect, the *Tuatha* became gods and goddesses of the underworld with some of their number (such as the giant Finn macCool, who is credited with building the Giant's Causeway) developing mythologies of their own.[4]

In opposition to the theory that the *Tuatha de Danaan* were the "people of the goddess Danu," there is a much more straightforward one: *Tuatha de Danaan* means, quite simply, "Tribe of Dan"—this being the name of one of the twelve tribes of Israel (about which more will be said later). Since uniquely among the Israelites the tribe of Dan was comprised of seafarers, this makes more than a little sense. Curiously, contained in the Edgar Cayce readings, there is indirect support for such a migration. For those readers unfamiliar with this resource, Edgar Cayce was an American from Hopkinsville, Kentucky, who had unique psychic abilities. Either because of a childhood accident or for some other reason, he was able, when asleep, to enter an altered state of consciousness. While in this state, he would answer questions of the most intimate kind concerning a person's health. Displaying a remarkable knowledge of medicine that he did not have while awake, he would prescribe treatments that today we might recognize as complimentary medicine but at the time were quite unknown. When he awoke, he would have no recollection of what he had said and would be as mystified as everyone else when he came to read the notes of his stenographer.

The "readings" refer to another talent of his: the ability while asleep to access the Akashic Records or as Christians would call it "the Book of Life." A devout, Bible-reading Christian while awake, in his sleeping state Cayce taught that we have each of us lived other lives before the present. According to this teaching, our souls come back, sometimes many times, in order to gain a wide experience of life. The sleeping Cayce was able to read the invisible records of a person's previous lives, giving details of who they were, what they did, and how, for good or ill, the unconscious memory of these past lives might be affecting them in the present. Over four thousand of these "life readings" were recorded which now form the basis of an archive. Thus while Edgar Cayce died in 1945, his eyewitness accounts still provide a unique database for those (like myself) who wish to investigate the past.

Concerning migrations, there are three relevant Cayce readings. They refer to a group of refugees from the Holy Land who travelled to England and set up "altars" in the vicinity of Salisbury. Since this is the nearest major conurbation to Stonehenge, it is generally thought that what Cayce refers to as "altars" is to be identified as this Stone-Age/Bronze-Age monument.

> Before that the entity was in the English land during those periods when there was the breaking up of the tribes of Israel . . . The entity was a granddaughter of Hezekiah the king, and among those who set sail to escape when the activities brought the rest of the people into servitude in the Persian land. Then the entity was among those who landed and set up the seat of customs as indicated in the altars built near what is now Salisbury, England (Stonehenge?). These were the early traditions carried into those activities. The name then was Elemeshia . . .
>
> .   3590-1

> Before that the entity was in England with the daughters of Hezekiah . . .   5276-1

> Before that the entity was in the Holy Land when there were those breakings up in the periods when the land was being sacked by the Chaldeans and Persians. The entity was among those groups who escaped in the ships that settled in portions of the English land near what is now Salisbury, and there builded those altars that were to represent the dedications of individuals to a service of a living God . . . (Stonehenge?) Thus the entity aided in giving the records and teachings that may help others in the present, in giving to others that helping hand—who may be as a record keeper. The name then was Mayra.
>
> 3645-1

A fourth reading refers to migrants from Israel (presumably with the same daughters of Hezekiah) moving to Somerset. This county is next to Devon and being on the coast of the Bristol Channel provides relatively easy access to Ireland.

> Before that we find the entity was in the English land in
> the early settlings (Stonehenge?) of the children of Israel
> who were foregathered with the daughters of Hezekiah in
> what is now Somerland, Somerhill or Somerset. There the
> entity saw group organization for the preservation of te-
> nets and truths of the living God, just as those admoni-
> tions would be for the entity in the present as it begins
> that social service with children . . . The name then was
> Ruth."   5384-1

These readings are very interesting as they give us a rough date for
these events. Hezekiah was king of Judah from about 716–687 BC. At the
start of his reign there were actually two kingdoms of Israelites. The
southern kingdom of Judah, which Hezekiah ruled, consisted of the two
tribes of Judah and Benjamin. The northern kingdom, called "Israel,"
"Samaria," or "Ephraim," had split off from Judah following the death of
Solomon (931 BC). It consisted of the remaining ten tribes, including the
tribe of Dan. In 722 BC Samaria, the capital of this northern kingdom of
Israel, fell to the Assyrians—then the region's greatest power. The majority of the people of the ten tribes were taken into captivity, with most
of them being deported to the Caspian Sea region in what is now Iran
or "Persia."

Now the tribe of Dan was rather different from all the rest. It held
land on the coast of Israel and was maritime in its outlook; like the
better known Phoenicians, the Danites were traders whose ships travelled all over the Mediterranean. It is not unlikely, therefore, that ships
belonging to the Tribe of Dan went as far as Britain or even to Ireland.
Britain was then the major source of tin (needed for making bronze) as
well as a supplier of other precious metals. Assyria, whose capital of
Nineveh was near Mosul in Northern Iraq, was not a naval power. One
can therefore assume that on hearing of the fall of Samaria, at least
some of the Danites got into their ships and sought sanctuary elsewhere. Those who couldn't escape by sea would very likely have turned
to their kinsmen, the Judeans, with whom they shared a common border, to seek sanctuary.

This would only have been a temporary respite for soon the Judeans
themselves were also under attack from the Assyrians. Eight years after
the fall of Samaria, Sennacherib, king of Assyria, seized all the fortified
cities of Judah with the exception of Jerusalem. Hiding behind the walls

of the city, Hezekiah tried to buy off the Assyrians with gold and silver, but still they threatened to take Jerusalem too. Then, because of disease, divine intervention,[5] or the fact that the Assyrians were distracted with problems elsewhere in their empire, Jerusalem was spared. As a result, the kingdom of Judah survived for another hundred or so years before its eventual destruction at the hands of the Babylonians.

In 687 King Hezekiah was succeeded by his twelve-year-old son Manasseh. He was a tyrant, and during his reign a lot of innocent blood was shed in Jerusalem. The Bible tells us, "He did evil in the sight of the Lord" (2 Chronicles 33), but despite his shortcomings he was able to reign for fifty-five years. We may safely assume, therefore, that during his reign (if not before) there must have been some people in Jerusalem who were anxious to escape from the Middle East altogether. If we are to believe Cayce's somniavoyant (i.e., seeing in your dreams) insights, then Manasseh's sisters, the "daughters of Hezekiah," were among these emigrants. According to him they fled to Britain, at first making their way to the Salisbury area of Wiltshire—where he says they built altars—and then proceeding onwards to the neighboring county of Somerset. Yet they could not have made this journey on their own; it, therefore, makes sense that they were brought over to England in ships belonging to members of the tribe of Dan. If they then proceeded onwards to Ireland, this migration could be the one referred to in Irish annals as the coming of the *Tuatha de Danaan*. In other words, these migrants to Britain and Ireland would appear to have been a remnant of the Israelites.

A further interesting clue that we can glean from Edgar Cayce is contained in the first reading listed here where it says: "Then the entity was among those who landed and set up the seat of customs as indicated in the altars built near what is now Salisbury, England." He doesn't tell us what the "seat of customs" was, but it does seem a significant statement when seen in the context of the legend that the Stone of Destiny, also known as Jacob's Pillow Stone, is traditionally used as a seat in coronations. Could Cayce's "seat of customs" be yet another name for this stone? Might it have been brought to southern Britain before being transported onwards to Ireland? Although our current understanding of Stonehenge is that even its last stage (Stonehenge IIIc), predates any supposed Danite migration to Britain by at least four hundred years, any "altars" built near Salisbury would certainly appear to be a reference to this monument. It is curious, though, that archaeologists have discovered during the last phase of building the so-called "Altar Stone" was stood on its end at the apex of the innermost horseshoe. This stone seems to have been removed from where it had stood in phase II. It is certainly not impossible, therefore, that the Altar Stone was either raised or reraised at the time Cayce states—ca. 650 or thereabouts. If so, then could the "seat of customs" have been a ceremonial chair that was placed in the center of the monument in line with the summer solstice rising sun?

We may never know the answer to this question, for despite centuries of archaeological research, Stonehenge itself remains an enigma. What we do know is that the monument, as a whole, functioned as a very accurate calendar with exact alignments towards significant rising and setting positions of both the sun and moon. The layout of its concentric rings of stones was also done in a very exact fashion, indicating that its builders had knowledge of sacred geometry as well as astronomy—more will be said about this in a later chapter. What is clear is that in its heyday (second millennium BC), it functioned as some sort of national shrine for the whole island of Britain rather as Westminster Abbey does today. It is, therefore, not out of the question that the "daughters of Hezekiah" and their attendants knew this and reused the old—by then abandoned monument—for the purposes of some sort of ceremony involving a "seat of customs."

The ceremony they performed probably involved observing sunrise at midsummer: the central event of the Stonehenge calendar. However, alignments through other archways indicate that it was probably designed to be used at other times in the year too. This was certainly the conclusion of Dr. Gerald S. Hawkins in his remarkable book *Stonehenge Decoded*, where he wrote: "Once the Stonehengers had got the solstices, or summer-winter extremes aligned—what was more natural than that they would try for the midpoints? With equinoxes and solstices they could quarter the year. They *could* have gotten these halfway points by bisecting the angles between solstice lines. Such a geometric method, familiar since long before Euclid, would have been easier than any observational technique. However it was done, the stones are aligned to equinoxes with remarkable accuracy."[6]

The supposed Irish connection is even more intriguing as it suggests a distant memory, perhaps handed down by the Druids, connecting Stonehenge with the mysteries of Ireland. In the Welsh *Brut Tysilio*, which is almost certainly the text which Geoffrey translated into Latin, the Giants' Ring is taken from "Killara Mountain,"[7] placed Killair (Killara) in

County Meath. This is the county that includes the River Boyne and such important Stone–Age Irish antiquities such as New Grange. It is also the royal county that surrounded the Hill of Tara, which Camden was inclined to see as being referred to as the "navel" of Ireland and hence Mount Killair. The translator of the *Brut*, the Rev. Peter Roberts, begins by quoting Camden and then presents arguments of his own linking the story of Merlin moving the Giants' Ring to Wiltshire with the secret transportation of the Stone of Destiny itself from Tara to Stonehenge:

"They say that Killair, a castle in these parts, is, as it were, the *navel* of Ireland, for *lair*, in Irish, signifies a navel." This tradition can, from the situation, be true in no other sense than that of the ὀμφαλός (omphalos) or place of divination; a sense that has at least the advantage of concurring with the reference of Merddyn (Merlin) to that place. There is another circumstance which makes this the more probable. O'Flaherty, in his *Ogygia* (part 3d. ch.6) says, that the Taltenian games were celebrated annually on Talten Mountain in Meath; and if I understand him rightly, the Timor, or great temple, was there also at least it was in Meath, and hence if, as I presume, it was an oracular temple, it was one that would be represented as the ὀμφαλός. At this time the Druids seem to have exerted themselves in opposition to Christianity, and Merddyn to have referred to the Timor for the means of effecting his purpose, and establishing the credit of his party, and probably restoring the rites of Stonehenge.

What these means were, it is now perhaps impossible to ascertain, but I will beg leave to hazard a conjecture which has occurred to me on the subject of this strange legend.

The convocation on Salisbury Plain is said to have had in view not merely the memorial of the British nobles assassinated there, but the grand objects of legislation, and the coronation of Ambrosius (viz. King Arthur's uncle, elder brother of Uther Pendragon). The title for the crown was also disputed by Pasgen (viz. third son of the traitor-king, Vortigern, who invited the Saxons to settle in Britain in the first place). To confer it in favour of Ambrosius was therefore of essential consequence, if it could be done. At that time the celebrated stone on which the kings were crowned was probably at Timor abovementioned, and the tradition concerning it is that, when the possessor of the throne by right sat on it, a voice issued from it in confirmation of the right, and that when any other sat on it, the stone was silent. Fordun says, this stone (viz. the Stone of Destiny) was brought from thence to Scone, by the Irish colonists, and yet it is not very probable that it would have been suffered to go with a colony, or without a contest. It is also evident, that Merddyn could not depend on his science alone, and that his object required the aid of a strong military force, and if it was this stone, it was sufficient as being a stone brought to Salisbury Plain, for tradition to confound it with the others. Such an evidence as its *speaking*, though of no very deep artifice, may have been of very great importance, and I am inclined to think this was so, and that the stone was, for the sake of security, carried in Scotland, either by Uther, or the remaining Druids, and perhaps by the direction of Merddyn himself."[8]

The "Timor" mentioned above is, of course, the same place as *Teamuir* or Tara, the ancient capital of Ireland where, according to the Irish Annals, the *Lia-fail* or Stone of Destiny was kept. The Rev. Williams' contention that the story of the transportation of Giants' Ring from Ireland is a fabrication to conceal the bringing of the Stone of Destiny to Wiltshire, and that later it was taken from there to Scotland is, of course, purely conjectural. However, what is of great interest is the link he makes among Stonehenge, Tara, and the Druids; for there can be little doubt that though the Druids were not involved in the building of Stonehenge, they almost certainly made use of it.

If, as seems likely, Stonehenge was built as a ceremonial center for the whole of Britain, then it suggests that many "Druid" ideas predate Caesar's Druids by many centuries. There is, however, a further tradition in Britain that the Druidic religion itself is Hebrew in origin. Curiously, we read in the Bible of Moses himself constructing what appears to have been a stone circle arranged around a central altar. He appears to have used this as a place of sacrifice and the renewal of the Israelites' covenant with God:

"And Moses wrote all the words of the Lord. And he rose early in the morning, and built an altar at the foot of the mountain, and twelve pillars, according to the twelve tribes of Israel. And he sent young men of the people of Israel, who offered burnt offerings and sacrificed peace offerings of oxen to the Lord. And Moses took half of the blood and put it in basins, and half of the blood he threw against the altar. Then he took the book of the covenant, and read it in the hearing of the people; and they said, 'All that the Lord has spoken we will do, and we will be obedient.' And Moses took the blood and threw it upon the people, and said, 'Behold the blood of the covenant which the Lord has made with you in accordance with all these words.'" (Exod. 24:4-8)

We don't know exactly the way that Moses arranged his stone circle, but it seems very likely that the stones he used as pillars were, like those of Stonehenge, undressed. In Deuteronomy we read of him commanding the Israelites to set up just such undressed stones when they arrive in the Promised Land.

"Now Moses and the elders of Israel commanded the people, saying, 'Keep all of the commandments, which I command you this day. And on the day you pass over the Jordan to the land which the Lord your God gives you, you shall set up large stones, and plaster them with plaster; and you shall write upon them all the words of this law, when you pass over to enter the land which the Lord your God gives you, a land flowing with milk and honey, as the Lord, the God of your fathers, has promised you. And when you have passed over the Jordan, you shall set up these stones, concerning which I command you this day, on Mount Ebal, and you shall plaster them with plaster. And there you shall build an altar to the Lord your God, an altar of stones; you shall lift up no iron tool upon them. You shall build an altar to the Lord your God of unhewn stones; and you shall offer burnt offerings on it to the Lord your God; and you shall sacrifice peace offerings, and shall eat there; and you shall rejoice to the Lord your God. And you shall write upon the stones all the words of this law very plainly.'" (Deut. 27:1-8).

Now one of the characteristics of Stonehenge—and indeed of every other Neolithic or Bronze Age stone monument in Britain—is that it consists of undressed stones. They are all rough cut even though the complex alignments according to astronomy, the geometry of their arrangement in circles, and the knowledge of mechanics that their setting up would require indicate that the people who put them up would have been quite capable of sculpting them into smooth pillars if they had wished to. Also, all over Britain there are "Druidic" altars—usually called *cromlechs*—that comprise of a large, flat table stone supported on three or more vertical stones. All of these stones are invariably undressed while the raising of the flat table stone must have taken a great deal of effort. In the archaeological literature these monuments are usually described as the skeletal remains of long barrows that have weathered away. However, this is clearly not the case. For a start there are plenty of long barrows that have not "weathered away" and at all of the *cromlechs* I have visited there is no evidence (such as remains of a ditch or remnants of an earth bank near the stones) to suggest these "skeletons" were ever covered with soil or turf. It therefore seems to me more likely that the *cromlechs* were altars and that animals were sacrificed on top of their flat table stones.

Cromlechs also seem to have some connection with the calendar. There is a relatively small one on the Dorset coast that is known locally as the Hellstone—not a reference to the underworld ruled over by the devil but rather to Sol, the Roman sun god. The chamber under this *cromlech* faces south, towards the sea. It would probably not be a mistake, therefore, to think that it functioned as a local center for rituals linked to the midday sun. The closest *cromlech* to where I live is another one that is today called "Kit's Coty House." This one does not face south but rather towards the setting point of the sun on May 1 (i.e., Beltane as it was called in the old calendar of the Druids). In Druidic times bonfires would be lit all over Britain on this day at sacred sites such as this, and no doubt sacrifices were made on top of this *cromlech*. All of this is highly reminiscent of the forms of worship practiced not only at Stonehenge, where it is very likely the Druids also sacrificed animals, but also according to the ways of the Hebrews.

Whether or not the *cromlechs* of Britain were once covered with plaster and inscribed with the laws of Moses, we will never know. However, there is some tangential evidence that they might once have been whitewashed for special occasions. A few years ago I visited a friend in Belgium, and he took me to see a collection of similar Neolithic monuments at a place called Weris—the Belgian "Stonehenge." It lies in the Ardennes Forest and in its vicinity there are quite a number of such monuments. Among those that I saw were a dolmen chamber that was not dissimilar from similar ones in Britain and a stone slab called "The Devil's Bed." On top of a nearby hill and therefore visible for miles around was a very tall, upright menhir called "The Stone of Henna."[9] This stone seems to have served as an *omphalus* or "navel" stone for the surrounding area and its astronomical connections are very obvious. Looking from it, there are east-west alignments to other stones, while sitting at the base of the dolmen chamber, the solstice sun can be seen to rise over the Stone of Henna. Now by tradition this stone is said to plug a portal leading to hell. It is also the focus of a curious tradition that may go back to Druid times when, of course, Belgium was inhabited by the same *Fir Bolg* tribes who lived in southern England and adhered to the Druidic religion. The tradition is that once a year at the spring equinox the local villagers from Weris give the Stone of Henna a coat of whitewash. They do this to purify the stone so that it will continue to plug the portal to the underworld.

We do not know if it was also once the custom to whitewash the stones of Stonehenge, but as it stands on chalk upland, there would be no shortage of the material to do just that. Thus if the "daughters of Hezekiah" really did visit Stonehenge, then perhaps the ritual Cayce says they carried out involved whitewashing the standing stones that were already in place, restoring any that were fallen, and, as instructed in the book of Deuteronomy, writing the laws of Moses upon them. They may also have carried out the blood sacrifice of a sheep on the recumbent Slaughter Stone.[10] Then, leaving the Salisbury area, they may have moved through Somerset to the Bristol Channel. Here they could have met up again with the Danite sailors who had brought them to Britain. Together the princesses and the *Tuatha de Danaan* may then have sailed on to Ireland. They could have brought with them a sacred stone (Jacob's Pillow) for we are told they "framed" (i.e., set inside a throne) such a stone and placed it on the hilltop of Taragh to signify their conquest of the land.

> "This people Twathy de Danann were most notable Magicians and would work wonderful things thereby; when they pleased, they would troble both sea and land, darken both Sonn and Moone at their pleasures. They did frame a great broade stone which they called Lya Fail, or the stone of Ireland, by theire art and placed the same at Tarragh."[11]

All this, I have to confess, is conjecture, but it does at least provide us with some useful dates. If the princesses sailed from the coast of Israel during the reign of Hezekiah's son Manasseh, then the migration of the Danites or *Tuatha de Danaan* would have to have taken place between 722 and 643 BC. Most likely it was near to 650 BC when Manasseh was becoming intolerable. The *Fir Bolg* are said to have arrived in Ireland thirty-seven years before the *Tuatha de Danaan*, which gives them an arrival date of probably around 700–685 BC, with 687 BC fitting the above picture. This, as we will see in a later chapter, is very possible. It leaves just couple of generations after the revised date for the fall of Troy. This event probably occurred around 750 BC rather than 1175 BC— the favored but erroneous date of academia. There will be more on this discussion later.

The last waves of emigrants from the Mediterranean area said to have arrived in Ireland are called the Milesians. In its earliest form, this migration legend is described in Nennius' *Historia Britonnum*, a book thought to date from the tenth century but to be based on much earlier sources.

> "If anyone wants to know when Ireland was inhabited and when it was deserted, this is what the Irish scholars have told me [Nennius]. When the children of Israel crossed through the Red Sea, the Egyptians came and pursued them and were drowned, as may be read in the Law (i.e., The Torah). Among the Egyptians was a nobleman of Scythia, with a great following, who had been expelled from his kingdom, and was there when the Egyptians were drowned, but did not join in the pursuit of the children of God. The survivors took counsel to expel him, lest he should attack their kingdom and occupy it, for their strength had been drowned in the Red Sea; for his wife

was Scota, the daughter of Pharaoh, from whom Scotia, Ireland is said to be named.[12] He was expelled and wandered for 42 years through Africa, and they came to the altars of the Philistines, by the Salt Lake, and through Rusicade and Mountains of Axaria, and by the river Muluya, and crossed through Morocco to the Pillars of Hercules, and sailed over the Tyrrhene Sea, and came to Spain, and there they lived for many years, and grew and multiplied exceedingly. After they had come to Spain, and 1002 years after the Egyptians had been drowned in the Red Sea, they came to the country of Dal Riada . . . "

A similar story of this migration is to be found in the *Annals of Clonmacnoise*, possibly the earliest and certainly the most complete of the medieval Irish Chronicles. Here the wandering Scythians are referred to as "Milesians," apparently because they were led by a prince called Miletus (Miledh in Irish):

"The most part of our Irish Chronicles agree that the sons of Miletus came to this land in the beginning of the destruction of Troy, and that Hermon and Heber sons of the said Miletus reigned together jointly when Agamemnon with his Gretians came to that destruction. The occasion of their coming is as followeth. In the yeare after the flood (of Noah) 1245 being about the 12th year of the reign of David king of Israel and Judah, Gallo the son of Billus king of Scythia after surnamed Miletus of Spain for his many and great exploits, hearing of the great wars which the Egyptians held then with their neighbouring countries, being before in some displeasure at home for the strife that grew between him and his kinsmen for the kingdom of Scythia and being also himself much given to war, ambitious of honour and desirous to increase his name (as the manner of his country was) passed out of Scythia with a number of his friends, kinsmen and followers into Egypt, where he was no sooner arrived than well entertained by the Egyptians, & in short time after did so well acquit himself in their service, that he was made general of their armies and withall married the daughter of Symedes then the greatest prince in Egypt or Pharao as they did then commonly call their monarch, his other daughter was married to Solomon, King of Jerusalem. This Symedes or Symenides by other authors is called also Silagh and became so great and mighty, that he had in his army 1200 chariots, 60,000 horses, and 400,000 footmen.

After the death of King Solomon and also after the departure of Gallo out of Egypt he [viz. Symedes] entered with the same [viz. His great army] into the city of Jerusalem, ransacked the city spoiled the Jews, and carried away all their treasure and jewels with him into Egypt".[13]

Now at first sight this is all very confusing and conflicting. Who, one might ask, was this Gallo (or Gathelus as he is called elsewhere) and why was he surnamed Miletus? What does it mean when it says he was a Scythian, and if he was, what was this sacking of Jerusalem after the death of Solomon? Furthermore what, if any, connection does this Gallo/Miletus have with Troy, Agamemnon, and the Trojan Wars?

The answers to all these questions and many others become clear once we can establish the real time frame in when Gallo might have lived, which turns out to be neither at the time of Moses (ca.1300 BC) nor of David and Solomon (ca.1000–950 BC). Unraveling this puzzle, which will be the task of the next chapter is, I believe, the key to understanding the truth behind the legend of the Stone of Destiny.

5

Turmoil in the East

*H*istory is a difficult subject, not because there is a lack of records from the past (often these are in abundance) but rather because we frequently misread them. All too often "consensus opinion" does not take into account all of the facts and indeed clings to falsehoods. Even where these falsehoods are abundantly obvious (for example, that the ancient Britons were painted savages), once an idea has taken root, it is extremely difficult to change. Indeed, sometimes even to challenge "consensus opinion" is to put at risk a promising academic career, for nobody, least of all a professor with a seat in a leading university, likes to be exposed as ignorant of the truth. So while a "consensus opinion" might have started life as nothing more than an idle conjecture floated by some long-dead professor, once it has been around for a while, it can morph into an unchallengeable article of faith.

One area where this has had dramatic and extremely damaging consequences is in our understanding of the chronology of ancient Egypt. Our primary source for dating ancient Egypt is a small book called *Aegyptiaca*,[1] which was written by Manetho: a Greek priest who lived in Alexandria during the third century BC. In fact, even this is an exaggeration, for, desirable as it would be, we don't have Manetho's actual book in hand as this has been lost for at least a thousand years. All we have today are epitomes: extracts made by later, mostly Christian, writers who made use of *Aegyptiaca's* contents to bolster arguments of their own. Nevertheless, from these extracts it has been possible to reconstruct a large part of Manetho's book including, most importantly, his king lists of ancient pharaohs. These are arranged chronologically in the form of "dynasties" (thirty–one in all) that stretch from the time of King Menes, who is said to have been the first to unify Upper and Lower Egypt, to Darius III, the Persian king who was ejected from his throne and later killed by Alexander the Great. Afterwards in 332 BC, Alexander took over Egypt, leading to the founding of the Greek dynasty of Ptolemy in 325 BC. So to the thirty–one dynasties of Manetho we can add two more: the Greek dynasty (which terminated with the death of Queen Cleopatra in 40 BC) and the Roman dynasty that began in the same year with the accession of the Emperor Augustus as ruler of Egypt.

By providing a skeleton on which to hang known events, Manetho's system of dynasties has given coherence to the study of Egyptology. Yet for all its usefulness, his chronology does have flaws. One of these is that in compiling his lists of dynasties (presumably drawn from records kept in the Library of Alexandria as well as from inscriptions on the walls of various temples) he clearly made mistakes. The most glaring of these was to treat concurrent, parallel dynasties from different parts of the country as though they came one after the other. Another is duplication, particularly where kings known by one set of names in one dynasty appear under slightly different ones in another, perhaps later dynasty. Normally, except to those scholars whose field it is to study ancient Egyptian history, such errors would not matter very much. However, in a way that Manetho himself could never have expected, his lists of kings and their dynastic sequence have become the bedrock of the archaeological dating system of the entire Near East. As a result, the errors made by Manetho have not only caused immense damage to our understanding of the chronology of Egypt but have led to mistakes in the reporting of the archaeology of neighboring states too.[2]

Unfortunately, because their own understanding of Egyptian history is so closely tied up with Manetho's system of dynasties, there is little incentive among Egyptologists to abandon it. Immanuel Velikovsky was one person who did challenge consensus opinion—and very strongly at that. Best known for his extraordinary and, it must be admitted in places, deeply flawed book, *Worlds in Collision*, Velikovsky was the ultimate bête noire of the establishment throughout the 1950s and '60s. Though *Worlds in Collision* was his most famous book,[3] he wrote many others, mostly challenging the consensus opinions of Egyptology. Blessed with a powerful intellect and ever willing to rush in where more timid authors feared to tread, Velikovsky was only too happy to grab the sacred cow of Manetho's chronology by the horns and plunge his sword into its very heart. Though he is seldom given any credit for his work, his attack on Manetho's dating system was a blow to its status from which Egyptology has never really recovered.

Velikovsky was Jewish, and not surprisingly, therefore, the driving force behind his work was a desire to prove that the Old Testament of the Bible gave a truthful account of history. He was particularly interested in the period from the supposed Exodus of the Israelites from Egypt (generally dated to the fourteenth century BC) to the fall of Jerusalem to the Babylonians (in 586 BC). He quickly discovered that the dating system based on the Egyptian chronology of Manetho was in his way. Undeterred by what many people would have regarded as an impossible task, he bit by bit unearthed evidence, which any unbiased reader can see proves that Manetho's lists (and hence the framework on which modern Egyptology is based) is out of kilter with real history, sometimes by as much as six to eight hundred years.

One example of this new approach was his redating of an event depicted on the walls of the mortuary temple of Pharaoh Rameses III at Medinet Habu, West Luxor. In this temple, which I have myself visited, huge murals describe how Egypt was invaded by an alliance of two groups of foreigners: the "Pereset" and the "Sea-Peoples." According to consensus opinion, the Pereset are identifiable as the biblical Philistines: a people who lived on the coastlands of what is now Israel. Meanwhile the Sea Peoples are thought to have been Mycenaeans: probably Greeks on their way home from the sack of Troy. Following the accepted chronology, the sack of Troy took place around 1200 BC. Accordingly, it is assumed that Rameses III must have lived around this time.

Velikovsky challenged this assumption. He pointed out what should have been obvious—the costumes worn by Rameses' Pereset are clearly Persian. Since in other contexts the Egyptian for "Persian" is P–r–s–tt,[4] and Greek historians, such as Diodorus of Sicily, describe a war fought by the Egyptians against an allied invasion force of Greeks and Persians, it is not unreasonable to suppose that the temple murals of Rameses III document this same event. The only trouble is that this war actually took place in 376 BC and not 1200: a discrepancy of over eight hundred years! Also, the reigning pharaoh, who defeated the invaders, is called Nectanebo in the Greek accounts and not Rameses. Undeterred, Velikovsky investigated further and discovered that though Egyptologists have settled on the name "Ramessu" (Rameses) for this pharaoh, in common with other pharaohs he has multiple names inscribed on his temple. One of these, his "Horus name," is *Neckt-a-neb*, which is remarkably similar to the Greek rendition of Nectanebo. To Velikovsky at least it was clear: "Rameses III" was none other than Egypt's last, truly great pharaoh Nectanabo, who, though praised by the Greeks for his exploits, is otherwise unknown to Egyptian archaeology. The only problem was that to accept this rather obvious fact means that the chronology of the entire history of ancient Egypt needs a thorough reevaluation. For if Rameses III lived around 375 BC and not 1200, what impact does this redating have on our dates for every other pharaoh?

Velikovsky was himself well aware of the hornets' nest he was opening when he wrote about all this in his book *Peoples of the Sea*:

> "We can stop here, perplexed by the evidently inadmissible thought that there could be a mistake of eight hundred years, or frightened at the sight of the perturbation into which this inquiry may lead us. But should we not make up our minds to try to probe a little further and may we not perchance feel relieved if some new evidence should exonerate the centuries-old concept of ancient history? For this must be clearly understood: we cannot let Rameses III fight with the Persians and keep the hinges of world history in their former places. What a slide, what an avalanche, must accompany such a disclosure: kingdoms must topple, empires must glide over centuries, descendants and ancestors must change places. And in addition to all this, how many books must become obsolete, how many scholarly pursuits must be restarted, how much in-

ertia must be overcome? It is not merely an avalanche but a complete overturning of supposedly everlasting massifs."[5]

Needless to say, Velikovsky was scorned by the academic world which sought to portray him as a crank. His critics loathed him for trespassing into areas of research that they believed only they were qualified to investigate. Since to admit that their chronology of Egyptian history could be wrong by not just a few decades but maybe by as much as eight hundred years, they had no alternative but to metaphorically close their eyes, put their fingers in their ears, and hum whenever his work was mentioned. Fortunately, not everyone has taken this approach. There are a few researchers who have tried to take his work further, notably Peter James and his colleagues in their seminal work *Centuries of Darkness*. Nevertheless even they found it necessary to distance themselves from Velikovsky lest their own work be considered tainted by association. Accordingly, they write: "His [Velikovsky's] model for a 're-vised chronology', based on a new series of links between Egyptian and Israelite history, proved to be disastrously extreme. Involving a reduction of Egyptian dates by a full eight centuries at one point, it produced a rash of new problems far more severe than those it hoped to solve. Sadly, while he pointed the way to a solution by challenging Egyptian chronology, Velikovsky understood little of archaeology and nothing of stratigraphy."[6]

Unfortunately, Velikovsky was already dead when these words were written and was therefore in no position to reply. However, what we can say with some certainty is that he would have refuted the charge that he understood nothing of stratigraphy; he would have said that he merely disagreed with the way it is generally applied. In any case stratig-raphy is not, to use a cliché, rocket science. It is basically a method of dating archaeological strata according to contents found within them. Simply put, if you find a piece of pot of a type you know dates from the twelfth century BC, then you can date strata at other sites that contain the same type of pottery as belonging to the same period. In this way different types of pots (and certain other objects) provide a useful yard-stick by which the various strata of an archaeological site can be dated. However, what if the yardstick is itself wrong? What if the pot type that is supposed to date from the twelfth century is really from the sixth or even fourth? This was Velikovsky's real complaint: that archaeologists and historians of the nineteenth and twentieth centuries have made glaring errors in their understanding of stratigraphy and that this has had a catastrophic effect on our understanding of ancient history. If we could only sort out the discrepancies in the stratigraphic time line, then much other data, (for example, texts such as the Bible and "anomalous" finds such as Persian armor of the fifth century that we see depicted in temple reliefs dated to the twelfth century BC instead of the fifth) would disappear.

Fortunately for our purposes, we don't need to engage in these arguments—at least not very much. For the most part the dates that we will be using are anchored firmly to three key events in antiquity, the dates of which are contained in contemporary archives: the fall of Jerusalem in 586 BC, the fall of Babylon in 539 BC, and the first conquest of Egypt by the Persians in 525 BC. These dates are not in dispute and consequently they provide us with reliable fixed points for the discussions that follow. What is also worth noticing is that under the "new dating" system (pioneered by Velikovsky and since revised further by Peter James and his colleagues) the Trojan War moves forward in time. This is important because it is one of the key events against which ancient Greek authors sort to anchor their history. Under the new chronology we discover that it probably took place in the ninth or even eighth century BC and not in the twelfth as is generally supposed. We discover that the Mycenaean Greeks (who sieged Troy) were the immediate forebears of the Classical Greeks who founded the great city of Athens and later colonized the coast of Ionia in Turkey. Indeed, the siege of Troy may be seen as part of this process of Greek expansion into Anatolia and not as some sort of isolated incident that took place hundreds of years before Homer, who lived sometime between 800 and 700 BC, wrote about it. The "Bronze Age Dark Age," which scholars have constructed in order to make stratigraphy fit with Manetho's Egyptian king lists, simple does not exist. As Peter James and his colleagues put it:

> "With a background of research in many different but related fields (specifically prehistoric Britain, Minoan Crete, Mycenaean Greece, biblical archaeology and Pharaonic Nubia), we pooled our resources and began an in depth investigation of the archaeological chronology of the entire ancient Mediterranean and Near East. Everything we found confirmed our suspicion that the original spanner in

> the works was the Egyptian time-scale, and that the 'cen-
> turies of darkness' inserted into the histories of so many
> areas between 1200 and 700 BC were largely illusory."[7]

The mention of prehistoric Britain is apposite, for the ancient history of the British Isles is also embroiled in a saga of confused dating. Expert opinion on the historicity of the early Irish Annals is that these are works of colorful fancy, if not of downright fiction. After all, it doesn't take an expert to see that in linking the invasion of Ireland with the Exodus of Moses, *The Annals of Clonmacnoise* get hopelessly confused. This is not helped when we read in the annals themselves that at the time of the Exodus, someone called Neale mcFenius, the "ancestor of the Clanna Miley," while living in Egypt met up with Aaron and Moses in the desert. Did he really invite the Jews back to his own camp for supper? Did Moses subsequently heal Neale's young son Gathelus after he had a strange encounter with a snake? Such stories have all the hallmarks of pious fiction. We can only conclude that the story of the snake was included in the *Annals* in anticipation of St. Patrick's later alleged banishing of snakes from Ireland. Given such embroidering, it is not surprising that archaeologists and historians tend to steer well clear of this literature; turning their backs on traditional history, they prefer to put their trust in what their shovels reveal.

The same conundrum faced me too, when I first read in *The Annals of Clonmacnoise* the account of Moses' meeting with Neale and his son Gathelus. However I also had an intuition (call it a gut instinct) that the subsequent story of Gathelus and his Milesians had buried within it a true account of a late Bronze Age (or even early Iron Age) invasion of Ireland. For this to be so, we must first dispense with the obvious fiction that such an invasion took place around the time of Moses' Exodus, for this is generally thought to have taken place during the reign of Rameses II of the Eighteenth Dynasty of Egypt (1567–1320 BC) with the most frequently quoted date being around 1447 BC. Even by Velikovsky's revised system of Egyptian dating the Exodus would still have happened by 1200 at the very latest, and this is far too early for the last migration to Ireland: the Milesian. This is clearly synonymous with the arrival of the "Celts" or Gaels—which archaeology tells us must have taken place between 600 BC and 500 BC.[8] Taking into account these considerations, it is clear that the key to unraveling the mystery of this last migration is working out who these Milesians really were and when such a people might really have been in Egypt.

This, actually, is not as hard to do as it may first appear, for although there is no connection with the Exodus of Moses, there were indeed people called Milesians living in Egypt during our target period of 600–500 BC. They were there just after the destruction of the kingdom of Judah and at the start of the Babylonian exile of the Jews. This was a time of turmoil not just in Judea but throughout the Middle East; for from the late seventh through to the late sixth centuries BC, first the Assyrian and then the Egyptian Empires were overthrown by the Babylonians before they in turn succumbed to the Medo–Persians. It turns out that the history of these turbulent times is crucial for the light it throws on the legends surround the Stone of Destiny. It also adds credence to the possibility that a stone such as this could indeed have once belonged to the ancient Israelites before being taken to Ireland.

As we discussed earlier, Manetho's system of king lists, though used by Egyptologists as a handy skeleton for developing a timeline, is actually anything but accurate and is in desperate need of revision. We are fortunate, however, that the period we are interested in (late seventh to late sixth centuries BC) contains some dates that are well documented elsewhere. As these dates refer to events that took place during Manetho's Twenty-Sixth Dynasty, we are able to fix this dynasty with some considerable accuracy into the contemporary timeline of Middle Eastern history.

The first important contemporary event is the fall of Jerusalem to the Egyptians. Manetho records that Nechao II [the biblical Pharaoh Neco] "took Jerusalem, and led King Ioachaz (Jehoahaz II) captive into Egypt." These events are told in more detail in the Bible where we read the following:

> "In his [King Josiah's] days Pharaoh Neco king of Egypt went up to the king of Assyria to the river Euphrates. King Josiah [of Judah] went to meet him; and Pharaoh Neco slew him [Josiah] at Megiddo, when he saw him. And his servants carried him dead in a chariot from Megiddo, and brought him to Jerusalem, and buried him in his own tomb. And the people of the land took Jehoahaz the son of Josiah, and anointed him, and made him king in his father's stead.
>
> Jehoahaz was twenty-three years old when he began

to reign; and he reigned three months in Jerusalem. His mother's name was Hamutal, the daughter of Jeremiah of Libnah. And he did that which was evil in the sight of the Lord, according to all that his fathers had done. And Pharaoh Neco put him in bonds at Riblah in the land of Hamath, that he might not reign in Jerusalem, and laid upon the land a tribute of an hundred talents of silver and a talent of gold. And Pharaoh Neco made Eliakim the son of Josiah king in the place of Josiah his father, and changed his name to Jehoiakim. But he took Jehoahaz away; and he came to Egypt and died there. And Jehoiakim gave the silver and the gold to Pharaoh; but he taxed the land to give the money according to the commandment of Pharaoh. He exacted the silver and the gold of the people of the land, and of every one according to his taxation, to give it to Pharaoh Neco.

Johoiakim was twenty-five years old when he began to reign; and he reigned eleven years in Jerusalem." (II Kings 23: 29-36)

We can work out from other dates given in the Bible that Neco's Judean campaign must have taken place in 609 BC: in this year Josiah died, Jehoahaz II was deposed, and Jehoiakim was set up as an Egyptian puppet. What the Bible doesn't tell us is that this war of Neco's was part of a much larger conflict that embraced almost the whole of the Middle East. During that time several major powers were jostling for supremacy. There were the Assyrians (with whom Neco, the Egyptian king, was in alliance); the Neo–Babylonians (who had already taken Nineveh and were in the process of finishing off the Assyrian Empire); the Medo–Persians (who would later incorporate both Babylonia and Egypt in their massive empire); and finally the Greeks, who at this time were divided into small city–states but would later defeat the Persians at the Battles of Marathon (490 BC) and Salamis (480 BC) and eventually (some two and a half centuries later under Alexander the Great) establish the largest empire of them all.

To understand how the interaction of these empires is connected to the story of a Gaelic migration to Ireland, it is first necessary to build an historical framework. For although the Old Testament of the Bible (in particular in the second book of Kings, the second book of Chronicles,

Isaiah, Jeremiah, Ezekiel, and Daniel) gives a moving description of these times as seen from the point of view of the Jews, this is incomplete. In reality, events in Palestine were a sideshow compared with the much larger conflicts raging between the competing empires that encircled the tiny kingdom of Judah. Indeed King Josiah would have been wise to have kept out of the way of Neco whose real quarrel was with Nabopolassar, the King of Babylon, and not with him. The fact that Josiah interfered cost him his life and the land of Judah a huge amount in taxes paid to the Egyptians.

Ages and Empires

According to the consensus dating of the Near East, civilization, at least in the form we generally recognize it, goes back to about 3500 BC. Just around then a literate, urban culture developed in Mesopotamia (modern day Iraq) and a similar culture appeared in Egypt at around the same time. By 3100 BC the cuneiform script was developed in Mesopotamia. At the same time a king, whom Manetho calls "Menes" but who is elsewhere referred to by the name "Narmer," united the lands of Upper and Lower Egypt under a single crown. Menes came from Upper Egypt, but for the sake of unity, he moved his capital to Memphis, which is just a few miles to the south of modern day Cairo. Within a few centuries the Egyptians, who had already mastered the skill of writing hieroglyphs, began building their first pyramids. The Sumerians, meanwhile, were perfecting their language and building the first of their ziggurats in the region of southern Mesopotamia.

As the centuries rolled by, both countries, though not yet in conflict, developed their infrastructures and consequently military strength. At first this was deployed quite locally, but by 1560 BC the Egyptian "New Kingdom" was in full swing. Under pharaohs such as Tuthmosis III, Seti I, and Rameses II, Egypt developed an empire that spread along the coast of the Levant as far north as Syria. Meanwhile, further east in Mesopotamia, the old kingdoms of Akkad, Sumer, and Babylon had been superceded by an emerging power: Assyria. This had its capital at Nineveh, a city on the River Tigris, on the opposite bank to Mosul, in what is now Iraqi Kurdistan. North of both these empires was that of the Hittites, whose capital Boğazköy was in what is now central Turkey.

It was inevitable that as these empires grew, there would be rivalry between them and so it proved to be. By the end of the second millennium BC, a "great game" was underway with several players struggling for control of the small but strategically important country of Israel. For about a century afterwards, during the reigns of King David and his son Solomon, these outside forces were held at bay, and indeed Israel itself increased in power and influence. However, following Solomon's death (ca. 932 BC), the kingdom of Israel split in two. The timing of this was very unfortunate, for to the east Assyria was growing to its peak of power.

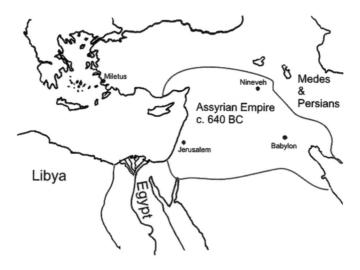

MAP 6: ASSYRIAN EMPIRE

Meanwhile in what is now Turkey, there were other dramas being played out. Eastern Anatolia, which had been dominated by the Hittite Empire, was now mostly part of the Assyrian Empire. West of the River Halys there was a collection of smaller, related states. The largest of these were Phrygia and Lydia, the latter growing extremely rich. As the first millennium BC progressed, so the pattern changed further with the Greeks setting up city–states on the coast, and other invaders, such as the Cimmerians and Scythians, entering Anatolia from the north and east.[9]

Chronologies of the Kings

The jostling for power between competing Middle Eastern empires

reached a peak in the seventh to sixth centuries BC. However, to properly understand how this worked out and its relevance to the migration
legends of the Scots and Irish (and hence to the Stone of Destiny), it is
helpful if we first build a skeleton of chronologies of the various kingdoms and their kings.

The first chronology to consider is that of Egypt. We don't here need
to concern ourselves with what happened during the times of Egypt's
greatness: the Old and New Kingdoms. The period that concerns us is
from the seventh to the end of the sixth centuries BC. This was long
after Egypt's Golden Age. During this time Egypt was conquered by first
the Assyrians, then the Babylonians, and finally the Persians.[10] Though
finding dates for pharaohs belonging to earlier dynasties is difficult to
do with any accuracy, we can easily identify those belonging to the
Twenty-Sixth Dynasty (the time in question) for these kings, along with
their periods of rule, are listed in the works of Manetho. As we also
know that the Twenty-Sixth Dynasty came to an end in 525 BC, we can
use this anchor date to backtrack the accession dates of the pharaohs
and thereby work out an accurate chronology. From this data we can
draw up the following table:

Egypt's Twenty-Sixth Dynasty (according to Manetho):

Ammeris	(12 years)	695–683 BC
Stephinathis	(7 years)	683–676 BC
Nechepsos	(6 years)	676–670 BC
Nechao I	(8 years)	670–662 BC
Psammeticus I	(45 years)	662–617 BC
Nechao II	(8 years)	617–609 BC
Psammeticus II	(17 years)	609–592 BC
Aphries	(25 years)	592–567 BC
Amosis	(42 years)	567–525 BC

525 BC marks the end of Twenty-Sixth Dynasty. In this year Egypt
was brought into the Persian Empire by Cambyses II who now, as far as
the Egyptians were concerned, became the first pharaoh of the Twenty-
Sixth Dynasty.

The dates for the corresponding kings of Judah are also easy to establish by using another important date: the fall of Jerusalem. This can
be dated accurately from Assyrian and Babylonian records as 586 BC.
Using this anchor date and the duration of reigns as given in the Bible,

we can create the following table for:

The later kings of Judah:

Hezekiah	716–687 BC
Manasseh	687–643 BC
Amon	643–641 BC
Josiah	641–609 BC (Killed by Neco)
Jehoahaz II	609 BC (Taken captive to Egypt by Neco)
Jehoiakim	609–598 BC
Jehoiachin	598–597 BC (Taken captive to Babylon)
Zedekiah	597–586 BC (Taken captive to Babylon. End of the kingdom of Judah)

The Old Assyrian Empire need not concern us here except to say that after a period of decline, it was followed at around 1000 BC by the New Assyrian Empire. Records of the kingdom reveal the names of rulers and the duration of their reigns. This Empire was finally and terminally overthrown in 606 BC. For our period of interest we can draw up the following table:

Assyrian Rulers: 727–606 BC

Shalmaneser V	727–705 BC (Sacked Samaria and deported the Israelites)
Sennacherib	705–681 BC (invaded Judea but army decimated by an "angel")
Esarhaddon	680–669 BC (in 670 Manasseh, king of Judah, paid him tribute)
Assurbanipal	668–626 BC
Assur–etil–ilâni	626–621 BC
Sin–shar–ishkun	620–612 BC (Fall of Nineveh)
Assur–uballit II	611–606 BC (End of Assyrian Empire)

The Neo–Babylonian Empire, which took over from the Assyrian, though of quite short duration, was also critical in the history of Judea. Babylon itself fell in 539 BC to a confederation of the Medes and Persians. By using this as another anchor date, we are able to put together the following chronology for the Babylonian Empire:

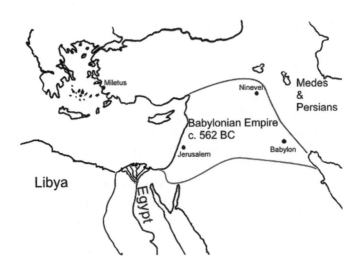

MAP 7: BABYLONIAN EMPIRE

Babylonian Rulers: pre–625–539 BC

Sin–shar–ishkun	(Assyrian but controlling part of Babylonia for several years)
Nabopolassar	625–605 BC
Nebuchadnezzar	605–562 BC (597 deposed Jehoiachin and took him to Babylon. In 586 BC sacked Jerusalem taking Zedechiah and the remaining Jews into captivity)
Amel–Marduk	561–560 BC
Neriglissar	559–556 BC
Labashi–Marduk	556 BC
Nabu–na'id	555–539 BC (Capture of Babylon by the Medes and Persians)

The Medo–Persian Empire also began during Assyrian times. At first the Kings of the Medes were the overlords with the Persian or Elamite dynasty as the junior partner. However, in 550 BC Cyrus II, the Persian king, rebelled and overthrew Astyages the Mede; thereafter Persia became the dominant partner. The Persians eventually established a huge empire that stretched from India in the east to parts of Greece and Egypt in the west.

Kings of the Medes

Deioces	728–675 BC
Phraotes	675–653 BC
Madius the Scythian	653–625 BC
Cyaxares	625–585 BC
Astyages	585–550 BC (Medes eclipsed by the Persians)

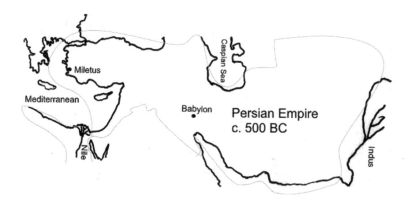

MAP 8: PERSIAN EMPIRE

Kings of the Persians

Achaimenes	700–675 BC (Founder of the Achaemenian Dynasty)
Teispes	675–640 BC
Cyrus I	640–600 BC
Cambyses I	600–559 BC
Cyrus II	559–529 BC (Conquered Babylon 539 BC)
Cambyses II	529–522 BC (Conquered Egypt in 525 BC)
Darius I	522–486 BC (Made first attempt at conquest of Greece)

These king lists of the seventh and sixth centuries BC give us a framework for placing in perspective the history of the Holy Land (and hence the supposed removal of the Stone of Destiny to Ireland). However, if we are to properly understand the confused statements contained in the *Annals of Clonmacnoise*, there are two other nations whose role in the sixth century BC needs to be considered: the Greeks and the Scythians. Minor characters on the stage, their role in the unfolding of sixth cen-

Miletus the Great—City of the Greeks

One of the most confusing aspects of the story contained in the Irish Annals is their insistence that the leader of the Gaels was a Scythian, sometimes called Gathelus and at other times Miletus (Miledh), who was, nevertheless, the son of a Greek king called Neale and yet lived in Egypt at the time of Moses and aided the Israelites. This is all very puzzling. However, once any connection with Moses and the Exodus is discounted and the real history of Egypt is analyzed, it becomes possible to see how "Gallo the Scythian/Milesian" might indeed have been a real personage. The key to this revelation is in Gallo's surname "Miletus"; for a Greek city of this name on the coast of what is now Turkey stood out like a beacon in the Late Bronze/Early Iron Age.

MAP 9: ORIGINS OF MILESIAN INVASION

Miletus, whose ruins are near modern-day Kusadasi, was the southernmost city of the Ionian league. This was a group of twelve Greek

city-states (the *dodekapolis*) which included Ephesus and the islands of
Samos and Chios. During the seventh and sixth centuries BC, Miletus
was the most brilliant city in the entire Greek world. Far outstripping
Athens for its wealth, it was also famous for its schools of philosophy.[11]
It was also the first city in the ancient world to adopt a grid street plan
(an idea later copied by the Romans). Right up until it was destroyed by
the Persians in 494 BC, Miletus remained the leading city of Ionia—and
indeed of the Greek world, in general. It is, therefore, sensible to investigate its history, and how, if at all, Milesians could have been involved
in a migration from Egypt to Ireland.

To properly appreciate the position of Miletus, we must first understand a little bit of early Greek history. It is a common misconception to
think that the Greeks (more properly called the Hellenes) were one uni-
fied nation. In fact, in the ancient world, the cities and people of Greece
belonged to four distinct subethnicities, each with their own dialects.
These were the Ionians, the Aeolians, the Dorians, and the Achaeans.
These different ethnicities came about as a result of successive waves of
invasions of the Greek islands and mainland. Thus while the four groups
were all Greeks, they also had their own identities and this often led to
intense rivalries. During the Late Bronze Age (ca. 900–600 BC), the Greeks
set up colony cities on the coast of mainland Turkey, displacing the
earlier "Luvian" population in the process.[12] Miletus was one such
colony. It looked towards Athens as its mother city because it was from
here that the Milesians' founding father, Neleus, was said to have come.
This seems to be the source of the legend, told in the *Annals of
Clonmacnoise*, that Gathelus was a son of Neale and was "surnamed"
Miletus.

The Milesians were seafarers and traders. As such, they themselves
established many other cities and colonies all over the ancient world.
Some of these were on the coast of the Black Sea in the region that was
then called Scythia: the term "Scythian" being applied by the Greeks to
all of the barbarian nations living north of Thrace. One of these colonies, Istria, lay at the mouth of the River Danube on the borders of
Scythia, but there were many other colonies all around the south coast
of the Black Sea.

The Milesians also went to Egypt where, along with other Greeks and
Carians,[13] they offered their services as mercenaries. Herodotus tells us
how they helped Necho's father, Psammeticus I, gain his revenge on
eleven "kings" who had driven him from his throne. The Greek merce-

naries proved to be crucial in helping him to regain his kingdom from usurpers:

> "When he [Psammetichus I] sent a query to the city of Buto, the home of the most reliable Egyptian oracle, he received in return a prophecy to the effect that his revenge would come in the form of bronze men rising from the sea. The idea of bronze men coming to help him struck him as extremely implausible, but a short while later some Ionian and Carian raiders, who had left home in search of rich pickings, found that they could not avoid being driven on to the coast of Egypt, and disembarked in their bronze armour. An Egyptian who had never before seen men dressed in bronze armour went to the marshes and told Psammetichus that bronze men had come from the sea and were plundering the plain. Psammetichus realised that the oracle was coming true. He got on friendly terms with the Ionians and Carians and, with promises of generous rewards, persuaded them to support him. Then, with the help of his Egyptian partisans and these allies of his he deposed the kings."[14]

By the time Psammetichus' son Necho (617–609 BC) came onto the throne, there was already a sizeable force of Greek mercenaries in Egypt to accompany him in his invasion of Judaea. We also know that Necho thought particularly highly of Miletus, for Herodotus tells us that following the battle of "Cadytis" (*Kadesh*) in 609 BC, he sent the clothes he was wearing to the oracle center of Brachidae, which was in Miletus [Herodotus 2.159]. In ca. 600 BC, Necho's son, Psammetichus II, formalized the friendly arrangement his father had with the mercenaries by allowing the Greeks to settle permanently in Egypt in a colony called Naucratis.[15] The city grew rapidly so that by around 550 BC, when King Amosis gave Naucratis its autonomy, it was already the major trading station of Egypt.[16]

Psammeticus II needed all the allies he could get, for although Necho had won the battles of Megiddo and Kadesh, the wars in the Middle East were very far from over. In 606 BC Harran was retaken by the Babylonians, signaling the final end of the Assyrian Empire. This meant that the Babylonians were now free to turn their attentions westwards.

In 605 BC they crossed the Euphrates and surprised the Egyptian garrison at Carchemish. The entire force, the cream of the Egyptian army, was destroyed with not a single man returning home. It was a disaster that for a time put an end to Egyptian ambitions in Syria and the Levant.

The Babylonians were led by Prince Nebuchadnezzar (also called Nebuchadrezzar) who while still in the field was informed of his father's death and his own elevation to the throne of Babylon. Jehoiakim, the king of Judah, installed by the Egyptians, found that he had little choice but to placate the new power on the block. In 604 BC he broke his promise to Necho and swore allegiance to Nebuchadnezzar. This left the Babylonians free to move south against Egypt itself. Around 601 BC the two nations fought a major battle in the vicinity of Gaza, with both sides suffering huge casualties. Jehoiakim evidently saw Egypt as the victor of the battle and tried to profit from this Babylonian setback by changing sides again.

Seething with anger at this betrayal, Nebuchadnezzar returned and placed Jerusalem under siege. Luckily for him, Jehoiakim died before he could be held to account for his treachery. Instead it fell to his son, an eighteen-year-old prince called Jehoiachin ("Jah establishes"), to pay the price.

In 597 BC with the Babylonian army surrounding the city and cutting off all escape, he had no choice but to throw himself on Nebuchadnezzar's mercy. King for only a few months, Johoiachin as well as his mother, the royal princes, his servants, his palace officials, and the treasures of the temple were taken back to Babylon. Also taken captive was the cream of the aristocracy along with the artisans whose skill brought wealth to the city. All that was left of Judah was a remnant, mainly composed of the common people. Then, taking a leaf out of Necho's book, Nebuchadnezzar appointed a puppet king of his own: Jehoiachin's uncle Mattaniah ("gift of Jah"), changing his name to Zedekiah ("Jah is might").

With the Egyptians responsible for the death of his father and elder brother, Nebuchadnezzar could be excused for thinking Zedekiah would be unlikely to rebel against Babylon. He was wrong, for almost as soon as he had heard that Psammeticus II had died, Zedekiah made overtures to his successor: Uapries or "Pharaoh Hophra" as he is called in the Bible. Nebuchadnezzar was furious, and unfortunately for Zedekiah (as the prophet Jeremiah had predicted), Egypt turned out to be an untrustworthy ally:

"In the ninth year of his (Zedekiah's reign) (587 BC), in the
tenth month, on the tenth day of the month, Nebuchadnezzar king of Babylon came with all his army against
Jerusalem, and laid siege to it; . . . so the city was be-
sieged till the eleventh year of King Zedekiah (586 BC) . . .
Then they captured the king, and brought him up to the
king of Babylon at Riblah, who passed sentence on him.
They slew the sons of Zedekiah before his eyes and, put
out the eyes of Zedekiah, and bound him in fetters, and
took him to Babylon."(2 Kings 25:1-7)

These traumatic events brought to an end the Judean monarchy and
even seemed to be the end of the House of David. However this, it
would appear, was not entirely the case. Speaking in the cryptic terminology of prophecy, the book of Ezekiel tells us of a sequel to this story.
Here, by means of an allegory, we are told the story of the struggle
between Egypt and Babylon for the submission of the Judean kingdom.
In the seventeenth chapter Ezekiel describes how two great eagles (symbolic of Babylon and Egypt) each seek to take control of Judea. As a
result, the King of Judah is to be taken to Babylon where God will pass
judgment on him for his treason. However, then in a following passage
we are told, again in symbolic language, that provision is to be made to
preserve the royal line:

"Thus says the Lord God: 'I myself will take a sprig from
the lofty top of the cedar, and will set it out; I will break off
from the topmost of its young twigs a tender one, and I
myself will plant it upon a high and lofty mountain; on the
mountain heights of Israel will I plant it, that it may bring
forth boughs and bear fruit, and become a noble cedar;
and under it will dwell all kinds of beasts; in the shade of
its branches birds of every sort will nest. All the trees of
the field shall know that I the Lord bring low the high tree,
and make high the low tree, dry up the green tree, and
make the dry tree flourish. I the Lord have spoken, and I
will do it.' " (Ezek. 17:22-4)

The interpretation of this parable is that the cedar represents the
family tree of the Royal House of Judah. The "topmost of its twigs, a

tender one" is symbolic of a daughter of Zedekiah, his sons having all
been killed in front of him before he was blinded and taken away into
captivity.

This story links up with another, told this time by the prophet
Jeremiah. Following the Babylonian destruction of Jerusalem, he warned
the remnant of the Jews, who, like himself, were left behind, that they
should not flee but rather put their trust in God. They didn't heed his
warning but instead fled to Egypt, taking the unwilling Jeremiah with them:

> "But Johanan the son of Kareah and all the commanders
> of the forces took all the remnant of Judah who had re-
> turned to live in the land of Judah from all the nations to
> which they had been driven—the men, the women, the
> children, the princesses, . . . also Jeremiah the prophet
> and Baruch the son of Neriah. And they came into the
> land of Egypt, for they did not obey the word of the Lord.
> And they arrived in Tahpanhes." (Jer. 43: 5-7).

This passage is important because it reveals that the princesses, the
daughters of King Zedekiah, were taken to Egypt. The pharaoh ruling
Egypt at the time of the Babylonian sack of Jerusalem was Apries or
"Pharaoh Hophra" as he is called in the Bible. He, like his father
Psammeticus II, employed a mercenary army which he had sent into
Judah with the intention of helping Zedekiah. However, on seeing the
strength of the Babylonians, this army turned tail and withdrew back
into Egypt without engaging the enemy. The only help that Apries could
offer the Jews was to allow those who had not been taken to Babylon to
cross the border too.

The place they went to, Tahpanhes (*Daphnae* in Greek), was a frontier
fortress on the Pelusian branch of the River Nile. It was here that, prior
to the founding of Naucritis, the majority of the Greek mercenaries
(mostly Milesians) were stationed. Consequently Jeremiah and the royal
princesses of Judah would there, if not before, have come into contact
with the Milesians.

When the Jews arrived at Daphnae, they would undoubtedly have
also come across many Scythians warriors: the remnant of a great horde
that once dominated Asia. In ca. 620 BC this horde had entered Arme-
nia, which lies to the west of the Caspian Sea. Moving south, they con-
fronted Cyaxares (the king of the Medes), who was then engaged in the

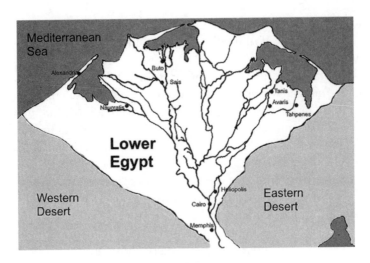

MAP 10: LOWER EGYPT

siege of Nineveh. After defeating him and seizing the possessions of the Medes, the Scythians made their way west and south—probably on horseback—through what is now eastern Turkey and Syria. From the outset, their intention was to invade Egypt, which was still the richest nation on earth. However Pharaoh Psammeticus I met with them and dissuaded them from this endeavor:

> "From there (Kurdistan) they (the Scythians) marched on Egypt. When they reached Syrian Palestine, the Egyptian king Psammetichus (viz. Psammetichus I) came to meet them. With a combination of bribery and entreaty he persuaded them not to go on any further and they turned back."[17]

Herodotus goes on to tell us that:

> "The Scythian domination of Asia lasted twenty-eight years, and their expulsion came about because of their abusive and disdainful attitude . . . Cyaxares and the Medes invited a great many of them to a feast, got them drunk, and then killed them. So the Medes regained their

empire and took control again of the same peoples as
before. They also took Ninus (Nineveh) and subdued all of
Assyria except for Babylon and its territory. Sometime later
Cyaxares died, after a reign of forty years (including the
years of Scythian domination)."[18]

Cyaxares died in 585 BC and the Scythian invasion seems to have
taken place near the beginning of his reign—perhaps around 620 BC.
This would suggest that the expulsion of the Scythians from Medea
took place around 592 BC, or maybe a few years earlier, (i.e., towards the
end of the reign of Psammeticus II—the son rather than the father of
Necho). Given the favorable reception accorded to them twenty-eight
years earlier by his grandfather, it seems very likely that following the
butchery of the drunks at Cyaxares' party, those Scythians who survived would have had every incentive to join the mercenary army of
the Egyptians. Discounting the red herring that these events took place
during the reign of David, king of Israel and Judah (who ruled from
ca.1000–965 BC), this agreement between Psammeticus II and the
Scythians seems to be what is behind the report in the *Annals of
Clonmacnoise* that "Gallo" (i.e., Gathelus/Miletus) was a son of the king of
Scythia:

> "In the year after the flood 1245 being about the 12th year
> of the reign of David king of Israel & Judea, Gallo the son
> of Billus king of Scythia after named Miletus of Spain for
> his many and great exploits, hearing of the great wars
> which the Egyptians held then with their neighbouring
> countries, being before in some displeasure at home for
> the strife that grew between him and kinsman for the king-
> dom of Scythia and being also himself much given to war,
> ambitious of honour and desirous to increase his name
> (as the manner of his country was) passed out of Scythia
> with a number of his friends, kinsmen and followers into
> Egypt, where he was no sooner arrived then well enter-
> tained by the Egyptians, and in short time after did so well
> acquit himself in their service, that he was made General
> of their armies and withal married the daughter of
> Symedes the greatest prince in Egypt or Pharaoh as they
> did then commonly call their monarch, his other daughter

was after married to Solomon, King of Jerusalem. This Symedes or Symenides by other authors is called also Silagh and became so great and mighty, that he had in his army 1200 chariots, 60,000 horses, and 400,000 footmen."[19]

Given that the Scythians were noted horse warriors, it is likely that they made up the bulk of Symedes' cavalry with the Greeks and Carians providing battalions of infantry and the Egyptians the chariots. So perhaps the boast that Symedes (clearly Psammeticus II) had "1200 chariots, 60,000 horses and 400,000 footmen" in his army is not quite the gross exaggeration it at first appears. It follows that Gathelus/Miletus, who is referred to in the Irish and Scottish Annals as the father of the Gallic Scots, must have been a general in Psammeticus' mercenary army. If this is the case, then his job would have been to defend Egypt against the threat of invasion by the Babylonians.

We may infer that the marriage of Gallo/Miletus to pharaoh's daughter, (whom we later discover was called "Scota"), took place at around this time. Gallo/Miletus would then have been stationed at Tahpanhes: today called *Tell Defeneh*. The identity of any sister of Scota who may have married a king of Judah is impossible to tell. As far as the Egyptians of this period were concerned, Judea, as well as supplying tax revenues, was a useful buffer state against the growing power of Babylon. It is therefore not impossible (and it is even probable) that as a gesture of goodwill towards a friendly client state, a sister of Scota was married off to a king of Judah. Clearly her husband would not have been Solomon, who reigned more than three hundred years earlier; however, he may have been Jehoiakim: the king that Necho had installed at Jerusalem in 609 BC. We may infer that the marriage took place early on in Jehoiakim's reign, perhaps around 608 BC. The intention would have been that the children of this marriage, being grandsons of the pharaoh, would be natural allies.

This is, of course, conjecture, but it does make some sense. It could well be that at least one of the Jewish princesses who accompanied Jeremiah the prophet when he was taken to Egypt was, in fact, a daughter of Scota's unnamed sister. What we can be more certain about is that if there really was a Scythian/Milesian general called "Gallo," he would undoubtedly have met Jeremiah the prophet at Daphnae and therefore also the Judean princesses who accompanied him. A small memory of their visit is still preserved at *Tell Defeneh* to this day in the name of a hill called *Qatsir Bint il Yahudi* or "the palace of the Jew's daughter." This is presumably where the Jewish princesses were housed during their stay in Egypt.

The fall of Jerusalem and the flight of the Jewish princesses was not the end of the story as far as the Babylonians were concerned. In 567 BC Pharaoh Apries was overthrown by Amasis, a rebel Egyptian general. The cause of the rebellion was failure in a war against the Greeks of the city of Cyrene in Libya. The native Egyptians in Apries' army resented that they had had to fight and die while the Greek mercenaries were excused from battle. Battle lines were drawn up with Apries supported by his mercenaries and Amasis by his Egyptians. Greater numbers ensured a win to Amasis and Apries was deposed. These events, however, do not seem to have pleased Nebuchadnezzar of Babylon who now invaded Egypt with a substantial force himself. In what to an Egyptian pharaoh must have seemed like terrible humiliation, Amasis was forced to accept Babylonian authority.

Taking all of these matters together, a recognizable picture emerges. We know that the city of Naucritis was largely Milesian in origin, and we can therefore postulate that a young nobleman called Gallo, perhaps even a Scythian from one of the sixty or so Milesian colonies on the Black Sea, came to Egypt to seek fame and fortune. If so, then in 609 BC he would have accompanied Pharaoh Necho. This pharaoh died and was succeeded by Necho's son Psamettichus II. He was on exceedingly good terms with his Greek mercenaries, so it is not inconceivable that Gallo "the Milesian," who was evidently the leader of the mercenaries, was on such friendly terms with the royal family of Egypt that he was allowed to marry one of the pharaoh's daughters. She may even, as tradition states, have been called "Scota." If a sister of hers had married Jehoiakim, King of Judah, then Gallo's children would have been first cousins of any royal progeny from this marriage.

But what about Jeremiah's role in this story? Is there any connection between him and a stone that could, conceivably, have been the coronation stone we have today? Well, the Bible tells us explicitly that he was taken to Egypt along with the princesses of Judah. Curiously, it invokes the image of him hiding symbolic stones. As the place where this took place was Tahpenhes, a castle garrisoned by Ionian (i.e. Milesian) mercenaries, Gallo would have been there. It is therefore entirely possible that Jeremiah and the princesses should have met with

Gallo/Miletus and even that his son, Heremon, should have married Tea Tephi, one of the said princesses—though more likely in Egypt rather than Ireland.

We know from Herodotus that there was continued friction between Pharaoh Amases and the Greek mercenaries who had worked for his rival Apries, son of Psamettichus II. If Gallo really had married a daughter of Psametticus, then he and Apries would have been brothers-in-law. That means that after Apries was murdered by the mob, Gallo and his men may very well have found it prudent to flee from Egypt rather risk the same fate. Their departure would most likely have been in 569 BC or thereabouts, and they would have headed westwards from Egypt, away from domination by the Babylonians. The Milesians and Scythians (we may assume the two groups of mercenaries amalgamated their forces) may then, as the Irish Annals state, have journeyed overland through Libya to the Pillars of Hercules. Acquiring ships, they could have sailed up the coast of Spain and at first settled in the province of Gallicia where, according to other legends, they founded the city of Braganza which we now know as Santiago de Compostella. This is where Gallo/Miletus is supposed to have planted his throne and where he eventually died. Geographically, however, this area of Northwest Spain is directly south of Ireland. It is therefore not impossible or even unlikely that after Gallo's death his son Heremon and his brothers (perhaps accompanied by their mother Scota) could have launched an invasion of Ireland. As a further twist to fate, it seems likely that the "Tea" who according to the Annals became Heremon's wife and after whom was name "Teamhair" (or "Tara"), the capital of Ireland, was probably one of the princesses who escaped from Jerusalem. This, at any rate, is what popular legend has to say.[20]

Now it can be argued that this is all conjecture, but this theory and timescale fit both the Irish myth of the Milesian migration and the facts of the late Bronze Age/early Iron Age history of the Middle East. It is at least a plausible account of who the *Tuatha de Danaan*, the Milesians, and the Scythians were and how they might indeed have fitted into both Egyptian and Irish history. All this said, it is now time to turn our attention to what the Stone of Destiny itself has to tell us about its origins.

6

The Witness Stones of Jacob

So far we have been looking at how and when the Stone of Destiny could have been brought from the Middle East (probably Egypt) to the British Isles. However, there is also the legend that it is Jacob's Pillow/Pillar Stone to be considered. If there is any truth in this legend—and I admit given that we have no information outside of the pages of the Bible that a patriarch named "Jacob" even lived—it seems to me that there should be at least some evidence that such stones had an important role to play in the religious ideas of the Near East. I have found some evidence that this is so, but before we go into this, I think it is worth reading again the actual words of the Bible.

The story of Jacob and his "pillow" stone is contained in the book of Genesis. It is in two parts. The first part of the story is in Chapter 28. It concerns what happens while Jacob is on the road fleeing from his brother Esau after (with the help of their mother Rebecca) he has tricked him out of receiving their father's primary blessing. With no land or livestock and literally only the clothes in which he stands, Jacob is tired and frightened. His only hope for the future is if he can find employment with his mother's brother Laban who is in Haran.[1]

"Jacob left Beersheba, and went towards Haran. And he came to a certain place, and stayed there that night, because the sun had set. Taking one of the stones of the place, he put it under his head and lay down in that place to sleep. And he dreamed that there was a ladder set up on earth, and the top of it reached to heaven; and behold, the angels of God were ascending and descending on it! And behold the Lord stood above it and said, 'I am the Lord, the God of Abraham your father and the God of Isaac; the land on which you lie I will give to you and to your descendants; and your descendants shall be like the dust of the earth, and you shall spread abroad to the west and to the east and to the north and to the south; and by you and your descendants shall all the families of the earth bless themselves. Behold, I am with you and will keep you wherever you go, and will bring you back to this land; for I will not leave you until I have done that of which I have spoken to you.' Then Jacob awoke from his sleep and said, 'Surely the Lord is in this place; and I did not know it.' And he was afraid, and said, 'How awesome is this place! This is none other than the house of God, and this is the gate of heaven.'

So Jacob rose early in the morning, and he took the stone which he had put under his head and set it up for a pillar and poured oil on top of it.

He called the name of that place Bethel,[2] but the name of the city was Luz at the first. Then Jacob made a vow, saying, 'If God will be with me, and will keep me in this way that I go, and will give me bread to eat and clothing to wear, so that I may come again to my father's house in peace, then the Lord shall be my God, and this stone, which I have set up for a pillar, shall be God's house; and of all that thou givest me I will give the tenth to thee.'"
(Gen. 28:10-22)

The second part of the story occurs some twenty years later as Jacob, now a wealthy herdsman with a large family, returns from Paddan-Aram (the Harran region of northern Mesopotamia) on route to Canaan, the land of his birth. They pause again at Bethel where they make an altar and Jacob renews his contract with God:

> "God said to Jacob, 'Arise, go up to Bethel, and dwell there; and make there an altar to the God who appeared to you when you fled from your brother Esau.' So Jacob said to his household and to all who were with him, 'Put away the foreign gods that are among you, and purify yourselves, and change your garments; then let us arise and go up to Bethel, that I may make there an altar to the God who answered me in the day of my distress and has been with me wherever I have gone.' . . .
>
> . . . God appeared to Jacob again, when he came from Paddan-Aram, and blessed him. And God said to him, 'Your name is Jacob; no longer shall your name be called Jacob, but Israel shall be your name.' So his name was called Israel. And God said to him, 'I am God Almighty: be fruitful and multiply; a nation and a company of nations shall come from you, and kings shall spring from you. The land which I gave to Abraham and Isaac I will give to you, and I will give the land to your descendants after you.' Then God went up from him in the place where he had spoken with him. And Jacob set up a pillar in the place where he had spoken with him, a pillar of stone; and he poured out a drink offering on it, and poured oil on it. So Jacob called the name of the place where God had spoken with him, Bethel." (Gen. 35: 1-15)

There are some interesting points to note here. First of all there is no indication that the stone he raises this time is exactly the same one he had used twenty years earlier as his pillow. It may have been, but we cannot know this for certain. Secondly, this time the promise that is made to him concerns his inheritance. Previously he has only been promised title to the land on which he sleeps: the immediate vicinity of Luz/Bethel.[3] Now the promise is extended to the land previously given to Abraham and Isaac, (i.e., all of Canaan). This is a much bigger deal, and this perhaps explains why he felt it necessary to raise a new pillar, though, of course, this might also have been the same stone reused.

The pillar(s) at Bethel are not the only ones set up by Jacob, and Bethel is not the only place he raises one. In Chapter 31 he and his uncle Laban set up a heap of stones, with a pillar on top, as a witness of a contract between them that their families should not fight one another:

> "And Laban answered and said unto Jacob, 'These daughters are my daughters and these children are my children, and these cattle are my cattle, and all that thou seest is mine; and what can I do this day unto these my daughters, or unto their children which they have born?
>
> 'Now therefore come thou, let us make a covenant, I and thou; and let it be for a witness between me and thee.'
>
> And Jacob took a stone, and set it up for a pillar.
>
> And Jacob said unto his brethren, 'Gather stones'; and they took stones, and made an heap: and they did eat there upon the heap.
>
> And Laban called it Jegar-sahadutha (heap of testimony): but Jacob called it Galeed (heap of witness).
>
> And Laban said, 'This heap is a witness between me and thee this day. Therefore was the name of it called Galeed';
>
> And Mizpah (watch-tower); for he said, 'The Lord watch between me and thee, when we are absent from one another.
>
> 'If thou shalt afflict my daughters, or if thou shalt take other wives beside my daughters, no man is with us; see, God is witness between me and thee.'
>
> And Laban said to Jacob, 'Behold this heap, and behold this pillar, which I have cast betwixt me and thee;
>
> 'This heap be witness, and this pillar be witness, that I will not pass over this heap to thee, and that thou shalt not pass over this heap to me and this pillar unto me, for harm.
>
> 'The God of Abraham, and the God of Nahor, the God of their father, judge betwixt us. And Jacob sware by the fear of his father Isaac.'

> Then Jacob offered sacrifice upon the mount, and
> called his brethren to eat bread; and they did eat bread,
> and tarried all night in the mount. (Gen. 31: 43-54)

The concept of a "pillar of witness" is something that goes back a very long way and is indeed associated with the Harran region of northern Mesopotamia, "Paddan–Aram." There is also good reason for believing that Paddan–Aram was also the birthplace of the patriarch Abraham, Jacob's grandfather. According to the Bible, Abraham or "Abram" as he was then known was born in "Ur of the Chaldees." For reasons of archaeological politics as much as anything else, this has been falsely identified with Ur, a Sumerian city that was already in ruins at the time of Abraham. This city was excavated in the 1920s by Leonard Woolley, who perhaps for reasons of prestige, was keen to identify it with the Ur of the Chaldees of the Bible. However, Ur—a Middle Eastern word from which is derived the Latin word *urbs* and hence the English "urban"— means nothing more than "city." Furthermore, Ur in Sumeria was at its peak a thousand years or more before the birth of Abraham. This means we need to look elsewhere for our "Ur of the Chaldees" and that place turns out to be northern Mesopotamia.

In fact the city of Urfa (in southeast Turkey) is a much better candidate than Woolley's for the biblical Ur. At the time of Abraham, this city which the Greeks renamed Edessa was called *Orhay*. It belonged to the Kingdom of Mitanni, which prior to the rise of Assyria, dominated the region of northern Mesopotamia for centuries. Mittanni was founded by Hurrian invaders from Uratu: the region of Mount Ararat in eastern Turkey. Significantly, the Uratians were also known as *Chaldini* or Chaldeans and even a quick look at a map shows that the semiarid fields around Urfa were much more suited to the raising of sheep than southern Mesopotamia, which at the time of Abraham was more like the delta region of Egypt: well irrigated and intensively farmed. Thus to anyone with an open mind, it is quite clear that Urfa is the biblical "Ur of the Chaldees" and not Ur in Sumeria.

Further confirmation that Abraham came from these parts is that the Egyptians recorded an invasion of their country around this time (ca. 1675 BC) and their country was taken over by foreigners they called the *hyksos* or "shepherd kings." These foreigners were able to conquer Egypt because they had in their possession a superior weapon which till then had not been seen there: the war chariot. Significantly, we know that it was the Hurrians, originally from the steppes of Russia, who introduced the war chariot to the Middle East. It is, therefore, not difficult to see that Abraham's migration to Egypt was aided by the fact that the pharaoh he met with was, like himself, of Hurrian descent.

Now this is important for we know that for centuries and indeed well into the Christian era, the people of northern Mesopotamia followed a star religion which honored a chief deity called *Marilaha*, whose name meant "the Great Lord." According to Professor J.B. Segal in his definitive history of Urfa, *Edessa: ' The Blessed City',* the cult objects associated with *Marilaha* were a stool and pillar:

> "In the month of Shebat in the year 476 (i.e., February AD 165), I, Tirdat bar Adona, ruler of the Arab, built this altar and set a pillar to Marilaha for the life of my lord the king and his sons and for the life of Adona my father . . .
>   . . . In the month of Shebat in the year 476 . . . we set this pillar on this blessed mound and erected the stool for him whom my ruler feeds. He shall be *budar* after Tirdat the ruler and he shall give the stool to him whom he feeds. His recompense shall be from Marilaha. And if he withholds the stool, then the pillar will be ruined. He, the god, lives" [4]

Engraved stones bearing these inscriptions were found on a mound at a place called Sumatar Harabesi, which lies in the Tektek Mountains, 60 kilometers southeast of Urfa. This mound stands at the center of a complex of other buildings; it is surrounded to the north and east and at varying distances by an arc of eight subsidiary mounds on which stand the ruins of eight further "buildings." Each of these (two of them are caves) would appear to have been a shrine dedicated to one or another of the planets. From the inscriptions it is clear that the whole complex, which is now a squatter camp for itinerant Bedouin, was once a major center for the star religion known as Sabianism.

Historically, the Sabians are famous for preserving the late Egyptian texts known as the *Hermetica* at a time when these had disappeared from Egypt itself. Resisting all attempts at conversion by Christians, the Sabians continued to follow their own religious practices long into the period of Islamic domination. Their origins, however, go back much further than either of these religions. Indeed, it would seem that

Sabianism, or at least something similar to it, was the predominant religion of the region even before the arrival of the Hurrians of Mitanni; for in 1999 ruins of what appears to be some sort of temple complex were made at Gobeklitepe,[5] just ten miles north east of Urfa. The still ongoing archaeological investigation revealed a series of circular structures with stone-build walls and carefully carved T-shaped columns weighing up to twenty-five tons each. Sculpted onto these columns were figurative pictures of recognizable animals: boars, sheep, foxes, lions, herons, ducks, scorpions, ants, snakes—indeed a whole "Noah's Ark" of local wildlife. What, however, is really exciting is that the ruins date back to around 10,000 BC, which makes them far and away the oldest man-made structures yet discovered.

Analysis of these finds, which profoundly challenge our view of the origins of civilization, is still in its infancy. However, the selection of this hilltop with its panoramic view of the heavens and symbolic architecture reminds me of Laban and Jacob raising their pillar and pile as a reminder and signature of their peace covenant with one another. It also suggests that sky worship was a feature of whatever religion was practiced there in those far-off times. We don't know what the complex was used for or why the people who built it decorated the pillars with pictures of sculpted animals, but it does have strange resonances with the story of Noah's ark. The Bible tells us that this floating zoo eventually moored on top of Mount Ararat, which is located not that far northeast of Urfa. It is tempting to think, therefore, that the story of Noah's ark has something to do with the temple complex at Gobeklitepe which maybe celebrates this event. What is clear, though, is that it was some sort of clan monument. Standing high on a local peak, it was probably a ceremonial center where the people remembered their common ancestry from some "Noah-like" figure: that they were men, not animals, and as such had a duty to one another to maintain peace.

More than this we cannot say except that at least some of the elements we see at Gobeklitepe (e.g., the idea of a ceremonial center with satellite temples arranged on a hilltop around a central temple) are somewhat similar to the much later Sabian complex that we now call Sumatar Harabesi. We know that the Sabians, like the Assyrians before them, followed a star religion. Did the builders of the "zoo" at Gobeklitepe watch the stars too? Only further excavation will give us the answer.

The center of the Sabian cult, at least in later centuries, was in fact some forty kilometers south of Urfa in the city of Harran. It is first mentioned in the Bible as the place to which Abraham moved (after leaving Urfa) and where his father Terah died. We are told that Abraham's brothers, Haran and Nahor, remained in the region (Paddan-Aram), settling down to raise their families and tend sheep. However, although Abraham departed, the family connection continued. His son Isaac married his first cousin Rebecca, the daughter of Nahor. Then, in the next generation, their younger son Jacob returned to Haran. He worked as a shepherd for Rebecca's brother, Laban, on the understanding that if he did so for seven years, he would marry the latter's daughter Rachel. With a wry smile, the writer of the book of Genesis tells us how Jacob kept his side of the bargain, but when he asked for his bride, Laban gave him instead her less comely but older sister Leah; he had to work for a further seven years before Laban would let him marry Rachel too.

The importance of this is that it is likely that the tradition of setting up a ruler's "stool" and "pillar" to show endorsement by the local god is something Jacob was very familiar with. Thus the idea of unending his "pillow" stone and using it as an altar is not as strange as it first appears. By doing so he was making a statement: that he was the *budar* or priest of the deity who had communicated with him on that spot and with whom he had made a covenant.

Jacob's "Bethel" pillar was not the only such sacred stone in the ancient world; there were many. Mostly these were meteorites, one such being the *Kaaba* stone at Mecca, which was revered as sacred long before the advent of Mohammed and the establishment of Islam. This stone, black in color, is thought to be made of glass produced in a meteorite impact. The impact site was probably *Wabar* which is about 1,100 kilometers east of Mecca in the *Rub' al Khali* desert. Here a meteorite hit the earth with such force that the surrounding sand was melted and turned into glass beads of nickel–iron (from the meteorite) fusing with it.

Of course the idea that the *Kaaba* stone (called *Hajar al Aswad* in Arabic) came from this impact zone is only conjecture; in the near future no chemical tests have been, or are likely to be, carried out to prove the theory. The Islamic tradition is that the stone fell from heaven to show Adam and Eve where they should build the world's first temple. This temple and the stone were lost at the time of Noah's Flood, but both were rediscovered by Abraham and his son Ishmael, the latter being the patriarch of the Arabs. Having found the stone, father and son are said to have rebuilt the *Kaaba* temple in Mecca in order to rehouse it. Ages passed, or so the story continues, and the people of Mecca took to idolatry. Eventually Mohammed came along. He cleansed the *Kaaba* of its idols, and he himself placed the *Haja al Aswad* stone in the eastern corner.[6] Thus although the *Kaaba* itself has been rebuilt on several occasions, many devout Muslims believe it goes back to the time of Adam and that it is the oldest temple in the world.

Perhaps more important than the stone itself is the fact that Muslims associate both temple and stone with Ishmael. The Bible tells us how Abraham's wife Sarah had an Egyptian slave called Hagar for her personal lady-in-waiting. Apparently unable to bear children herself, Sarah encouraged her husband to impregnate Hagar so that he might have a son. This he did and so Ishmael was born. However, a couple of years later, though very old, Sarah herself bore a son whom she called Isaac, meaning "laughter." Determined to preserve Isaac's inheritance, she demanded that Abraham send Hagar and Ishmael away. It was a cruel decision for the family lived at Beersheba ("Well of the Oath") on the edge of the Negev Desert. By ordering Hagar and Ishmael to leave the security of their encampment and its well, Abraham and Sarah were condemning them to certain death. Indeed the Bible says they would have died had not God heard Hagar's prayers and he himself intervened with the following words:

> "'What troubles you Hagar? Fear not; for God has heard the voice of the lad where he is. Arise, lift up the lad, and hold him fast with your hand; for I will make him a great nation.' Then God opened her eyes, and she saw a well of water; and she went and filled the skin with water, and gave the lad a drink. And God was with the lad, and he grew up; he lived in the wilderness, and became an expert with the bow. He lived in the wilderness of Paran; and his mother took a wife for him from the land of Egypt."
> (Gen. 21: 17-21)

The wilderness of Paran is in the northeast of the Sinai Peninsula, south of the Negev desert and to the west of Eilat. It is a dry, inhospitable place inhabited only by itinerant Bedouins. This story, which may or may not be a simple folktale, has great repercussions in our own day; for just as the Jews claim descent from Isaac, so the Arabs believe they are descended from Ishmael. In the Bible Ishmael is little more than a footnote but in the Muslim world, as the patriarch of the whole Arab nation, he is a massively important figure. Indeed, in the holy books of Islam, it is Ishmael not Isaac who was about to be sacrificed by Abraham on Mount Moriah when an angel stayed his hand. Needless to say there is no evidence in the Bible that Abraham ever visited Mecca and rebuilt Adam and Eve's temple to house a holy stone. However, it does tell us that Ishmael had twelve sons and that their descendents "dwelt from Havilah [southwest Arabia] to Shur [northern Sinai abutting Egypt]." (Gen. 25:18) As Mecca is included in this desert region, it is not unreasonable to see a connection between the *Haja al Aswad* and the biblical story of Ishmael. It is very significant that this rock, towards which all Mosques are aligned, is the focal point of the Islamic faith. All Muslims direct their prayers to Mecca, and it is incumbent on them to, at least once in their lives, visit the holy shrine of the *Kaaba* and if possible touch or kiss the stone.

God's speaking to Hagar and revealing the location of a secret well seems to hark back to an earlier passage in the Bible where an angel makes a contract with Hagar during an earlier attempt by her to run away from Sarah's household: "The angel of the Lord found her [Hagar] by a spring of water in the wilderness, the spring on the way to Shur. And he said, 'Hagar, maid of Sarai, where have you come from and where are you going?' She said, 'I am fleeing from my mistress Sarai.' The angel of the Lord said to her, 'Return to your mistress and submit to her.' The angel of the Lord also said to her, 'I will so greatly multiply your descendants that they cannot be numbered.'" (Gen. 16: 7–10) The millions who gather at Mecca every year for the *Hadj* pilgrimage would suggest that God hasn't forgotten his promise.

The *Haja al Aswad* is not the only stone of meteoric origin that was known to the ancient world. In Greek such stones were given the name *baetylus*: a rendering of the Semitic word bethel. The most famous of these was the stone of Delphi, which was thought to be the very stone which Cronos, thinking it was the baby Zeus, had swallowed and later vomited.[7] It is clear that this stone symbolized Zeus and as a relic, was thought to act as a link that would enable devout followers to establish contact with the God himself.

There were other *baetyloi* linked to other gods and goddesses. One such was the stone of Amun that was kept at the Siwa Oasis in Egypt. People visited this oracle from all over the eastern Mediterranean region, the most famous pilgrim being Alexander the Great. The priests there told him, quite sensibly under the circumstances (he had just conquered Egypt), that he was right to believe that he was extra special. His mother had apparently not been impregnated by his father, Philip of Macedon, but rather by the god Amon himself. Like his hero Achilles, Alexander's exceptional genes came from the gods.

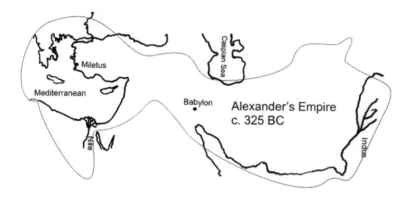

MAP 11: ALEXANDER'S EMPIRE

Probably the most famous *baetylus* of all was the stone of Cybele, which again was a meteorite. It was regarded as the incarnation of the Anatolian goddess of the same name, Cybele, and was kept at Pessinus—a city not far from Ephesus. Then, in 204 BC the Romans were told by their own Sibylline Oracle that if they wanted victory over Carthage, they must obtain this stone and bring it back to Rome. They did so and indeed won the war. Thereafter the stone remained in Rome though what happened to it in later centuries, after the Romans were converted to Christianity, is anyone's guess. Some people think (though without any evidence as far as I can tell) that it may have resurfaced as the *Haja al Aswad* of Mecca.

Unfortunately, the Cybele stone or indeed any of the other *baetyloi* of Greco–Roman times give us little in the way of clues concerning Jacob's Pillow/Pillar stone. Obviously, and taking the biblical story at face value, it is just possible that he found a large meteorite at Bethel and used it as his pillow; however this does not seem very likely. Such a stone would have been conical in shape, not a regular oblong like the British Stone of Destiny. It would also have been exceptionally heavy, knobbly, and have been anything but suitable as a pillow. We can probably discount, therefore, the possibility that Jacob's stone was a meteorite.

Yet another stone that has come down to us from ancient times is the so-called "Black Obelisk" put up by the Assyrian King Shalmaneser III (r. 852–824 BC) at Nimrud, the later capital of the Assyrian Empire. The ruins of Shalmaneser's palace lie somewhat to the south of Mosul in what is now Iraqi Kurdistan, and it was here that in 1846 the Black Obelisk was found. Now in the British Museum, it stands about six feet high and like all such stones is crowned by a miniature version of a ziggurat or Mesopotamian pyramid. It is heavily inscribed with cuneiform texts; however although these begin with invocations of all the major gods of Assyria and Babylonia: Assur, Anu, Enlil, Ea, Marduk, Ishtar, etc., its purpose was not primarily religious for it was clearly sculpted to reinforce his authority by boasting of Shalmaneser's many victories over his enemies

What makes this stone interesting from our point of view is that besides the long sequences of texts that give a year–by–year account of his campaigns, there are also small sculpted reliefs of subservient kings bringing Shalmaneser gifts. One of these is of *Iaua mâr Humrî* (Jehu son of Omri) who was king of Samaria (i.e., the northern Kingdom of Israel) from 841 to 814 BC. In the relief Jehu (or maybe one of his servants) is shown prostrating himself before Shalmaneser. The inscription reads: "Tribute of Jehu son of Omri. Silver, gold, a golden bowl, a golden beaker, golden goblets, pitchers of gold, lead, staves for the hand of the king, javelins, I received from him." Outside of the Bible, this is the earliest extant reference we have for the existence of the kingdom of Israel which in itself makes the black obelisk an extremely important document.

Clearly the Black Stone is not the same sort of memorial that might have been raised by Jacob and Laban to demarcate the border of their respective territories. It is, however, evidence that monumental stones with invocations to the gods were used by the Assyrian Empire, which from around 1365 to 609 BC dominated the area of northern Mesopotamia. This is hundreds of years after the time of Jacob, but fortunately there is evidence for such marker stones going back to before the rise of the Assyrian Empire. At roughly the same time that the Hurrians were invading Syria and founding the empire of Mitanni (ca. 1500 BC), another people, the Kassites, invaded Babylonia and left behind their marker stones.

The Kassites were an Iranian people thought to have emerged from the region of the Zagros Mountains of western Iran. Their invasion of Mesopotamia brought about the fall of the Old Babylonian Empire (ca. 2000–1531 BC), but rather than destroy what they had conquered, they adopted the language and ways of Babylon themselves. Accordingly, the new dynasty of Kassite kings honored the old gods of Babylon and even retrieved the statue of Marduk,[8] which had previously been captured by the Hittites. Thus the old pantheon of Babylon was respected with the tribal gods of the Kassites merely being added to their number.

Little remains of Kassite literature, which is why the four-hundred-year period of their rule is sometimes referred to as a "Dark Age" in Babylonian history. However, they did leave behind one type of memorial that is extremely pertinent to our own enquiry: marker stones. I went to see a collection of these in the British Museum where they are kept separately in their own glass case. Known as *kudurru*, these boundary stones recorded and made public the ownership of land. Usually they carry an inscription giving details of to whom the land belongs and how it was given to him by either a king or local governor. In addition to any dedicatory inscription, the *kudurru* were usually engraved with symbolic pictures representative of the gods under whose protection the stone was being placed. Thus on one boundary stone, we read of the granting of a piece of land by Eanna–shum–iddina, the local governor of "the Sealand" (southern coastal area of Iraq), to someone called Gula–eresh. At the top of this black, shiny stone are the symbols for the Sun (represented by a radiant four–pointed star), the Moon (represented by a crescent), and Venus (represented by an eight–pointed star). Below these are symbols for shrines, each surmounted by a glyph representative of one or another god. On the row below this are what appear to be proto–zodiacal figures—though these are not placed in any definite order. Prominent among these are a lion and a scorpion, which presumably represent the constellations of Leo and Scorpio, respectively.

A rather larger and more elaborately carved stone repeats most of these glyphs. Once again on the top are the symbols for the Sun, Moon, and Venus. Below these are symbols for shrines dedicated to the high gods: Anu, Enlil, and Ea. Below these are altars to Marduk (symbolized as a dragon) and the goatfish (Capricorn?) which was sacred to Nabu—the god of writing. In the lower two registers are a scorpion archer (Sagittarius?) and below this other symbols that might be in some way linked to zodiacal constellations. Stretching up the side of this stone as well as the other is a symbolic serpent, its head at the top and tail towards the bottom. The meaning of this is unknown, but it may represent rising energy or there again be symbolic of the Milky Way.

Now clearly the *kudurru* stones of Babylonia are much more elaborate in their design than the stones that Jacob is said to have erected, yet we can see a common purpose. The stone he jointly erected with his uncle Laban was intended to be a boundary between their respective family ranges. It sealed a contract between them, supposedly made with God as their witness, that other than with peaceful motives, neither Jacob's nor Laban's families should cross into each other's territories. Similarly, Jacob's stone at Bethel was first and foremost a witness stone to his contract with his God (who identifies himself as the same as the God of his father Isaac and grandfather Abraham) that in exchange for doing as he was told and paying a tithe of his goods, he will be protected and given possession of the land thereabouts. Both stones were probably unmarked and neither would have been considered legal documents in the sense that the *kudurru* stones were. Indeed they might not have even been easily identifiable to anyone not in the know. Nevertheless, they were obviously meaningful to his immediate family, and one presumes were treated with respect long after Jacob was dead and buried; in this sense they became heirlooms.

Now if we approach the story of Jacob's stones from the other end (i.e., from the British Isles), other than the Stone of Destiny itself, do we find any parallels? Well, curiously enough, we do. As it turns out, the idea of using a stone as a witness to a coronation was fairly common place in the Britain. In Saxon times the most famous such stone was one that is still to be seen in the marketplace of the Surrey town (now London suburb) of Kingston–upon–Thames. Like the Stone of Destiny, though larger and more irregular in shape, it is a block of sandstone. Seven kings are said to have been crowned on this stone: Edward the Elder (son of Alfred the Great); Athelstan (son of Edward the elder); Edmund (brother of Athelstan); Eadred (another brother of Athelstan and Edmund); Eadwig (son of Edmund); Edward the Martyr (son of Edgar and nephew of Eadwig, and finally Ethelred "the Unready" (brother of Edward the Martyr). The last mentioned, Ethelred "the Unready," died in 1016. He was, of course, the father of Edward the Confessor whose shrine is in Westminster Abbey.

Further down the Thames at the City of London,[9] there is an important monument known as the "London Stone." During Roman times this stone, which once stood several hundred yards east of St Paul's Cathedral in the middle of Canon Street, was considered to be the *omphalus* or "navel stone" of Britain. All the Roman *millaria* or "milestones" throughout Britain were measured in relation to this central stone and marked as so many miles to London. Tradition states, though, that the London Stone predates the Roman occupation and that it was, in fact, the foundation stone of the city of Trinovantum—the old name for London. Since this was the capital of Britain as a whole, the capture of this stone symbolized conquest of the kingdom. For this reason in Shakespeare's *Henry VI, Part 2* the rebel leader Jack Cade uses the London Stone as witness to his usurpation of the throne. He strikes it with his sword and then, sitting on it, delivers a little speech:

> Cade: Now is Mortimer lord of this city. And here, sitting upon the London Stone, I charge and command that, of the city's cost, the pissing-conduit run nothing but claret wine this first year of our reign. And henceforward it shall be treason for any that calls me other than Mortimer.[10]

Crossing the sea to Ireland we find other important ancient stones with claims to royal endorsement. At the hill of Tara, where the Stone of Destiny is said to have once resided, there is a small pillar or obelisk. According to the Irish this, not the Stone of Destiny, was the *Lia-fail* of legend. This claim, however, seems hard to substantiate as the top of the stone is rounded, making it difficult for a would-be king to have stood upon it. It could, however, have been used as some sort of altar stone for pouring libations onto, which could conceivably give it a symbolic if not actual link with Jacob's Pillar.

Further west in Ireland, in County Roscommon, there is another royal stone. During the Middle Ages, this one was used by the kings of Connacht, some of whom were also high kings of all Ireland. They belonged to the O'Conor family, and though they are no longer kings, the family head, the "O'Conor Don" as he is known, is still in possession of this stone. Today it rests in the family's stately home of Clonalis House in Castlerea, and I was able to exchange emails concerning its provenance with the current O'Conor Don: Mr. Piers O'Conor Nash. He assured me that the stone is absolutely genuine and that it had originally rested on a hilltop near Carnfree. This is near to Tulsk (also in County

Roscommon and was the traditional inauguration site of the Kings of Connacht). According to Mr. O'Conor Nash, there is a reference to a fifteenth-century inauguration (that of Felim O'Conor) which gives a detailed description of the ceremony. This is contained in a book by Professor Francis John Byrne called *Irish Kings and High Kings*. Byrne tells us that the ceremony was called the *Banaish ri* or "King's marriage"—the hilltop on which it took place overlooking the five counties (Gallway, Leitrim, Mayo, Roscommon, and Sligo) that make up Connacht. The Connacht stone itself is very rough in appearance and bears the mark of a footprint. However, it would seem that what we see today is only a fragment of the stone; originally there were two footprints chiseled into its surface. During the inauguration ceremony, the would-be king would place his feet into these, thereby symbolizing consummation of the marriage between the king and the land.

Connacht itself is, of course, the part of Ireland which tradition says the *Fir Bolg* retired to following their defeat at the hands of the *Tuatha de Danaan*. The *Fir Bolg* or "men in trousers (pants)" are generally credited with being the same people as the *Belgae*, who settled in large numbers in southern England. The arrival of the *Belgae* in Britain (at sometime during the Iron Age) would appear to be the event commemorated in traditional British history as the conquest of Brutus, the eponymous "Father of Britain" with his company of "Trojan" warriors. It is, therefore, interesting to see that in Britain itself there is—or rather was—a "Brutus Stone" that supposedly marked his first footfall on the island he was to conquer. This was at Totnes, a town on the river Dart, and even today there is a paving slab halfway up Fore Street that supposedly marks the spot. In actuality the original Brutus Stone would have almost certainly have been kept in the Totnes Castle, which controlled the high ground above the town. The castle remains we see today go back to Norman times, but there was undoubtedly an old British, Iron-Age lookout fort (or *tot*) on this site thousands of years earlier. We can therefore envisage Brutus and his men storming this "castle" at the start of their invasion of Britain. The Brutus Stone, (rather as the Plymouth Stone in the US symbolizes the arrival of the Pilgrims) would have symbolically marked his first footfall on the promised land of the island, then called *Alba* (the White Land) but renamed Britain in his honor.

In Ireland the *Tuatha de Danaan*, who displaced the *Fir Bolg* and drove them westward into the rather poor lands of Connacht, were in their turn overcome by the Milesians, the ancestors of the Scots. It is, there-

The Stone of Destiny

Coronation Chair of Edward I

Relic of St. Edmund

Emperor Hadrian

Hadrian's wall building inscription

Edinburgh Castle

St. Margaret of Scotland

St. Giles' Cathedral

New Scottish Parliament

Perth Roman military stone

Pictish hunting stone—copy

Scone Palace

Proclamation of Scottish king

Author seated on replica Stone of Destiny

Homer

Cup marks stone

Pictish head

Perth red sandstone

Queen Tashereteneset, mother of Pharaoh Amasis, Twenty-Sixth dynasty

Kassite stone

Black obelisk

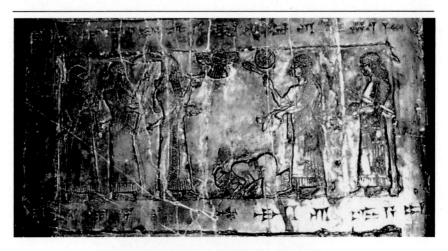

Jehu, king of Israel, prostrates to Assyrian king

Stela of Nabonidus

Ionian Greeks bringing gifts to the Persian king

Miletus amphitheater

Miletus temple ruins

Miletus great harbor monument

Iona

High cross of St. Martin, Iona

Iona abbey church

Iona abbey cloister

Grave effigies from Iona

Reilig Odhrain chapel, Iona

Way of the dead leading to chapel of Odhrain

St. Columba's pillow stone

Collace pictish stone, Perth

Perth-pict-cross

Orion rising over Mull

Window of St. Columkille, Iona

fore, interesting to note that when the Scots migrated to Britain—the northern part of which we now call Scotland but was then known as "Alba" or "Albion"—they established a capital on a hill called Dunadd. This is a rocky outcrop on the mainland of Argyll, south of Oban and close to Kilmartin. Archaeological excavations reveal that the site was, as at Totnes, already occupied by a hill fort dating from long before the arrival of the Scots. What is even more interesting is that a footprint is carved onto the bed rock making up the main body of the hill. It would seem, therefore, that carving a footprint implies not so much consummation with the goddess of the land as symbolizing conquest.

With this array of stones to consider, it is easy to dismiss the Stone of Scone as just another symbol of Celtic conquest. Yet there are differences. Unlike the footprint stone at Dunadd, which is carved into the solid rock of the hilltop, this stone is portable. Not only that, it differs from the Stone of Connacht or the King's Stone of the Saxons in that it was clearly at one time a regular block of precise proportions and not just a rough boulder. Curiously, this regularity in shape indicates, to those with the eyes to see it, that the Stone of Destiny may very well have come from the Middle East. To understand this we must go back to Egypt and reconsider what we know of its pyramid culture.

7

The Stone of the Phoenix

*I*n 1994 Robert Bauval and I coauthored a book entitled *The Orion Mystery*. This book, which has since been published in some twenty different languages and is still in print, was based on Bauval's, then novel, theory that the pyramids of Giza were intended to represent the "belt" of the constellation Orion. The evidence for this theory need not concern us here, but as an ancillary theme of the book, we also discussed the legend of the Egyptian phoenix or *bennu* bird. According to this legend, which in its later and probably corrupted form was recorded by the Greek historian Herodotus, the phoenix is a rarely seen bird that in appearance is similar to an eagle:

> "Another sacred bird is the one called the phoenix. Now, I (Herodotus) have not actually seen a phoenix, except in a painting, because they are quite infrequent visitors to the

country (Egypt); in fact, I was told in Heliopolis that they appear only at 500-year intervals. They say that it is the death of a phoenix's father which prompts its visit to Egypt. Anyway, if the painting was reliable, I can tell you something about the phoenix's size and qualities, namely that its feathers are partly of gold but mostly red, and that in appearance and size it is most like an eagle. There is a particular feat that they say the phoenix performs; I do not believe it myself, but they say that the bird sets out from its homeland in Arabia on a journey to the sanctuary of the sun, bringing its father sealed in myrrh, and buries its father there. The method it uses for carrying its father is as follows. First it forms out of myrrh as big an egg as it can manage to carry, and then it makes a trial flight to make sure it can carry the egg. When this has been tested, it hollows out the egg and puts its father inside, and then seals up with ore myrrh that part of the egg which it has hollowed out to hold its father. The egg now weighs the same, with its father lying inside, as it did before it was hollowed out. So when the phoenix has sealed the egg up again, it carries its father to the sanctuary of the sun in Egypt. That is what they say about the bird."[1]

Now there are several things to be said about this account, which seems to be another reference to sacred meteorites. First of all the "sanctuary of the sun" that Herodotus mentions is a building in Heliopolis (now a suburb of Cairo) known as the Temple of the Phoenix. Here there was a subterranean pit or sanctuary with an obelisk in the middle of it that was sacred to the Egyptian phoenix or *bennu* bird. Contrary to Herodotus' description, this is described in ancient Egyptian literature and in hieroglyphic form on temple walls as resembling a grey heron rather than an eagle. Over and above any legends concerning its role in burying its father at Heliopolis, its appearance was primarily seen as heralding the start of a new age or creation, and the periods between its appearances could be much longer than five–hundred years. Egyptologist R.T. Rundle Clark connected the appearance of the phoenix with dawn sunlight shining on a raised, pyramidal stone called the benben. The start of a new age corresponded to the beginning of a new day, a new year, a new cycle of Sirius[2] or any other period of cyclical time:

"For the Heliopolitans morning was marked by the shining
of light on an erect pillar or pyramidion on a support which
could reflect the rays of the rising sun. At the beginning (of
the age) a light-bird, the Phoenix, had alighted on the sacred stand, known as the Benben, to initiate the great age
of the visible God. The rising of the (Primeval) mound[3]
and the appearance of the Phoenix are not consecutive
events but parallel statements, two aspects of the su-
preme creative moment."[4]

In graphic art, the phoenix was depicted as a grey heron perching on
top of the sort of pyramidion–tipped pillar that Rundle Clark describes.
During the Egyptian Old Kingdom there had indeed been a column
standing in the Temple of the Phoenix at Heliopolis that was known as
the "Pillar of Atum," Atum being the local name for the sun god. Resting
on top of it was a pointed stone called the *Benben*, the combination of
the two together being the prototype of all the later obelisks.

Now the word *Benben* is itself interesting for in the ancient Egyptian
language the root word "ben" was linked with sexual reproduction (se-
men, copulation, to fertilize, etc.). Meanwhile, in Hebrew *ben* still means
"son of." The Egyptian phoenix is called the *bennu*, i.e. *ben-nu*, which looks
remarkably similar to *ben-nut*. Since Nut was the name of the sky goddess, the mother of Osiris and his siblings, *ben-nu* probably means "son
of the sky–goddess."[5] If this is the case, then the *bennu* was probably
connected with Osiris: the most important son of Nut, the sky goddess.
Meanwhile talk of the sky goddess and her children naturally brings us
back to meteorites and the likelihood that the original *benben* stone was
indeed one such cult object. We may surmise, though, that this was not
just some random meteorite found in the desert but was picked up
shortly after it was seen coming down to earth. Burning as it came
through the atmosphere it would have looked a lot like a "fire–bird."
However, when people arrived looking for it at the site of impact, there
would be no trace of the "bird." All they would find—and then only if
they were lucky—was the bird's egg: a now cooling meteorite. What,
however, they might have guessed is that such rocks originated in
comets.

In 1997 several years after the publication of *The Orion Mystery*, I had
the pleasure of meeting Dr. Victor Clube, then a senior lecturer in the
Astrophysics Department of Oxford University. An expert on the sub-

ject of comets and asteroids, he was then one of the few people to speak up about the possibility that in the near future the earth would be hit by one or more moderately sized asteroids. During our meeting Dr. Clube astounded me by talking about the likelihood that the Egyptians did, indeed, witness the impacts of meteorites. He explained that such events do not happen in isolation: they are usually associated with the appearance of a parent comet (or fragments of a comet) from which the meteorite(s) has (have) come. Comets, he said, begin life as bodies circling the sun with orbits well beyond the planetary solar system. Interactions with the gravitational attraction of other stars or simply collisions with other comets can, however, affect their trajectories. Such random events can even cause such radical changes to a comet's orbit that it now starts periodically visiting the inner solar system. Although when far away they are dark objects which are hard to spot with even a large telescope, these are the comets we see. This is because as they approach the sun that they become luminous. Solar energy melts some of the ice and other, more volatile chemicals that bind them together, and as this material evaporates, so the comet develops one or more long "tail." When stripped of its more volatile components, the rest of the cometary mass then splits up to make a "swarm" of rocks. These can vary from pebbles the size of a pea or smaller to enormous boulders over a kilometer in diameter. Should the Earth be hit by one of the latter, then it is likely to cause a life-extinction event such as is believed to have brought about the demise of the dinosaurs. Fortunately for us such events do not seem to happen more than once in fifty- to a hundred-million years. Nevertheless, smaller events happen much more frequently than this; the Earth will, on average, be hit by a hundred-meter sized boulder about once every hundred years.

Dr. Clube then told me of how for a number of years his team had been following one particular cometary cluster. This, he said, represented the remnants of a super comet which, according to their calculations, had first entered the inner solar system around 30,000 BC. All of the volatile components of this comet have long since been blown away by the solar wind. What is left is a now fairly dispersed cluster of rocks. From a close analysis of data recorded by ancient Chinese astronomers, it is clear that this cluster crosses over the Earth's orbit every five hundred or so years. Each time it does so there is a high probability that some of the rocks would collide with the Earth as meteorites. This phenomenon, he said, is what seems to be behind the meteorite cults of the

Egyptians and other peoples. In addition to meteorites large enough to survive their passage through the atmosphere, there would many others that burnt up as meteors, lighting up the sky with a veritable firework display. Anyone witnessing such events might assume that these were stars falling out of the sky. To then find a rocky remnant of such a "star" would be taken as a sign the gods had laid an egg: the egg of the phoenix.

Although it seems likely, we don't know for sure that the *benben* was a meteorite coming from this cluster. However, whatever it was, by the start of the Middle Kingdom (ca. 1991 BC), both it and the pillar of Atum on which it once stood appear to have gone missing. The likelihood is that this happened during the Old Kingdom and prior to the start of the Fifth Dynasty (ca. 2494–2345 BC). In *The Orion Mystery* we drew attention to the fact that the kings of this dynasty built their pyramids at Abusir. This is a site somewhat to the south of Giza which, if we accept the thesis that the Giza pyramids represented the belt of Orion, corresponds, more or less, to his "head." The head of Orion is actually composed of three rather dim but close together stars: Lambda, Phi 1, and Phi 2 Orionis, while curiously, the first three pharaohs to build pyramids at Abusir were triplets. In addition to building pyramids, they also each built a temple to the sun god Rē. These temples, which consist of an enclosure surrounding a mound with a stump–like obelisk on top, were clearly modeled on the old Temple of the Phoenix. Why they built these temples is one of the great mysteries of Egyptology, but at least part of the answer (and some clues to the real origins of the Stone of Destiny) is contained in the Westcar Papyrus.

This Westcar takes its name from Henry Westcar, who acquired it in 1824 and in 1839 gave it to Karl Richard Lepsius, the leading German Egyptologist of the day. Kept today at the Egyptian Museum in Berlin, it is without doubt one the most remarkable Egyptian documents to have survived to the present times. It is thought to date from the Second Intermediate Period (ca. 1786–1567 BC), which coincidentally is also the era during which Abraham, Isaac, Jacob, and the other patriarchs of Israel are believed to have lived. It is, however, almost certainly a copy of an even older papyrus that would have been written several hundred years earlier during the Middle Kingdom. The stories it narrates, however, take place in even more archaic times: during the Fourth and Fifth Dynasties of the Old Kingdom, i.e., the Pyramid Age.

Robert Bauval and I visited Heliopolis in 1993, examining for ourselves the famous Temple of the Phoenix. Though the obelisk that once had pride of place in its midst is now gone, we could see the plinth that it once stood on.[6]

What interested us about this temple was a story in the Westcar that concerned Khufu, the builder of the Great Pyramid of Giza. In this story his son Djedefrē brings to court a magician called Djedi. This man has unusual powers: he is one hundred ten years old, can put the severed head back on a goose, and cause a lion to walk tamely behind him. On questioning, it also transpires that he has some important information: he knows about the *ipwt* (numbers) of the *wnt* (secret chamber) of Thoth at Heliopolis. Khufu demands that he tell him what these numbers are so that he can use the same in building his pyramid. Djedi replies that he doesn't know them himself, but he does know where the information can be found: it is in a flint box in a room called "repetition" in the sanctuary of Thoth at Heliopolis.[7] He continues to tell the king that it will not be he, Djedi, who brings him the information he desires but the eldest of the children contained in the womb of Reddjedet, the wife of a *wab* priest of Rē. According to Djedi, these children have been sired by the sun god Rē himself, and they will one day occupy the greatest office in the land: i.e., be pharaohs.

Now this story brings us back neatly to the triplets who built the sun temples at Abusir for it is they whom the prophecy concerned. Khufu was succeeded by several other pharaohs of the Fourth Dynasty but eventually Userkaf, the eldest of the triplets, did indeed take the throne, thereby inaugurating the Fifth Dynasty. History doesn't record whether prior to this he did indeed bring Khufu the requested information, but the Djedi's story is nonetheless intriguing and in my opinion the state-ment that the *Ipwt* of the *Wnt* of Thoth are to be found in a "flint box" deserves even closer attention.

On the face of it, the suggestion that a box was made of flint seems very strange. There were certainly flint mines in the eastern desert of Egypt, and right up until the Iron Age, flints continued to be used for certain tools and surgical instruments. However, from a practical view, the idea that flint would have been used at any period for the manufac-ture of a box in which to keep secret information seems highly unlikely. For one thing it does not lend itself to such a purpose. By its very nature it is brittle, and while flints can be used in place of bricks as a building material,[8] it was mostly used for making weapons such as spear and arrow heads. My feeling, therefore, is that in this respect the accepted translation of the Westcar Papyrus is wrong; the word "ds", which here is translated as "flint" and given the determinative of a knife sharpener, means some other material. What could this be?

Well, it may seem strange and a bit of a long shot, but a more plausible explanation would be if the "flint box" was neither a box nor made of flint. In fact I believe it was probably a block of sandstone that was hard enough to be used for sharpening knives while still soft enough to be shaped. This sounds remarkably like the Stone of Destiny, or at any rate if not the stone we know by this name today, one very like it. My reasons for saying this are based on geometry; the "numbers of Thoth" are the system of proportions which governed the building of the Great Pyramid. For as amazing as it may seem, the Stone of Destiny provides us with a geometric way of generating such a pyramid.

Geometry of the Stone of Destiny

Physically, the Stone of Destiny is a rough block of sandstone. It has two iron rings inserted in its sides, presumably so that it can be carried more easily from place to place. The guidebook I bought in 1973 says it weighs 336 lb. and has the dimensions 26" x 16" x 10.5" but these figures have to be taken as rough approximations as it is somewhat irregular and show signs of wearing. This wear and tear in itself speaks of the stone's great antiquity as for the past seven-hundred years it has been protected by King Edward's Coronation Chair and has probably not received any wear at all.

On close inspection the stone seems quite unprepossessing, indeed boring. However, a careful analysis of its dimensions reveals a link with Egypt, or at any rate, the Egyptian system of measures. The height of the stone at 10.5" is exactly half an Egyptian royal cubit of 21". One-and-a-half cubits would be 31.5" and half of this would be almost 16"—effectively the depth, from front to back, of the stone. Two-and-a-half cubits would be 52.5" and a half of this would be just over 26"—the width of the stone. We can therefore say that the stone is a block which if measured in units of half an Egyptian cubit has the dimensions 2.5 x 1.5 x 1.

Now this in itself is very interesting, for if we consult the Bible (Exodus 25) we discover that the Ark of the Covenant, which was in essence simply a wooden box in which to keep the tablets of the law as received by Moses, had dimensions of 2.5 x 1.5 x 1.5 cubits. On top of this box was placed a golden "mercy seat" and this had a surface area of 2.5 x 1.5

cubits. This seat, we are told, was to be the throne of God himself:

> "And thou shalt make a mercy seat of pure gold: two cu-
> bits and a half shall be the length thereof, and a cubit and
> a half the breadth thereof . . .
>
> . . . And thou shalt put the mercy seat above upon the
> ark; and in the ark thou shalt put the testimony that I shall
> give thee.
>
> And there I will meet with thee, and I will commune
> with thee from above the mercy seat, from between the
> two cherubims which are upon the ark of the testimony,
> of all things which I will give thee in commandment unto
> the children of Israel." (Exod. 25:17, 21-22)

THE ARK OF THE COVENANT

We can see immediately from the above dimensions that the mercy
seat had the same proportions as the top of the Stone of Scone: 2.5 x 1.5
units; the difference being that it was measured in whole rather than
half cubits. Could it be that Moses, having seen a stone with these proportions in Egypt, decided that 2.5 x 1.5 was dimensionally the correct
proportion for God's throne? Certainly his choice of these measures is
suggestive of a link between the Stone of Destiny and the Ark of the
Covenant. Indeed it is not impossible that one of the reasons Moses had
the Ark made was so that it could be used for carrying the Stone. The
difference in scale can be attributed to the fact that were the stone
measured in cubits instead of half cubits it would have weighed eight

times as much, (i.e., 8 x 336 lb. = 24 cwt. or 1.2 tons). Such a large block of stone would not have been very portable.

Measures based on the Stone of Scone

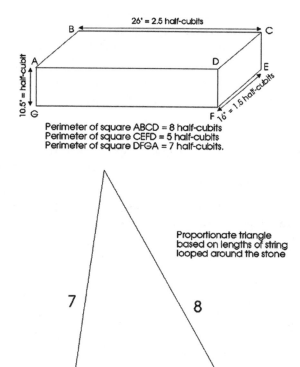

Perimeter of square ABCD = 8 half-cubits
Perimeter of square CEFD = 5 half-cubits
Perimeter of square DFGA = 7 half-cubits.

Proportionate triangle based on lengths of string looped around the stone

There is more, however, to the shape of the Stone of Scone than its similarity to the mercy seat on the Ark of the Covenant. As mentioned earlier, the dimensions of the Stone as measured in half cubits is 1 x 1.5 x 2.5. Now as can easily be visualized; if we take a piece of string, we can wind it round the block in three different ways. If we lay the block down flat (as it normally is), then one winding of the string will require a length of: 1.5 + 2.5 + 1.5 + 2.5 = 8.

If we now stand the block on its back side and wind string round

. . . .

again, we require a length of 1 + 2.5 + 1 + 2.5 = 7. If we then stand the block on its side and wind string around it in this position, we will need a length of 1 + 1.5 + 1 + 1.5 = 5. All these lengths are in half cubits, but if we use two windings for each length, we will get lengths of string in the proportions 8: 7: 5 which is a royal cubit.

Now at first sight these lengths may not seem to mean very much, but in actual fact they are very precise and chosen for a particular reason. If the pieces of string are joined together and pulled straight, they will make a triangle of sides 8, 5 and 7. (See diagram 1). By dropping a perpendicular the side of length 8 cubits is easily divided in a ratio of 5.5: 2.5. Using the length 5.5 we can easily draw a square of side 11. This square will have the same perimeter (44 units) as a circle drawn using the side of length 7 units as a radius. In other words the triangle generated from the lengths of string enables us very easily to "square the circle" (see diagram 2). Furthermore, if we draw a line of length 7, perpendicular to the plane of the square and join the top of this line to the corners of the square, then it will create a pyramid shape.

How the triangle formed from "string-lengths" taken around the Stone of Scone can be used to square the circle and draw a pyramid.

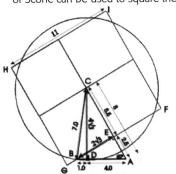

CA = 8 cubits
AB = 5 cubits
BC = 7 cubits
Perpendicular DE divides CA exactly into 5.5 + 2.5 cubits
GE, perpendicular to CA, is 5.5 cubits
GF = 2 x GE = 11 cubits

Perimeter of circle CB = 2 x (22/7) x 7 = 44 cubits
Perimeter of square FGHIF = 4 x 11 = 44 cubits
Therefore the square has same perimeter as the circle.

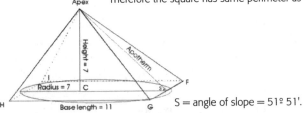

S = angle of slope = 51º 51'.

If the radius of the circle, 7 cubits, is used to define the height of a pyramid on the square base FGHI, then it will have a slope of 51º 51'. This is the slope of the Great Pyramid of Giza.

This pyramid will be of the same shape as the Great Pyramid of Giza, having the "Pi" angle of 51° 51'.

If we now recall the story of King Khufu and the magician Djedi as told in the Westcar Papyrus, then it becomes very obvious that the "flint box containing the numbers of Thoth" must have been a block similar to if not exactly the same as the Stone of Destiny. The "numbers of Thoth," 7 and 11, are those which enable the building of a pyramid similar in shape to the Great Pyramid of Khufu. For those who know how to use it, a stone shaped like the Stone of Destiny does indeed contain the secret numbers of the sanctuary of Thoth.

This, however, is not the end of the story for we have definitive proof that the ancient Druids possessed knowledge of the same "sacred" 5:7:8 triangle needed to give the measures of the pyramid. The first classical author to write about Britain with any sort of personal experience was Julius Caesar. He made two attempts at invading the island, the first in 55 BC and the second a year later in 54. He wrote about his exploits in his book *de Bello Gallico*: his British campaigns being ancillary to his much more important war in Gaul. Although he probably exaggerates the scale of his successes and the tribute he was able to extract from Britain's kings, he did at least set foot on Britain and explore as far as the north bank of the river Thames. Initially Caesar had little direct intelligence concerning the island, but later he informs us concerning its shape and dimensions:

> "The island is triangular, with one side facing Gaul. One corner of this side, on the coast of Kent, is the landing-place for nearly all the ships from Gaul, and points east; the lower corner points south. The length of this side is about 475 miles. Another side faces west, towards Spain. In this direction is Ireland, which is supposed to be half the size of Britain, and lies at the same distance from it as Gaul.
> . . . This side of Britain, according to the natives' estimate, is 665 miles long. The third side faces north, no land lies opposite it, but the eastern corner points roughly in the direction of Germany. Its length is estimated at 760 miles. Thus the whole island is 1,900 miles in circumference.[9]

The importance of Caesar's description of Britain is not geographical but symbolic. As even he must have known, the island of Britain is not actually triangular in shape but rather irregular. However, if we divide each of the supposed lengths of the coastlines of this triangle as recorded by him (475, 665, and 760 miles) by 95 then we discover its shape is actually a triangle of proportions 5, 7, and 8. Though much larger, Caesar's triangle is similar in shape to that generated by the Stone of Destiny. Since Caesar tells us earlier that neither he nor the Gallic traders he met before going to Britain had any knowledge concerning the extent of the island or its shape, we can only conclude that he was given all of the above information by the same "natives" he mentions above. These, it would seem were educated men, perhaps Druids, who were perhaps in possession of secret knowledge concerning the Stone of Destiny.

We can therefore see that not only is the stone measured in half royal cubits (an Egyptian measure) but gives in coded form the dimensions of the perfect pyramid. However if, as now seems likely, the Stone is one and the same as the "flint box" described by Djedi, then the following scenario presents itself. First of all, some mathematical genius, who for argument's sake we can call Thoth, invented the Pi pyramid as a symbol. The essential nature of such a pyramid is that contains within it the Pi relationship: that the perimeter of its base is the same as a circle drawn using its height as the radius. Then, either through serendipity or sheer genius, he encoded the measurements needed to construct such a pyramid by using a block of stone. This he concealed in a secret room at Heliopolis where it lay hidden until the time of King Khufu. He, or rather his architects, found the stone and used it to rediscover the "numbers of Thoth": i.e., the Pi proportion of 22/7. They then used this information for the construction of the Great Pyramid. The question then is how such a stone could have got to the British Isles.

This brings us back to the Irish migrations that we discussed in the previous chapter. However, we should also remind ourselves that the period in which the Westcar Papyrus was penned corresponds to the Second Intermediate Period when the "shepherd kings," Semitic invaders from the direction of Syria, held sway over Egypt. This is the period when first Abraham and later Jacob and his family visited and settled in Egypt. If the Bible is to be believed, then Jacob's son Joseph became no less a figure than the vizier of all Egypt and even married the daughter of Potiphera, the High Priest of On (Heliopolis). With these sorts of connections, he, if anyone, must have known the location of the "flint box" mentioned in the Westcar.

By the time of Moses the Intermediate Period was over, and the Israelites were living as slaves. The masters of Egypt were no longer the Semitic shepherd kings but the pharaohs of the New Kingdom. These rulers, who are listed by Manetho under the Eighteenth to Twentieth Dynasties, were from Upper as opposed to Lower Egypt. For them the "high god" was Amun, and his principle sanctuary was at Luxor. The New Kingdom pharaohs were not as interested in the gods of Heliopolis which fell in status as a religious center. It is, therefore, not unlikely that when Moses and the Israelites either escaped or were ejected from Egypt, they took the Stone of Destiny with them. This was very likely already in the possession of Joseph's descendants: the tribes of Ephraim and Manasseh. These "Israelites" were, after all, in part descended from Potiphera, the High Priest of Heliopolis. They would very likely have regarded such an important stone as a family heirloom.

There is, admittedly, no direct evidence to show that this is the case. However, it is surely no coincidence that when Moses ordered the making of the Ark of the Covenant, the dimensions of its top were proportionately the same as the Stone. The Ark itself was, of course, primarily a box for carrying things. In this it was little different from similar boxes that the Egyptians used for carrying around statues of their gods and goddesses. The Israelites, of course, believed in only one God and he was not to be symbolized by statues. So instead of carrying a statue, they used the Ark to transport important symbols of their own faith: most notably the stones of the Law which Moses brought down from Mount Sinai. There was, however, plenty of room in the Ark for the Stone to be put within it too if that had been Moses intention. His only reason for doing so would be if he regarded it as a token of an earlier Covenant. This would be the case if the "flint box" was considered to be one and the same as Jacob's Pillow Stone. We don't know if this is the case, but removal of the Heliopolitan Stone by the Israelites at the time of the Exodus would explain its apparent disappearance around this time. It would also explain why the Irish Annals, among others, link the migration of Miletus and his Scythian Greeks to the Exodus when clearly it would have to have taken place centuries later when there were Milesian and Scythian mercenaries living in Egypt. That in biblical times there probably was a migration of the British Isles is borne out by certain similarities in language and customs between the ancient Egyptians and those most mysterious priests: the Druids.

8

The Origins of Druidism

*A*s we have seen in several of his readings, the "sleeping prophet" Edgar Cayce mentioned the presence of a party of Jews that included at least two princesses erecting altars in the vicinity of Salisbury, England. These princesses are said by him to have been daughters of Hezekiah, the king who reigned over Judah between 716 and 687 BC. He didn't mention Stonehenge by name but almost certainly, by saying "altars that were to represent the dedications of individuals to a service of a living God (3645-1)," this monument is what he meant. It is the single most important Neolithic monument in Europe while there is really nothing else in the vicinity of Salisbury that could qualify. Unfortunately, the famous trilithon arches and other structures that we see at Stonehenge today predate Hezekiah by at least a thousand years. Not only that, carbon dating tells us that the construction of the earth bank around the monument and the aligning of its entrance

135

towards the rising point of the summer solstice sun goes back even further in time; for it seems that the first stage of the monument (generally called Stonehenge I) dates from around 3100 BC. This makes it roughly contemporaneous with the reign of King Menes of Egypt (First Dynasty) and several hundred years older than the very first Egyptian pyramid—the Step Pyramid at Saqqara. By 700 BC (the time of Hezekiah), it would already have been in existence for 2400 years. Assuming Cayce's report was accurate and given that he made many other statements which, though they seemed wrong at the time, have since proved correct, this means that the main structure of Stonehenge must already have been there at the time of the princesses' arrival. Consequently, whatever "altars" were put up at the time of the Jewish princesses must have been somewhat different from the stone circles we see today. We don't see these structures today, so we therefore need to use our own imaginations if we are to make any sense of Cayce's cryptic statements on this subject.

These thoughts were going through my own head when in 2008 I found myself standing in front of Stonehenge. It was not my first visit, of course; indeed, there was a time when I used to drive past it at least once a month, and long before this I first examined it close up in about 1966. At that time the stone circles were open to the public and visiting them was free; indeed, you could walk right up to the stones, sit on the fallen ones, and even have a picnic if you so pleased. Now, following the explosion of global tourism and the notoriety of Stonehenge as probably the most important Neolithic monument in the world, this sort of free-and-easy attitude is simply not possible anymore. Today you have to pay a not-inconsiderable amount to go inside the Stonehenge area. Even then the bulk of the monument is out-of-bounds, and you need a special scientific permit to enter the inner rings of stone where we were once able to sit and eat sandwiches.

Being kept back from the stones is not, however, an entirely bad thing. One thing I do remember from that first visit in 1966 was just how disappointed we were at the relatively small scale of the monument when viewed from inside. Yes, it was nice being able to walk at will and play peekaboo through the trilithons, but it didn't really help us understand the monument any better and in some respects took away from its mystique. It was like visiting the National Gallery in London and looking at an old master from too close-up: yes, if you stand right next to a painting, you can see the brush strokes of the artist and get a better view of how, with time, the varnish has cracked, but it doesn't help you see the whole picture. So it is with Stonehenge: by standing back from it you get a much better perspective; not only that, you see it in the context of its broader landscape.

As I wandered round the perimeter, keeping to the prescribed path, I thought about Edgar Cayce and what it was that he might have been referring to when he said "the entity was among those who landed and set up the *seat of customs* {my italics} as indicated in the altars built near what is now Salisbury." (3590-1) I wondered if these words could be a cryptic reference to the Stone of Destiny. If so, what might be the *customs* and how might they have been indicated by the *altars*? These were questions which invited further study; accordingly, with these matters in mind, I decided to take another look at the enigma that is Stonehenge.

How this monument came to be built is one of the world's greatest mysteries. Given the fact that its Neolithic builders had little in the way of machinery, the raising of huge sarsen stones (some weighing as much as fifty tons) is itself surprising. Yet this is only a part of the Stonehenge enigma and by no means the most important. More interesting is that the stones were laid out in such a way as to mark not just the midsummer sunrise but also a number of other significant positions of the sun and moon.[1] Then, as if this were not enough, the positioning of the stones in relation to the center of the monument indicates knowledge of sacred geometry and the use of the same units of measurement as were employed in Egypt. How the Neolithic Britons came by the astronomical, geometric, and mechanical knowledge needed to construct such a complex monument is one of the most puzzling enigmas of ancient history.

The ruins we call Stonehenge have, of course, been the subject of curiosity and speculation for at least a thousand years. In his book *The History of the Kings of Britain*, which was published in 1136 and is in essence a translation of an older Welsh language Chronicle, Geoffrey of Monmouth claimed that Stonehenge was a war memorial. According to him, the stones were erected in honor of the 460 British noblemen, who were murdered by the Saxons while attending a peace conference at nearby Amesbury.[2] In his book, Geoffrey calls the monument the Giants' Dance, and he claims that Merlin used magic powers to bring the stones from Ireland. It is, of course, easy to dismiss such an idea as nonsense, particularly since the geology of the sarsen stones that make up the trilithons and surrounding circuit of archways indicates that they come not from Ireland but rather from the Marlborough Downs which is about thirty miles to the north of Stonehenge. Nevertheless, it could be that Geoffrey's story is not entirely fabricated. We now know that the smaller "bluestones," which are mostly arranged in circles between the rings of great sarsen stones, were brought to the site from the Prescelly Mountains of Pembrokeshire in West Wales. Though we don't know the reason for their transportation, it seems likely that they were brought to the Stonehenge area by sea and river. The supposed Irish connection is even more intriguing as it suggests a distant memory that Stonehenge, though Neolithic in its construction, was later used by the Druids who many now believe had their center in Ireland.

Now the Druids (*derwydd* in Welsh) are said to take their name from *derwen*: the Welsh for oak tree. It is known that groves of oaks were held as sacred by the Druids not least because these trees acted as natural hosts for mistletoe, the cutting of which was a sacred ritual. However, recent archaeological research reveals that even in Neolithic times oak trees (though not necessarily Druids) had an important place in the religion of Britain. Just a few miles to the northeast of Stonehenge is "Woodhenge." This monument consists of six elliptical rings of holes that once held oak posts. It was discovered in a series of digs conducted between 1926–8, is roughly contemporaneous with Stonehenge, and almost certainly, like its more famous neighbor, featured "lintels," i.e., crossbeams supported by uprights.

Since 1928 a number of other "woodhenges" have been found, both in Wiltshire and in other places such as Norfolk—the easternmost county of England. In 1999 an even more remarkable structure, dubbed "Seahenge" was discovered on the seashore of Suffolk, Norfolk's neighbor. A relatively small monument, it consists of a circle of upended oak logs arranged around the lowest part of an oak tree. For reasons unknown, the top end of this central "stump" had been buried so that the tree's roots were pointing towards the sky. What is particularly interesting about this discovery is that through both carbon and tree-ring dating it has been ascertained that Seahenge was constructed in 2050–49 BC and that no fewer than thirty different bronze axes were used in its construction. The year 2050 BC is roughly the time that the second phase of Stonehenge was completed though before the raising of the circle of sarsen stones or the great trilithons. The implication has to be that the stone circles we see at Stonehenge and other such monuments were simply more permanent versions of earlier wooden monuments such as Woodhenge and Seahenge. The question remains, though. Why were any of these monuments built?

In the case of Stonehenge, it is well known that its major axis points towards the position of sunrise on the summer solstice—a date that was clearly of great importance to the predominantly agricultural people who built the monument. A similar solar orientation is less easy to prove at Woodhenge. However, Professor Alexander Thom of Glasgow University made a careful survey of the monument in the 1960s, and this revealed that it, too, was aligned on the summer solstice sunrise.[3] We can therefore say, unequivocally, that if these monuments were re- ligious in intent, then the sun played a significant role in the beliefs of the Stonehenge and Woodhenge builders.

What both astronomers and archaeologists would really like, of course, is written evidence to back up this assumption. Unfortunately, as far as we know, the Neolithic and Early Bronze Age peoples of Britain did not make use of a written language, or if they did, examples of it have not survived and come down to our day. For written evidence of the past we have to turn to outside of the British Isles. Rather surpris- ingly Julius Caesar, who attempted the conquest of Britain in 55-54 BC, is our chief classical source. For, although he fought wars in both Britain and Gaul, he also seems to have actually met some Druids and dis- cussed with them their religious beliefs. In his book *de Bello Gallico* he tells us that although Druidism was widely practiced in Gaul, Britain was considered to be the center of the religion and was very likely its point of origin. He also informs us that young men studying to become Druids were "required to memorize large numbers of verses" and that their religion forbade them from committing their teachings to writing. However they were clearly not illiterate for he also states that for ordi- nary purposes the Gauls made use of the Greek alphabet.[4]

As to their teachings, Caesar writes that the Gauls believed in rein- carnation and made a special study of the heavenly bodies and their movements (astrology?). Using mathematics, they also computed the size of the universe and of the Earth. Their favorite god, he said, was Mercury to whom they attributed the invention of the arts, with guid- ing them on journeys, and helping them in commerce.[5] After him they next venerated Apollo, Mars, Jupiter, and Minerva (Roman equivalent of the Greek goddess Athena). Caesar, writing for a Roman audience, is, of course, using the names of equivalent Roman gods. He understood perfectly well that the Gauls and Britons had names of their own for all these deities.

For centuries Caesar's report was pretty much all that anyone knew about the Druids; however it would seem that not everything was lost. Besides the numerous medieval chronicles that still exist, there is evidence that an oral tradition, of an antiquity we can only guess at, was preserved in Wales right up until quite recent times. The transmitters of this knowledge were the bards, one of three pre-Christian colleges of wise men (the other two colleges being the Druids and the Ovates). It was the job of the bards to preserve the history, language, and culture of the ancient Britons. According to a remarkable book, written in Welsh and called *Barddas* (Bardism), the Welsh bards preserved an unbroken lineage of teachers and students who went right back to pre-Christian times. At some time between 1580 and 1616, their lore was finally written down in manuscript form by a senior bard called Llewellyn Sion. It was this manuscript that in 1862 was finally published under the title *Barddas*. In addition to the Welsh text, it contained an English translation, a useful preface, and accompanying footnotes. This book, a copy of which I obtained in 1996, throws a lot of light on the subject of henge monuments—wood or stone. It also divulges certain secrets of the Druidic religion which make it clear that it had much in common with ancient Judaism, thereby adding some credibility to Cayce's report that Jewish princesses went to Stonehenge.

The central doctrine of the religion turns out to be the identification of God, (whose name cannot be spoken), with light. Thus we read:

> "When God pronounced His name, with the word sprang the light and the life; for previously there was no life except God Himself. And the mode in which it was spoken was of God's direction. His name was pronounced, and with the utterance was the springing of light and vitality, and man and every other living thing; that is to say, each and all sprang together. And *Menw* the aged (the first man or 'Adam'), son of *Menwyd* (mind, as in Latin *mens*), beheld the springing of the light, and its form and appearance, not otherwise than thus, /|\, in three columns; and in the rays of light the vocalization—for one were the hearing and seeing, one unitedly the form and sound; and one unitedly with the form and sound was life, and one unitedly with these three was power, which power was God the Father. And since each of these was one unitedly, he

understood that every voice, and hearing, and living, and
being, and sight, and seeing, were one unitedly with God;
nor is the least thing other than God. And by seeing the
form, and in it hearing the voice—not otherwise—he knew
what form and appearance voice should have. And having obtained earth under him coinstantaneously with the
light, he drew the form of the voice and light on the earth.
And it was on hearing the sound of the voice, which had
in it the kind and utterance of the three notes, that he obtained the three letters and knew the sign that was suitable to one and other of them. Thus he made in form and
sign the Name of God, after the semblance of rays of light,
and perceived that they were the figure and form and sign
of life; one also with them was life, and there is no life but
God, and there is no God but life."[6]

It would be wrong to think that these writings, evocative as they are,
are word for word the teachings of the bards alive at the time of Julius
Caesar. However, there are some themes which are clearly very ancient.
The first is that God manifests as a trinity, with a name that while it
cannot be pronounced can be thought of as manifesting like columns
of Light. Later on we are told that these bars, drawn as /|\ and known as
the symbol of *Awen* (literally "poesy" or the muse of creativity) represent
sounds of the vowels "O," "I," and "V" (the last pronounced like "U"). This
is remarkably similar to the teachings of the Bible where the
tetragrammaton or name of God, spelt Yod–Heh–Vav–He, is similarly
unpronounceable. In fact if we change the order of the letters but
slightly it gives us "IOV": the name of God the Father in the Roman
tradition.[7]

In the Welsh–Celtic tradition, *Awen* is also the name of a goddess:
their equivalent of the Roman goddess Minerva (Greek Athena), viz:

The Druids of Gaul, according to Caesar, were of opinion
that it was this goddess who "instructed them in the prin-
ciples of works and arts." It is very likely that she was the
same originally with the Awen, (A wen, /|\[8]), the word of
God that proceedeth out of the His mouth, even as
Minerva is said to have sprung out of the brain of Jupiter
(viz. Jove). It was from Awen that all knowledge was de-

rived—in like manner Minerva was considered as the goddess of wisdom.[9]

From the three strokes that make up her name, *Awen*, is created a
whole alphabet of letters that the bards call *coelbren y Beirdd*. This is a
long and complex study that goes well beyond our interest here. However, suffice it to say that the *coelbren* letters are very similar to the
Pelasgian alphabet that was invented in Anatolia and predates the Greek
alphabet, which it somewhat resembles. We may therefore infer that the
teachings concerning *Awen* and the origins of a pre–Roman alphabet in
Gaul and Britain comes from that part of the world.

Elsewhere we are told that the three lines of light that make up the
Awen symbol are derived from positions of the sun: "Thus are they
made;—the first of the signs is a small cutting or line inclining with the
sun at eventide, thus, /; the second is another cutting, in the form of a
perpendicular, upright post, thus, |and the third is a cutting of the same
amount of inclination as the first, but in an opposite direction, that is,
against the sun, thus \; and the three placed together, thus, /|\.[10]

In a different book, *The Iolo MSS*, we are told how the bards used to
meet together in a *gorsedd*, literally a circle of seats with a higher seat
placed in its center:

> "A *gorsedd* of the bards of the island of Britain must be
> held in a conspicuous place, in full view and hearing of
> the country and aristocracy, and in the face of the sun and
> the eye of Light; it being unlawful to hold such meetings
> either under cover, at night, or under any circumstance
> otherwise than while the sun shall be visible in the sky:
> or, as otherwise expressed,—
>
> A chair and *gorsedd* of the British bards shall be held
> conspicuously, in the face of the sun, in the eye of Light,
> and under the expansive freedom of the sky, that all may
> see and hear . . .
>
> . . . It is an institutional usage to form a conventional
> circle of stones, on the summit of some conspicuous
> ground; so as to enclose any requisite area of green-
> sward; the stones being so placed as to allow sufficient
> space for a man to stand between each two of them;
> except that the two stones of the circle which most di-

rectly confront the eastern sun, should be sufficiently apart to allow at least ample space for three men between them; thus affording an easy ingress to the circle. This larger space is called the entrance or portal; in front of which, at the distance of three fathoms, or of three times three fathoms, a stone called *station stone*, should be so placed as to indicate the eastern cardinal point; to the north of which, another stone should be placed, so as to face the eye of the rising sun, at the longest summer's day; and, to the south of it, an additional one, pointing to the position of the rising sun, at the shortest winter's day. These three are called station stones: but, in the center of the circle, a stone, larger than the others, should be so placed, that diverging lines, drawn from its middle to the three station stones, may point severally, and directly, to the three particular positions of the rising sun, which they indicate.

The stones of the circle are called sacred stones, and stones of testimony;—and the centre stone, is variously called the stone of presidency, the altar of the Gorsedd, the stone of compact, and the perfection stone. The whole circle, formed as described, is called the greensward-enclosing circle, the circle of the presidency, and the circle of sacred refuge; but it is called *trwn* (circle) in some countries. The bards assemble in convention within this circle; and it accords neither with usage nor decency for any other person to enter it, unless desired to do so by a bard."[11]

Of course the above was probably written no earlier than 1600, but nevertheless, reading these words immediately brings to mind Stonehenge and suggests that it was the meeting place for *gorseddau*. If this is so, then it was certainly a very advanced type of such structure. The archaeological evidence, which is growing all the time, indicates that it was actually part of a much larger "sacred landscape," the whole consisting of not just the henge monument itself but a collection of surrounding causeways and barrows, some of which were constructed in the Neolithic Period and others from the Bronze and maybe even Iron Ages. Furthermore, several skeletons have been found in recent years and the picture that is now emerging is that Stonehenge was more than a local attraction: it was built as a national monument where all the tribes of Britain could meet together. For what purpose is not entirely clear but the proximity of large burial mounds in the vicinity suggests that, like the pyramids of Egypt, it was connected royalty and with ideas to do with death and transformation. Indeed it may well have been regarded as marking a sort of portal through which either the souls of the dead could pass or kingship be conferred on the living. I was surprised to discover that further clues to this use and its undoubted connections with Egypt can be gained by study of the patterning of its stones and their underlying geometry.

The Patterns of Stonehenge

This remarkable monument has received more than its fair share of attention over the years and indeed many researchers, professional and amateur, have written whole books on the subject. There are, however, three researchers whose work stands head and shoulders above all other in terms of perceptiveness and originality of thought. The first of these was one of England's most famous archaeologists, indeed the man who is sometimes regarded as the "father" of modern Egyptology: William Flinders Petrie. More famous for his survey of the Great Pyramid, which he carried out in 1880, he had prior to this, in 1877, made an accurate survey of Stonehenge. The purpose of this survey was twofold. First of all, he wanted to put on paper an accurate representation of the monument so that researchers could investigate it further, and secondly, he was anxious to put into practice his own system of "inductive metrology" by means of which it was, he believed, possible to recover the units of measure used by ancient builders and thereby ascertain if countries and cultures borrowed these from one another.

For this work, Petrie designed some special surveying equipment including a purpose-made chain for extremely accurate work. Using this equipment he measured the diameters of the various stone circles, their heights, and also the diameter of the earth bank and other features. Applying inductive metrology to all this base data he discovered the following units had been used in the setting out of the monument:

1) A "cubit" of 22.48 inches, which was close enough to the "Phoenician" cubit of 22.51 inches that was already known.

2) A "foot" of either 11.68 or 11.72 inches, which was close to the

"Roman" foot which varies from 11.64 inches in Rome to 11.68 in Greece and Africa.

This did not mean the monument was Roman in construction. In his opinion: " . . . the unit was the great Etrurian or Cyclopean unit, originally derived from Egypt, and it may have been introduced at any date into Britain."[12]

Petrie carried out detailed work on measuring the diameters of the outer bank and ditch of the monument; indeed it was these measures that allowed him to inductively infer that the builders used a unit of measure of 22.48" and therefore more or less equal to the Phoenician cubit. He measured diameters based on the inner edge of the bank, the neutral point between it and the ditch and the outer edge of the ditch. These came to 3595, 4045, and 4495 inches, respectively. Dividing the first by eighteen gave a figure of 224.68, dividing the second by eighteen gave him 224.72, and the last by twenty gave 224.75. From these measures he was able to deduce that in setting out the earliest monument, Stonehenge I, the builders used a "chain" that was ten cubits in length (i.e., approx 10 x 22.48). To draw these circles on the ground prior to digging, they used radii of 8, 9, and 10 chains: i.e., half the measured diameters.

With this success under his belt, he was able to apply himself now to the stone circles. Because many of the stones have moved around a lot, this was not an easy thing to do, but because parts of these are well preserved, he was highly successful in measuring the diameters of the inner blue stone circle and comparing this with the diameter of the outer sarsen circle. He found that the diameter of the sarsen circle was 1167.9" (+/- .7) and that of the inner bluestones 472.7" (+/- .5). This meant that within the tolerance that could be expected, both circles were laid out in "feet" with the outer circle being 100 and the inner 40.

All these measures Petrie presented with painstaking clarity in his book *Stonehenge: Plans, Description, and Theories.* Just as important he provided detailed maps of the monument which were sufficiently accurate for other investigators to use to unlock more of Stonehenge's secrets. The second investigator, Gerald Hawkins, whom we have already met, did just that. His careful examination of Petrie's survey coupled with his own investigations on site enabled him to prove, once and for all, that the ancient Britons were superb astronomers. Not only that, his work indicated that the location of Stonehenge was not chosen at random but was specifically related to astronomy. Indeed, it could be used as a machine for the prediction of eclipses.

The astronomical aspect of Stonehenge seems to have been important right from the earliest days of construction, for the prime alignment of the monument is towards the summer and, perhaps more
importantly, the winter solstices. The actual location of the site on latitude 51º 10" 44" is also important, and Hawkins found proof for this in
the arrangement of four "station stones" that are placed strategically on
the outer bank. These stones are thought to be part of the second phase
of building (referred to as Stonehenge II) which is thought to date to
around 2150–2000 BC, though they may be part of Stonehenge I (3100–
2300 BC). In any event, they predate the erection of the sarsen circle, the
great trilithons, and even the placement of the bluestones in their
present arrangement. What Hawkins discovered is that the positioning
of these rather inconspicuous station stones not only forms a rectangle
but that the sides of this have an extraordinary significance. First of all,
two sides are aligned towards the midsummer and midwinter solstice
sunrises. Given that the whole monument has this alignment—it is after
all the one which ensures that the sun rises over the Friar's Heelstone
on midsummer—this is not surprising. However, what Hawkins also
found was that at the time the monument was built, the other two sides
of the station–stone rectangle pointed directly towards extreme rising
and setting positions of the moon. Meanwhile the diagonals of the rectangle crossed over very close to the center of the monument while also
pointing to important lunar rising and setting positions at midsummer.
What was so astounding about this was that at any other latitude, while
stones could be positioned to align with the sun and moon in this way,
they would not form a rectangle. It is clear, therefore, that Stonehenge
was located where it is for just this purpose.

Hawkins book was published in 1965, and it caused a sensation. However, he was not the only investigator actively searching for the meaning of these enigmatic stones, and soon there would be a very crowded
field of "alternative" theorists. Undoubtedly the most important of these
was our third man: John Michell.

Educated at Eton College and Trinity College, Cambridge, his was not
the sort of background (wealthy, aristocratic) from which one would
expect such an esoteric genius to emerge. Yet Michell was far from ordinary and had a view of the world that was genuinely "alternative" in
that he seemed able to perceive hidden patterns that eluded more orthodox intellects. A founder member of R.I.L.K.O. (Research into Lost

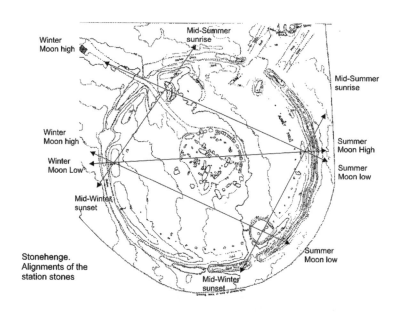

Winter
Moon high

Mid-Summer
sunrise

Mid-Summer
sunrise

Winter
Moon high

Summer
Moon High

Winter
Moon Low

Summer
Moon low

Mid-Winter
sunset

Stonehenge.
Alignments of the
station stones

Summer
Moon low

Mid-Winter
sunset

Knowledge Organization), he became profoundly interested in the concept of the New Jerusalem: the visionary city whose manifestation on earth is the culminating event of the book of Revelation and therefore of the Bible as a whole.

"And I saw the holy city, New Jerusalem, coming down out of heaven from God, prepared as a bride adorned for her husband . . .

. . . And in the Spirit he carried me away to a great, high mountain and showed me the holy city Jerusalem coming down out of heaven from God, having the glory of God, its radiance like a most rare jewel, like a jasper, clear as crystal.

It had a great, high wall, with twelve gates, and at the gates twelve angels, and on the gates the names of the twelve tribes of the sons of Israel were inscribed; on the east three gates, on the north three gates, on the south three gates, and on the west three gates. And the wall of the city had twelve foundations, and on them the twelve names of the twelve apostles of the lamb.

And he who talked to me had a measuring rod of gold

to measure the city and its gates and walls. The city lies
foursquare, its length the same as its breadth; and he
measured the city with his rod, twelve thousand stadia;
its length and breadth and height are equal. He also measured its wall, a hundred and forty-four cubits by a man's
measure, that is an angel's. (Rev. 21: 12-17)

Michell recognized that the design of this city to come is actually a
geometric construct of profound significance. The basis of this diagram
is squaring the circle, and there are three ways of doing this. The first is
to draw a square around a circle so that they touch midway along each
side; the second is to draw a circle around a square so that they touch at
the corners; and the third is to draw a square and circle that are the
same perimeter.

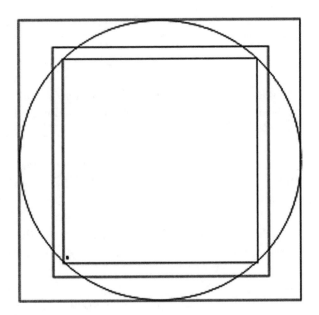

The third option is the most perfect as it is the so-called "pyramid"
relationship. It is called this because, as we have seen, if you use the
square as the pyramid's base and the radius of the circle as its height,
you obtain a pyramid similar in shape to the Great Pyramid of Giza.

Michell realized that in ancient times, squaring the circle in this way
was the central proposition of the architectural canon (i.e., the sacred

laws of architecture). This is because squares symbolize materiality while circles represent spirit. Thus the squared circle symbolizes the unity of spirit and matter: the marriage of heaven and earth which is the very basis of life.

> "The architectural form of the canon is the cosmic temple, the instrument by which the ideal concept of the marriage of heaven and earth, expressed in the symbol of the squared circle, was translated into actual reality. In the old geometric cosmologies the earth was represented by a square, the heavens by a circle, and the two forms were harmonised in the groundplan and architectural features of the temple. So it is that at the foundation of every cosmic temple is the figure of the circle squared."[13]

Michell goes on to describe how the squared circle underpins the construction of Stonehenge, which is itself a manifestation in stone of the New Jerusalem plan:

> "Of all ancient monuments, that which can be most certainly identified as an example of the cosmic temple is Stonehenge. The dimensions of its stone circles are numerically the same, though on a reduced scale, as those of the New Jerusalem, and the geometry of its ground plan differs in but one respect from St John's model city: that whereas the city takes its form of a square, Stonehenge is circular. In their measurements, however, temple and city are identical, and both derive from one scheme of proportion which is the lost canon of the ancient world. The fact is that St John's vision of the New Jerusalem was prefigured at least 2000 years earlier in the British temple, Stonehenge."[14]

Michell summarized these finding in a diagram. (See page 150).

Now what is important for us to note here is that the same construction, squaring the circle and creating a pyramid with the proportions of the "New Jerusalem" can be elaborated from a 5:7:8 triangle and this can be obtained either theoretically from the dimensions of Caesar's

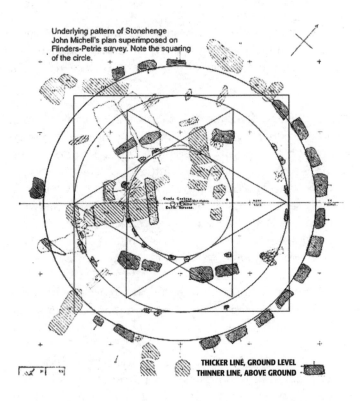

Underlying pattern of Stonehenge
John Michell's plan superimposed on
Flinders-Petrie survey. Note the squaring
of the circle.

THICKER LINE, GROUND LEVEL
THINNER LINE, ABOVE GROUND

map of Britain or, as we have also seen, practically from the Stone of
Destiny. This provides us with another unexpected link between
Stonehenge, the Stone of Destiny, and the visiting princesses from
Jerusalem. It also explains why they may have visited this ancient British temple of the Sun and Moon. Not only was it built using Middle
Eastern measures (feet and cubits) and perfectly positioned geographically to record the most important risings and settings of sun and moon
as they happened at right angles to each other, but it was built to be a
perfect representation of the New Jerusalem. The inescapable conclusion is that whoever built it was connected with the same civilization as
flourished in Egypt. We don't know who the architects were (quite possibly sages from Ancient Egypt), but we do know they must have been
in possession of the same arcane knowledge as would later inspire King
Solomon in his building of the Temple of Jerusalem and then St. John
with his vision of the Holy City from the sky: the New Jerusalem.

There is one other message that we can now read from these silent
stones, and this has to do with British monarchy. The Stone of Destiny,

we now discover, is not only a geometric talisman of huge symbolic significance, but it is also intimately connected with the idea of "New Jerusalem": i.e., the founding of the perfect civilization for the new age. In this sense we can call it the foundation stone of the celestial city.

Walking around the perimeter of Stonehenge, I could feel something of this. Although I had not yet elaborated just why this ancient monument is so important and has such a draw for millions of people, at a deeper level I was aware of how, like the Pyramids of Giza, it was somehow alive even now. Without any proof I felt certain that its main purpose had not been agricultural, cultic, or even as a place of worship of the most visible of ancient "gods": the sun and moon. Pure and simple it was a statement of faith in the divine dressed in stone. Its builders— and there must have been many over long ages—were initiates of a secret tradition that links Britain with Egypt and Israel. But like Westminster Abbey today, it was not just a collection of stones. It was a national shrine that almost certainly witnessed the crowning of kings in times so ancient that we have lost all trace of their existence, let alone their names. As such, Stonehenge would have been a fitting place for the princesses of Jerusalem to have visited, perhaps for a time installing their own throne stone among the ruins of the broken monument. This was a pleasant thought to entertain, but now, as the days were growing shorter, I had no time to tarry. I needed to get to Iona to see for myself the island to which the Stone of Destiny is said to have been brought by none other than St. Columba.

9

Iona—Isle of the Blessed

*M*y quest for the meaning of the Stone of Destiny and its relationship to the destiny of world, as a whole, and Britain, in particular, was coming to an end. Back in Edinburgh after my brief visit to Perth and Scone, I paid my hotel bill and made my way to Edinburgh Waverley Station. It was still early in the morning, and most of the shops along the north side of the Prince's Street were closed. On the other side of the road was Prince's Street Gardens, once an open sewer but converted by the Victorians into an oasis of calm. Towering above the Gardens was the Scott memorial, a colossal Gothic folly to Scotland's preeminent Victorian author: Sir Walter Scott. In another setting it would have seemed out of time and place, but here in Edinburgh, with the great bulk of the hill on which sits the Old Town and Castle, it looked just right. I could imagine eminent Scottish Victorians like Alexander Graham Bell, David Livingstone, and Earl Haig clambering up the hundreds of steps inside the monument so that they could take a last glimpse of Edinburgh before taking the train from Waverley to London, or rival Scottish authors such as Robert Louis Stevenson, Arthur Conan Doyle, and John Buchan throwing the monument envious glances as they rushed along Prince's Street in their horse-drawn taxis.

Though not yet ready to return to London, I, too, was leaving Edinburgh, and my own journey was scarcely less exciting: my first ever trip to the Hebrides. Leaving the Scott Monument behind me, I walked down a ramp from the bridge and soon found myself in the Stygian gloom of Waverley Station. My reverie over Edinburgh in the morning light was abruptly interrupted as my nostrils were assailed by the stench of diesel taxis mixed in with the miasma of ancient soot and rotten bananas that, for some reason, seems to permeate every major station in Britain. My train, too, was a disappointment. Far from the sleek express of my imagination, it turned out to be little more than a bus on railway tracks. Further disconsolation was to come. Because I was travelling by way of Glasgow, I had been hoping to catch, at least, a glimpse of what remains of the Roman wall raised by the Emperor Antoninus. However, as I looked out of the window, to my great disappointment, there was no sign of it. It seemed that the railway track followed a route some miles to the north of the wall or at least of the little that remains of it. Instead all I could see were dreary suburbs—Linlithgow, Falkirk, Cumbernauld, Muirhead—that looked little different from the outskirts of London or any other big city in England. It was not an auspicious start.

Presently we arrived in Glasgow Queen Street, which reminded me of Charing Cross Station: one of the smaller of the London terminals. One difference that stood out was that all signs seemed to be written in Gallic as well as English. I had noticed the same thing in Edinburgh: that everywhere signposts were duplicated. Given that Gallic, the old language of the Irish–Scots, has only ever been native to some of the Hebridean islands and the wilder parts of Argyllshire, it seemed odd that such notice was being taken of this almost extinct language. Indeed, since today there is only a handful of Scots for whom English is not their first language and even those would be fluent in the latter, dual signing in Hindi, Urdu, or Mandarin would have been of more practical use.[1]

The subject of language is, of course, as much a matter of national pride as convenience. The Gallic signs are there to advertise the idea that Scotland has a separate identity from England and that just as the Stone of Destiny has been removed from the English throne, so should Scotland itself now secede from the United Kingdom of Great Britain. The purpose of the signs, therefore, is not inclusiveness of a small and endangered minority. No, they are there to increase Scotland's sense of "otherness" in preparation for full political secession from the UK. However, to me as an observer who very seldom crosses the border, the real difference in Scotland is between lowland and highland Scotland. The first is almost identical in character with northern England while the latter has much more in common with Norway: a nation with which Scotland has much shared history. The Hebrides in particular—many of them mountainous and with wild, moorland landscapes—are among the unheralded treasures of Britain. They include the Island of Skye (made famous by its role in the escape of "Bonny Prince Charlie" after his defeat at the Battle of Culloden in 1746) and Harris, famous for its tweed cloth. These islands, and even the areas of mainland that face them, are worlds unto themselves and are as different from most of Britain as Canada is from Connecticut.

These differences in landscape became immediately clear as my next train made its way north. My destination was the coastal town of Oban, and once the next train had left behind the crowded suburbs of Glasgow, it began to thread its way along the north side of the river Clyde, going past the old Roman settlement of Dumbarton. Soon we were in a different world: one characterized by lochs, mountains, and deeply chiseled cuttings. The line threaded its way onwards, skirting alongside Gare Loch and Long Loch before joining the upper reaches of Loch Lomond. It then began to climb steadily to Crianlarich where the branch to Oban split off westwards from another that was going northwards to Fort William. The scenery round here was spectacular: brooding mountains, waterfalls, and here and there areas of forest. Yet it was a landscape that did not seem particularly friendly to man. In contrast to the lush but crowded lowlands, the land looked barren. What fields there were seemed small and capable of supporting only sheep. It was a reminder that not much has really changed since England's eighteenth-century sage, Dr. Johnson, journeyed in these same parts, with his friend and chronicler, James Boswell:

> "Sir Allan McLean bragged that Scotland had the advantage of England, by its having more water. JOHNSON, 'Sir,

we would not have your water, to take the vile bogs which produced it. You have too much! A man who is drowned has more water than either of us,' and then he laughed. (But this was surely robust sophistry: for the people of taste in England, who have seen Scotland, own that its variety of rivers and lakes makes it naturally more beautiful than England, in that respect.) Pursuing his victory over Sir Allan, he proceeded: 'Your country consists of two things, stone and water. There is, indeed, a little earth above the stone in some places, but a very little; and the stone is always appearing. It is like a man in rags; the naked skin is still peeping out.'"[2]

Looking at this wilderness around me, I could see just what he meant: there was much rock and water but only a little soil. However, I could also see how the mountains of rock had one advantage: they provided a natural means of defense. It was easy to understand how the Scots of Dalriada had managed to colonize the coastline of Argyll; for even if the Picts to the northwest or the Britons to the south had wanted to dislodge them, doing so would have been well nigh impossible. Access by land would have been extremely difficult while, without naval superiority, the coastal route would have been closed. On the other hand for the Dalriada Scots, the thinly soiled coastlands of Argyll could offer but a meager living. It would have been just a matter of time before they would want to burst out of this barren enclave to take over the better lands of the Picts to the north and Britons to the south. This, of course, is what eventually happened. Travelling by train through Argyll, therefore, was an interesting lesson in how landscape often dictates history, and it was for me in 2009, as for Dr. Johnson in 1773, an initiation.

At Oban I checked into a seafront hotel with the intention of the next day crossing over by the ferry to the Island of Mull. From there I was going to take a bus from Craignure on the east coast to Fionnphort on the southwest, and then a second ferry would take me over the narrow channel that separates the Ross of Mull from my eventual destination: the tiny island of Iona. The Fates, however, had other plans in mind. It was already raining when I got off the train, but by nightfall it was also blowing a gale. The sea in the harbor, one of the most protected in Britain, was whipped up into a frenzy, and the rain, by now torrential, was being driven so hard against the window of my room that it seeped between the putty and glass, making a pool on the windowsill. It continued to blow all night, and the following day it was still pouring with rain. I ate an early breakfast and rushed down to the ferry terminal, only to discover that sea conditions on the water were still so bad that no ships were sailing that day.

There was now nothing for me to do but retire back to my room where I spent the day reading books about Iona: an island paradise that it now seemed likely I would not actually see. Reading about it, while actually staying on the Argyll coast, gave me a much better grasp of the enormity of Columba's achievement. Scotland is not a large country and for the most part, even today, it is sparsely populated. However, in St. Columba's day, travelling in the Highlands was far more difficult than it is now. There were no railways then and north of Dumbarton no roads worthy of the name. There were no "climbing centers," no stately homes converted into hotels, no emergency helicopters, and, outside of his immediate community of Dalriada Scots, no one in Britain would have spoken the Gallic language. Even so, Columba did have one inestimable advantage over most of us: he came from a nation of sailors—people were used to using the sea as their highway. For him, then, the little island of Iona, separated as it is from the agriculturally richer parts of Scotland by dangerous seas and mountains, would not have appeared, as it does today, to be an isolated speck. Rather it was at the very hub of a buzzing, seafaring community of fishermen, adventurers, and pioneers. To the north lay the largest of the Hebridean islands: Lewis and Skye, as well as a string of other inhabitable isles: North Uist, South Uist, Rhun, Coll, and Tiree. To the south and east were the relatively large islands of Islay, Jura, Mull, and Aran as well as the island-like peninsula of Kintyre. South and within sight of this lay Columba's homeland of Ireland.

While looking on a map, these islands and coastlands appear isolated from one another, but for a seafaring people they are not; in many respects Iona was ideally situated to act as a religious center for the entire region. It was also, for someone whose stated intention was to Christianize the northern Picts, not a bad place to set out from. Their capital was at Inverness on the east coast of Scotland. If he had had to travel there overland, then even in summer this would have presented near insurmountable problems. However, on the other side of Mull from Iona lies the access point to the "Great Glen." This is a connecting chain of lochs and rivers that separate the most northerly part of Scotland

from the rest. Using a small boat Columba could have sailed straight up
Loch Linnhe, which in turn connects with Loch Eil. After disembarking
at the port we now call Fort William, a short trek (following the course
of the river Lochy) would have brought him to Loch Lochy. From the
north end of this loch, another short trek would have brought him to
the southern end of Loch Ness. After that it would quite literally be
plain sailing to the Pictish capital of Inverness.

In Columba's time and maybe even before, the Great Glen was one
of the principle trade routes of northern Scotland and with good reason: the Picts had much to gain from trading with the Scots. We can
imagine that Columba's people brought with them goods, perhaps gold
and quality tableware from Ireland and wine from the Mediterranean.
They would have traded these for horses and other livestock for the
breeding of which the Picts were famed.

They may also have traded the timber that was needed for the building of the boats in which other goods were carried. Seafaring was far
and away the most important activity of the Dalriada Scots, and it is
likely that at the time of Columba, Oban, with its protected harbor, was
even then the major port for the area. Even so, lying on my bed with
the rain crashing against the window, I couldn't help but feel sorry for
those sailors of the seventh century whose open boats would have offered little protection from the elements. Luckily for me, by the following morning the storm had passed, and the sun was once more shining.
This time when I went returned to the ferry terminal, I was able to book
return crossings to Mull and Iona with a scenic coach ride through the
southern arm of Mull linking my two ferry journeys.

Without further trouble, I soon arrived on Iona at the tiny port of
Baile Mor. I was half expecting Iona to be a major anticlimax; however
this proved not to be the case. As soon as I had disembarked, I could
feel the special atmosphere of the little island: a feeling that far from it
being at the edge of the world, it is in some special way connected to
the very center of creation. At this point I can do no better than to once
more quote the words of Dr. Samuel Johnson from the journal of his
travels in the Hebrides with his faithful companion and biographer
Bosworth, when they, too, arrived in Iona:

> "We were now treading that illustrious Island, which was
> once the luminary of the Caledonian regions, whence sav-
> age clans and roving barbarians derived the benefits of

knowledge, and the blessing of religion. To abstract the mind from all local emotion would be impossible, if it were endeavoured, and would be foolish, if it were possible. Whatever withdraws us from the power of our senses; whatever makes the past, the distant, or the future predominate over the present, advances us in the dignity of thinking beings. Far from me and my friends, be such frigid philosophy as may conduct us indifferent and unmoved over any ground which has been dignified by wisdom, bravery, or virtue. That man is little to be envied, whose patriotism would not gain force upon the plain of Marathon, or whose piety would not grow warmer among the ruins of Iona."[3]

The intense blue of the sea between Mull and Iona reminded me of the Mediterranean. In fact the village of Baile Mor itself reminded me of holidays spent on Greek islands in the early 1970s. There were rows of small cottages and one or two gift shops but nothing truly commercial, and unlike in Dr. Johnson's day when the village was teaming with illiterate crofters, except for tourists, the place seemed to be deserted. The only sign of industry was a pile of empty lobster pots.

Leaving the jetty where the ferry pulled in, I, like Dr. Johnson before me, walked up the cobbled path that leads from Baile Mor to what remains of Columba's ancient abbey. Turning right and walking along behind a row of cottages, I soon came upon the ruins of what had evidently been a nunnery. Judging by the very substantial remains, it must, in its prime, have been a grand foundation. My guide book told me that it was actually quite a late structure; it was built in around 1200 and therefore over six hundred years after the death of Columba. Most of the walls looked in pretty good condition so that given the will and money it could very easily be reroofed and brought back into use.

Next to the nunnery was the *Teampull Rònain* or St. Ronan's Chapel. It was a small, rather plain building that had been built in 1200 and until the time of the Reformation, had served as the island's parish church. Unlike the nunnery it has been restored, but as it is reserved for the private use of the Iona Community, I was not able to go inside.[4] According to the guide book there has been a chapel on this spot since the eighth century. This makes it one of the oldest foundations on the island. North of the *Teampull Rònain* lies the main abbey complex, but

between the two stands what for me turned out to be the most significant place of all: the *Reilig Odhrain* or St. Oran's graveyard. This was a
walled churchyard with magnificent views across the straights towards
Mull. According to a guidebook, which I purchased at the gate, many
kings of Scotland, Norway, and even some from Ireland were buried
here. These included Macbeth as well as Duncan, the king he is said by
Shakespeare to have murdered. At the center of the graveyard was another chapel, not dissimilar to the *Teampull Rònain*, only slightly more
ornate. This one was open to the public, so I was able to enter, and as I
like to do when in churches, light a couple of candles in remembrance
of deceased family members.

I will return to the subject of St. Oran's graveyard later, for it has a
bearing on our story. However it is worth noting that while the elaborate grave markers of the old kings of Scotland (and also of the "Lords of
the Isles" who came after them) have been removed to the safety of the
abbey museum and church, people continue to be buried in the graveyard. The most notable, recent arrival whose gravestone I found near to
the sea's edge was John Smith. He was the leader of the Labour Party
before Tony Blair, and although he never became Prime Minister himself, he had much to do with the revival of his party's fortunes in the
early 1990s. Also, by putting pressure on the Conservative government
of John Major over Scottish devolution, he had a hand in the return of
the Stone of Destiny to Edinburgh. Indeed, it can be said that John
Smith's death and subsequent burial in Iona created the atmosphere
that brought this about.

Leaving the graveyard of St. Oran, I made my way to the abbey complex itself. Although founded by St. Columba in the sixth century, the
buildings we see there today were all raised much later. Begun in ca.
1200 at the time when Reginald was "Lord of the Isles" (effectively King
of Argyll and the Hebrides), the church was built by monks from the
Benedictine order. During succeeding centuries their church was added
to and modified, right up until the time of the Reformation of 1560. At
that point the monks were expelled, and the abbey, like the convent,
was left to go derelict. An attempt in the 1630s to reverse this process—
the intention being that the church, at least, could serve as a Cathedral
of the Isles—came to nothing; for without a living community on Iona
there were simply not enough people to run or protect it.

All this changed in 1874 when the Duke of Argyll, the then Laird of
Iona, employed the famous architect Robert Rowand Anderson to see

what could be done to halt the further decline of the abbey ruins. Then in 1899 the abbey, along with various other important buildings, was given over to a new body called the Iona Cathedral Trust. The primary mission of the Trust was to restore the abbey building itself sufficiently for it to be used in public worship. The first service was held in 1902, and this phase of the work was completed in 1910. Then, nearly thirty years later, the real rebirth of Iona took place with the founding of the Iona community.

This time the initiative came not from the aristocracy but rather from ordinary people. The driving force and instigator of the community was the Rev. George MacLeod, minister for Govan Old Parish Church, which is one of the poorest neighborhoods in Glasgow. The idea was to bring trainee ministers and craftsmen to the island so that they could hone their skills on rebuilding the abbey as a preparation for working in deprived areas. The restoration was complete in 1965, but the community George MacLeod founded lived on. Today the Island of Iona belongs to the nation, but the abbey, the *Reilig Odhrain*, the *Teampull Rònain*, and the nunnery are in the care of the National Trust for Scotland. As a result, the buildings are better cared for now than they have been at any time since the Reformation.

Walking around the abbey, it was apparent at every turn that this building is not a museum but a living church. However, I found the cloister by far the most attractive area. In the parts where it has been rebuilt, the freshness of the sculpted limestone of pillars and gargoyles lie in stark contrast to older stonework from the thirteenth century. Likewise the walls of the cloister were decorated with dozens of tomb lids from the St. Oran's burial ground. They had been brought indoors into the abbey itself, so that they could better be preserved from the elements. Most of them were attractively decorated with Celtic knotwork and other such like design motifs, while some bore full-sized effigies of the person at one time buried beneath them. Unfortunately, as very few carried written inscriptions, most of the owners of the lids were unidentifiable; the tomb lids of the kings were indistinguishable from those of mere nobles. In death, unlike in life, all were equally anonymous.

I left the main church building and walked around outside. Although it was October, the sun was shining brightly and I felt curiously at peace with my surroundings. I then walked back towards the main avenue and stopped to admire the St. Martin's Cross. One of several High

Crosses on the island, at over four meters it towers like a totem pole above the green grass that surrounded it. I found that on one side it was decorated with sinuous vines that twist and turn up the shaft, threading their way through a simple design of stone bosses. The other side is both more elaborate and also more Christian in content. At the center of the crossing and surrounded by a stone halo is a depiction of the virgin and child. Below this are scenes taken from the Bible: Daniel in the lions' den, Abraham about to sacrifice his son Isaac, David with his harp, and again David with Goliath.

This cross and also another dedicated to St. John (a replica of which stands close to the main church entrance) are potent reminders that Iona was once a center for religious iconography. The artistry of the monks, which even today can be seen everywhere around the abbey, was not confined to stone carving; for centuries this island was the foremost center for the making of illuminated manuscripts. Indeed the famous Book of Kells, which is now kept at Trinity College Dublin, was made on Iona, possibly in part handwritten and illustrated by St. Columba himself.

All this history, though interesting, was not the reason I had come to Iona. What I wanted to know—and felt I would find out only by standing on the soil of the island myself—was how and in what way it was involved in the mystery surrounding the Stone of Destiny. What was clear was that this island had indeed been a place of burial for royalty as well as the site of the most significant religious foundation in northern Britain. However, I wanted to know more. Was the island holy is some intrinsic way or was it simply the association with the story of St. Columba that made it so?

Leaving the Cross of St. Martin, I walked around the outside of the abbey to a small courtyard on the other side. Here I discovered there was a museum containing more grave slabs from St. Oran's as well as a large selection of other stonework. I examined these stones carefully, especially the grave slab of one of the Lords of the Isles. Responsible for most of the building we see today, they took power in the aftermath of Viking rule. Starting in the ninth century, the Vikings had, at first, contented themselves with raiding the coasts of the British Isles. Iona itself was pillaged in 795, 802, 806, and 826 by these pirates in search of treasure. There was, however, also a sense of the hand of destiny in the pressure the Vikings exerted. It was as a result of their pressure that the kingdoms of the Picts and Scots were brought into union by Kenneth

MacAlpin. He, it is claimed, moved the Stone of Destiny from Iona to Scone. If there is any truth in the prophecy that wherever the stone is taken, the Scots will rule, it was found to be true in this instance. Because MacAlpin had as his mother a Pictish princess and for them the right to kingship came through the female line, he was able to unite the two kingdoms of Scotland and Pictavia with himself as king.

Following MacAlpin's unification of Scotland with Pictavia, the bones of St. Columba were moved to Dunkeld Abbey. This was probably done for reasons of safety as Dunkeld lies not far from Perth itself, and the Vikings were an ever-present threat to Iona. It seems probable that it was at this time that the Stone of Destiny was removed, too, and brought from Iona.

After this the Vikings did, indeed, take possession of Iona, many other of the Hebridean islands, and even much of Ireland. However, by this time the Norwegians were converting to Christianity so for them, too, Iona became a place of spiritual pilgrimage rather than pillage. Indeed, several of their kings were buried in St. Oran's burial ground. Then, as so often happens with conquerors, they began intermarrying with the local people. As a result a new, mixed race of Hebrideans—part Dalriada Scot, part Norwegian—emerged. Hardy and self-sufficient, they soon threw off the shackles of both Norway and Scotland proper to establish a new "Lord of the Isles."[5]

Although St. Columba's bones had been moved to Dunkeld, there was another relic which remained in Iona and which I now stumbled upon in the museum there. This was a rounded stone that had apparently been used as a pillow under his head when he was buried. Confusion about this stone, which today is kept very securely under a metal grill, seems to be the origin of a further legend that, as he was dying, he slept with his head on the Stone of Destiny itself.

So much for history and so much for mythology, at this distance in time it is difficult to know what is truth and what is wishful thinking. Nevertheless, walking around the monastery in the footsteps of Columba, I could feel in my bones a certain aura of sanctity. This was most pronounced in the enclosed St. Oran's graveyard. Accordingly, I made my way back there, pausing to meditate for a few minutes to make sure that I had a strong connection to its "spirit of place." Taking out the guide book I had bought earlier, I reread the section on St Oran's . . . and then it hit me: this graveyard and not the abbey was the most important center of power on the island of Iona. Indeed its location was probably the reason why St. Columba moved to the island in the first place.

To understand this, we need to consider the story of St. Oran. According to this legend, Columba needed someone to be buried in order to consecrate the ground. St. Oran, one of his monks, volunteered and was subsequently buried alive. Three days later the grave was opened, and much to everyone's surprise, he was still alive. Opening his eyes he told the bewildered monks that there was nothing to fear from death and that hell is not as bad as it is described. In order to stop him from saying anything else that might contradict Christian teachings on the subject, Columba quickly had him reburied. Thereafter St. Oran became the patron of the graveyard which, as we have seen, became the preferred place of burial for not just monks but even kings.

Now this story intrigued me firstly because the name "Oran" would seem to come from the same root as *Orendel*, a giant from north European mythology who equates to the constellation of Orion.[6] Giants are very prominent in the mythology of the Hebrides and indeed the tiny island of Staffa, which lies just six miles NNE of Iona, is home to Fingal's Cave. This is a natural wonder that is geologically linked to the Giant's Causeway in Northern Ireland. Composed of gigantic hexagonal cylinders of crystallized basalt, it looks something like a cathedral. Legend attributes it to the handiwork of a giant called Fionn mac Cumhail who is Finn macCool. Although I wasn't able to go to Staffa myself, guide books say that Fingal's Cave is perfectly aligned towards Iona Abbey. They say that from the back of the seventy meter cave, the abbey can be seen framed in the doorway. Since the graveyard of St. Oran lies on the other side of the abbey, it would seem that this must also be aligned with the cave and maybe it, too, could have been seen from there before the abbey was built.

All this is not as strange as it might at first appear. It is very clear to anyone with an open mind that Iona was already sacred from long before the advent of Christianity. The legend of St. Oran probably goes back to this period, when the cult of Orion and its connection with death and rebirth was integral to the religions of not just Britain but to all of Europe and Egypt too. The disappearance of Orion in summer time signified his death while the constellation's first reappearance at dawn was emblematic of rebirth. The chapel of St. Oran is aligned east-west so that provided the sky is clear of clouds, on this day at dawn the first star of Orion would be seen rising out of the opposing island of

Mull. Then, over the period of a couple of weeks, more and more of him would "climb out" of the earth before the stars became invisible in the daylight. This, I believe, to be the origin of the myth concerning St. Oran's burial and resurrection.

Curiously, the pathway leading from the shore to the graveyard was known as "the way of the dead." Based on traditions prevalent throughout Europe, this would suggest a symbolic connection between this pathway and the "roadway" of stars that we call the Milky Way.[7]

In one last curious twist to this story, the night after I returned home from Iona I had a strange dream. In this I was back on Iona, hiding behind a small hillock by the *Reilig Odhrain*. Three aliens dressed in silvery, tightly fitting suits appeared nearby, and I realized there was a sort of elevator there that could lift one to the stars if he knew the right code. I went into it and dialed up a device like the rotating wheels of a fruit machine, but unfortunately I woke up before going off to the stars.

Of course one can always overstate dreams and read into them more than is really there, but I can't help feeling that there is, indeed, some sort of special energy field, stargate, point of contact—call it what you will. This island is special. It has a feeling that the curtain between earthly reality and the world of spirit is especially thin here. Perhaps St. Columba himself knew this, and that is the reason why he located his community here, away from civilization out on the outermost fringes of the British Isles. If so, then the Stone of Destiny carries this connection for it is here that Columba is said to have crowned his friend King Aidan while the latter was either sitting or standing on the Stone. The question remains, however: Is the Stone of Destiny we see today the "real" one or is it a more modern copy? If so, can it nevertheless function as a stone of prophecy?

10

Talisman of Kings

*M*y quest had come a long way since I first set eyes on the Stone of Destiny that sunny morning in 1973. Whether or not it really is, as many believe, the selfsame stone on which Jacob rested his head at Bethel or the lost "flint box" (perhaps really a sandstone block) from which Djedi claimed the ideal dimensions of the Great Pyramid could be extracted, can only be a matter of conjecture. Tradition tells us that it is the former while the secret geometry of its shape implies the latter. However, without a written testimony in engraved hieroglyphs, cuneiform writing, or perhaps even early Hebrew characters, we cannot be sure of its provenance. Furthermore, there is also the little question of scholarly opinion which since the early nineteenth century has steered argument away from ancient traditions to a more prosaic solution: that the block was quarried from a sandstone pit in the vicinity of Perth and may therefore be of no great antiquity at all. Indeed a story

now repeated so frequently that it has become almost part of the leg–
end is that the stone taken by Edward I in 1296 was not the real one but
a substitute. According to this tale, when the abbot of Scone heard that
the English were approaching, he ordered that the real Stone of Destiny
be hidden and a substitute (actually a manhole cover) be put in its
place. To the glee of the gathered Scots, the king of England, believing
that the manhole cover was the real thing, took this back to Westminster
and kings of England have been sitting on it ever since.

Now while it cannot be denied that such a story has a pleasingly
comic ring to it, the evidence does not support it. In 1296 not even the
king of England and still less the monks of Scone Abbey had running
water on tap. People did not have flushing toilets (with their associated
drainage systems), still less electric cables or gas pipes entering their
properties through manholes. Under these circumstances it is difficult
to see what role "manhole covers" could have played in their lives. The
only real possibility is that the stone was the stopper for a well. How–
ever, given its relatively small size and its rectangular shape (it is, as we
have seen, only about 16½" x 26¾" in its largest section), it would seem
to be entirely unsuitable for the covering of a well with a better option
being a light wooden lid that could be easily lifted by women. More–
over, if the Stone was not the right one, then it seems strange that the
Scots made repeated protestations to Edward I and his successors that
they should return it to Scone. Would they have done that if they were
secretly smirking behind the King of England's back?

There is, however, another popular argument against its being the
actual Pillow Stone of Jacob. Critics point out that with 10½" as its short–
est measure, the Stone of Scone is much too deep to have functioned as
a pillow. Unless it was half buried at the time, this is certainly true, and
it is also true that its shape would not be particularly conducive to a
good night's sleep. A better choice for Jacob would have been a concave
stone: one just a couple of inches deep that would nestle better around
his head and not give him a crick in the neck. This argument, however,
ignores the second part of the story that tells us Jacob subsequently
raised the stone on its side and used it for an altar. For this purpose the
Stone of Scone would have been ideal and much better than a thin
concave one of whose existence we have simply no evidence.

The most damning piece of evidence against the stone's authenticity
as Jacob's Pillow is contained in William Skene's book *The Coronation
Stone*. He points out that none of the early chroniclers of Scotland make

any mention of the legend. Indeed, writing just after 1249, Fordun tells us no more than that the kings of Scotland were consecrated while sitting on the "regal chair—that is the stone" and that " . . . nor were any of them in wont to reign anywhere in Scotland, unless they had, on receiving the name of king, first sat upon this royal stone in Scone, which was constituted by ancient kings the 'sedes superior' or principal seat, that is to say, of Albania [Scotland]."[1] Fordun, Skene tells us, then goes on to say that when Fergus, son of Farquhar, led the Scots from Ireland to Scotland, he brought with him a royal chair and that this was cut out of marble.[2] The implication is that the Stone of Scone was somehow fitted into this marble chair, perhaps in the same way as it was later inserted into the coronation chair of Edward I.

Skene is emphatic that: "it is no part of the Scotch legend that the stone at Scone was Jacob's pillow."[3] However he does quotes Fordun on a story concerning the origins of the "marble chair" saying that it came from Spain. He repeats the by-now familiar story of how: "Neulus, a Greek, has a son Gaythelus, who goes to Egypt, marries Scota, daughter of Pharao, king of Egypt, and leads the remnant of the people who were not drowned in the Red Sea through Africa to Spain. One of his descendants, a king of Spain, has several sons, and sends one of them, Simon Brec, to Ireland, to whom he gave 'Marmorea Cathedra', the marble chair, diligently and carefully sculptured by ancient art."[4] Again quoting Fordun, Skene then adds that there are two accounts concerning the origins of the stone. One is that Gaythelus brought it from Egypt and the other that Simon Brec, having cast anchor on the shore of Ireland, raised a marble stone cut in the shape of a chair when weighing anchor.

This story of the anchor is very likely the source for a similar account in the *Chronicon Rythmicum* which, like Fordun's chronicle, is a primary source concerning Scottish history. According to this document, Gaythelus brought the *lapis Pharaonis* or "Pharaoh's Stone" from Egypt. He gives it the epithet *anchora vitae* (anchor of life). This seems to be the source of Fordun's confused account concerning the stone being raised with an anchor.

Now the Stone of Destiny is, of course, a block of sandstone. It is therefore difficult to reconcile this with Fordun's account concerning a marble chair. However, there are abundant sources of sandstone of all colors throughout the Middle East in Egypt, Jordan, and Israel.[5] Is it really so far-fetched, therefore, to think that a special "Pharaoh's Stone" was taken to Ireland from Egypt and later achieved iconic status as "Jacob's Pillow"?

I am not myself a geologist, and I don't know what sorts of tests (if any) have ever been applied to the Stone of Destiny to prove that it came from a quarry in the Perth area. All I can say is from just looking at it that it is not obvious to me it is local in origin. When I visited Perth Museum, there was a block of the local sandstone on display. This block was rather coarse-grained and purple in color; indeed it looked very much like the kind of stone used in the construction of Scone Palace and most of the old town area of Perth. Yet the Stone of Destiny does not look as though it is made from this material. It is certainly sandstone, but I would describe it as more creamy in color though with a bluish tinge. It seems curious, then, that Skene writes: "The coronation stone is described by Professor Ramsay as consisting 'of a dull reddish or purplish sandstone . . . The rock is calcareous, and is of the kind that masons would call freestone.'"[6] Anyone visiting the stone today can see with his own eyes that it is neither dull red nor purplish in color. In photographs it often looks rather grey, but this could be due to poor color balance; close up it looks much lighter. It is also not "calcareous" unless this term is being applied in general to all types of sedimentary rock including sandstone and not just to calcium containing rocks such as marble and limestone. So while one cannot dismiss the idea that the Stone of Destiny comes from the Perth area, it does seem strange that it does not resemble almost every other stone used in buildings in the area.

As far as I know, no tests have been carried out—for example making a comparative examination with a microscope or fingerprinting the concentrations of isotopes in the rock—that definitively rule out the possibility that the rock comes from either Egypt or Israel. If they have, then the results of such tests are not readily available for inspection. Most of the articles concerning the geology of the stone that are available for inspection on the Internet are, like the report of William Skene quoted above, secondhand accounts. They feed off one another, assuming that plausible tests have indeed been carried out that support the theory of its Perthshire origins. The Internet is awash with general statements such as: "It has been known for years that the Stone of Scone is an indigenous piece of Perthshire sandstone . . . " or "geological sampling would appear to confirm a match with the sandstone of Scone rather than the Palestinian limestone of Beitin [Bethel]." Unfortunately these statements are not backed up with the sort of hard scientific data that would resolve the question once and for all.

Nevertheless, the last comment quoted does seem to be based on an article published in the *London Sunday Times* on September 18, 2005.[7] Unlike all of the other articles I have read, this one does refer to some real chemical tests. Headlined "Stone's biblical past is exposed as a myth," it seems at first sight to demolish with one blow any idea that the Stone of Destiny might be anything other than a lump of Perthshire rock. After narrating in brief the legend of the stone, the article tells us how Jill, Duchess of Hamilton, went to Beitin—a Palestinian village considered by many to mark the spot of the biblical Bethel. Her mission there was to take samples of local rock so that geologists back in Scotland could compare these with the Stone of Destiny:

> "The samples, which are almost identical in composition to those at the time of Jacob's supposed visit more than 2,000 years ago, were analysed by scientists at the British Geological Survey in Edinburgh. They discovered that the samples contained fine-grained crystalline limestone, in stark contrast to the sandstone composition of the Stone of Destiny.
>
> Emrys Phillips, the geologist who carried out the tests, said the samples were as different as 'chalk and cheese'. The stone was instead hewn from the 400m-year-old (400 million-year-old) sandstone rocks around Scone."[8]

At first sight this would appear to be absolutely damning evidence that the Stone could not have come from the Middle East. However, if we examine the logic of this article a little more closely, we see that this is not really the case.

First of all, if the samples Lady Hamilton brought back from Beitin were limestone, you would not need to examine them under a microscope to tell they were different from the Stone of Destiny. A few drops of sulfuric acid (available from any car battery in the neighborhood of Beitin) would have shown this: limestone fizzes in the present of acid whereas sandstone doesn't. More to the point, just because Lady Hamilton's samples are made of limestone does not mean that every stone in the vicinity of Beitin is the same. In general, limestone and sandstone form sedimentary strata, and these can be recognized all over

the Middle East, from Egypt right up through the Dead Sea and to Leba-
non. Even at Petra, which is famous for its rose-colored sandstone, limestone can also be found. Not only that, there is nothing in the Bible to
suggest that the rock Jacob used as a pillow was actually local in origin.
It could have been brought to Bethel—perhaps for the building of an
even more ancient temple—at any time before Jacob's arrival; indeed, it
could even have been Egyptian in origin. There is even the outside
possibility that it was the self-same "flint box" that the magician Djedi is
said to have told King Khufu, which seems to have disappeared during
the chaotic "intermediate" period following the collapse of the "Old
Kingdom" (ca. 2,180 BC). Nobody knows what happened to this famous
"box," but it could as easily have been taken to Beitin as anywhere else.

All this is, of course, conjecture; for even if the Duchess of Hamilton
had found at Beitin a piece of what was unarguably sandstone of the
same type as the Stone of Destiny, this would still not prove that the
latter was used as a pillow by Jacob. The best that can be said is that
such a story is not impossible. However, there is another, just as important, factor to be taken into account which concerns the nature of relics
in general; for as a **symbol** it really makes no difference at all whether
or not the Stone of Destiny came from Palestine, Egypt, or indeed the
valley of the River Tay. For in the last resort, it is not the substance of the
stone that really matters but what it signifies. Or to put it another way,
the **idea** of using 'Jacob's Pillow as a coronation stone is more important than the actuality.

The *ka* and the Stone of Destiny

Before we go any further with this discussion, it is worth examining
a set of teachings that also takes us right back to ancient Egypt. The
connection between the stone and these teachings needs some explanation, but this can be understood if we first consider the role of por-
traiture in ancient Egypt. Now the Egyptians believed that in addition
to his or her physical body, a person (more importantly a pharaoh)
possessed a series of invisible or "subtle" bodies. These bodies were
thought of as forming a "Jacob's Ladder" or chain, stretching from the
densest to the most subtle. In Egyptian terminology, the lowest or densest of these subtle bodies was called the *ka*.

Looking after the *ka* of a deceased relative was a matter of some
importance to the Egyptians. Believing that it could feed off the inner

essence of food and drink, they used to bring gifts to the tombs of their ancestors. The *ka* was not necessarily confined to the tomb though. They believed that it was also possible for a portion of it to take up residence in a statue of the person. This is why we read about animated statues in the following, highly controversial, section of the Late Hermetic dialogue we call the *Asclepius*. The conversation is between Hermes Trismegistus (the Greek name for the Egyptian god Thoth) and his pupil Asclepius:

> "Trismegistus . . . Mankind is ever mindful of its own parentage and the source whence it has sprung, and steadfastly persists in following God's example; and consequently, just as the Father and Master made the gods of heaven eternal, that they might resemble Him who made them, even so do men also fashion their gods in the likeness of their own aspect.
>
> Asclepius Do you mean statues, Trismegistus?
>
> Trismegistus Yes, Asclepius. See how even you give way to doubt! I mean statues, but statues living and conscious, filled with the breath of life, and doing many mighty works; statues which have fore-knowledge, and predict future events by the drawing of lots, and by prophetic inspiration, and by dreams, and in many other ways; statues which inflict diseases and heal them, dispensing sorrow and joy according to men's deserts."[9]

This passage, which seems to condone idolatry as a virtue, was enough to cause the *Asclepius* dialogue to be banned by the church. Yet if we keep this doctrine in mind, it not only explains certain puzzling aspects of the Egyptian religion but by extension the function of talismanic relics such as the Stone and Spear of Destiny.

Now the purpose of mummification was to preserve after death as much as possible of the physical body. This was done not so much with the expectation that the pharaoh would rise again in a way analogous to Jesus Christ in the Gospels but rather to provide an anchoring point for the higher bodies of the deceased to return to earth. Besides the *ka*, the most important (or at least understandable) of these were the *ba* and the *khu*. The *ba* was usually depicted as a human-headed bird. Immediately after death it would hover over the dead body, but thereafter it would be free to depart from the tomb to take up residence elsewhere. In description it corresponds most closely to what Christians call the soul, though in occult literature it is more like what Theosophists and others call the "astral body." The *khu* (also called *akh*), which the Egyptians represented with the hieroglyph of a crested heron, was regarded as an even higher level of existence: one capable of returning to the source of all being. *Khu* is sometimes translated as "intelligence," "mental body," "higher being body," "*spiritus* body" or even "ghostly self". A better understanding, in my opinion, is to see it as the crystallized spark of the divine that, though it dwells in the heart of man, is also, in identity, the same as God himself. As such it is immortal: the physical body being confined to the earth and the *ba* only able to rise to the stars. The big questions then are: "What exactly is the *ka* and how does this "subtle body" fit in with the others?"

The hieroglyphic symbol for the *ka* is a pair of arms bent at the elbows. This is said to represent an embrace. According to Wallis Budge (former Keeper of the Egyptian and Assyrian collections at the British Museum) the *ka* is also the "genius" of the deceased.[10] More modern writers describe the *ka* as synonymous with personal life force. Mark Lehner puts it this way: "Perhaps the most succinct translation [of *ka*] is 'life force' . . . While residing discretely in each person the *ka* was characterised by its transferability and commonality. For the Egyptians an embrace transferred vital force between two people, or between gods and king . . . At death one's *ka* went back to rest, subsumed back into its generic folds. This return to commonality took place while the body was prepared and transformed into the mummy. The *ka* then needed to be reactivated so that the spiritual transformation of rebirth could take place and so that the link to the land of the living, through the tomb, could be established and maintained."[11]

Lehner's definition gets nearer to the truth but in my opinion still misses the point. I believe a better definition than "life force" (which in Egyptian art is anyway usually symbolized by the *ankh* or key of life) would be "atmosphere" or "aura"—a person's atmosphere being more or less synonymous with their aura. When you enter someone's house, you "feel" his or her atmosphere wrap around you. If that person is a friend or someone with whom you have a harmonious relationship, this can be a pleasant embrace. On the other hand, where the atmosphere is antagonistic to your own aura, you may feel magnetically repelled and want to leave the room immediately.

The idea of atmosphere is something the Egyptians seem to have understood not just intuitively, as we do, but as a recognizable reality. They believed that when people died not only did their "souls" (ba) and "spirits" (akh) leave their bodies, but their auras would have a tendency to disperse too. Yet, as we all know from visiting the houses of the famous dead, if a people's possessions are preserved and their personal space kept as it was, something of their atmosphere linger on—sometimes for many, many years.

The Egyptians sought to use this knowledge in a practical way. I believe it is the main reason why they tried to furnish the pyramid or tomb of the deceased with his or her familiar possessions. In doing so, they were attempting to invoke the atmosphere (ka) of the dead person. This was necessary so that the ba and khu, should the person decide to return to earth, would have a home to go to. He or she could not take up residence in the tomb unless supported and nourished by the ka or atmosphere of the deceased.

This, however, was only part of the story. The Egyptians believed that the ka of people, that is to say their distinguishing presence or aura, was not confined to the immediate vicinity of their mummies but could also be invoked by means of statues. In other words a person's likeness, sculpted or painted, could also carry a portion of the ka.[12] The closer the resemblance between portrait and person, the more powerfully connected the former would be to the ka of the sitter. To give added focus and to enhance the atmosphere of the tomb, they would frequently place one or more ka–statues at the entrance to its innermost chamber. We see examples of this in the ka statues of Tutankhamen which now reside in the Cairo Museum. Statues, however, were not only used in tombs. It was believed that a really good statue of a living pharaoh could function as a conduit and amplifier of his ka. It was for this reason that powerful pharaohs (most notably Rameses II) had so many statues made of themselves. This was not just a cult of the ego; they were attempting to spread their aura throughout the land and thereby make it easier to control. It is also why statues of earlier pharaohs were defaced by their successors. By breaking the nose or chin of a statue they were also breaking the link between it and the former pharaoh's ka.

Curiously, we see the cult of the ka statue even today. People visit Madame Tussaud's in London to look at waxworks. Where these are of high quality, they do indeed have something of the presence of the celebrity they are meant to represent. The same thing happens today in dictatorships where there is a cult of the leader. In preinvasion Iraq, Saddam Hussein's statues helped to spread his atmosphere and therefore keep the country under his spell. When on the April 9, 2003, the large statue of Saddam—the one that dominated Paradise Square in Baghdad—was toppled, it signified not just the end of his rule but the dispersal of his *ka*. To those of us watching the event on television, the dismemberment of Saddam's statue was reminiscent of scenes in Eastern Europe and the former USSR when many huge statues of Lenin, Stalin, and other "patriarchs" of Communism were similarly torn down. Again this symbolized a change of atmosphere: the removal of the unseen *ka* of a hated regime and its replacement with something else.

So what does any of this have to do with the Stone of Destiny? Well, it is really quite simple. It is not only people who manifest atmospheres, (i.e., have a tangible *ka*); every nation also has its own *ka*. That is what gives it a particular atmosphere that is both identifiable and recognizable in any place under the jurisdiction of that country. Not only that, but it is not only statues that can be vehicles of *ka*; other objects can personify the *ka* of the countries with which they are linked. Thus it is that while the famous Spear of Destiny may not be the actual weapon used to pierce the side of Christ, there is no doubting that in a very deep way it symbolizes Germany as the Holy Roman Empire. Centuries of usage in the rituals of the Holy Roman Emperors and the long established belief in the tradition that it is, indeed, the Spear of Longinus have imbued it with an atmosphere all of its own. Indeed this is so much the case that even were the real spear to come to light now, it would not have as strong an aura of mystery as is evident with the Hofburg Spear.

By visiting Vienna and taking the Spear into his possession, Adolf Hitler carried out a ritual that was deeply symbolic, resonating as it did with the German psyche at a most profound level. Had he been a good and honest man this might have led to great things. This, however, was not to be. His destiny was to plunge the world into perhaps the most terrible war even seen on this planet: one that was only brought to an end with the explosion of atomic weapons. It would be true to say that in making his grab for power, Hitler set off a train of events that has still to fully work through. The explosion of the first atomic bomb opened Pandora's box bringing mankind the apocalyptic power to destroy all life on earth.

The story of the Spear of Destiny is well documented, but unknown to most people; the Stone of Destiny is similarly imbued with mystic power. As a symbol, it is in a way irrelevant whether or not this particular block of sandstone actually comes from the Middle East or if the patriarch Jacob used it for his pillow. What is much more important is the fact that mythology links it with this event just as surely as the Hofburg Spear is linked to the crucifixion and death of Jesus Christ. It is in these terms that we need to look at the stone; for by intent and usage it can be said to carry the *ka* of the Old Testament prophecies linked to Jacob's dream at Bethel. As such it is at the epicenter of the tradition that Britain is the real Israel: the gathering point of the "lost" tribes who were dispersed from the northern kingdom by the Assyrians.

The association of the stone with an anchor (as we have discussed earlier) could also have resulted from later commentators, such as the author of the *Chronicon Rythmicum*, not understanding that the stone was associated in some way with the Egyptian concept of a "living stone" (i.e., one imbued with *ka*) and therefore containing *ankh* or life. The Irish legend that the stone would cry out if a trueborn king stood on it also seems connected with the idea that this stone is, in some curious way, alive. In other words, the stone has *ankh* as opposed to being an anchor.

As I have written about British Israel at some length in my book *The New Jerusalem*,[13] I won't say too much here about this belief. Suffice it to say that from at least the time of Gildas (sixth century AD), Britain has been regarded by some as the "reincarnation" of biblical Israel. There is, however, more to this than a romantic notion that the British (and hence those other nations of the British diaspora: the US, Canada, Australia, New Zealand, etc.) are descended from the Lost Tribes of Israel. The monarchy of Britain is also modeled on that of ancient Israel, the sovereign, like King David, being considered to have been chosen by God. The Royal Oath (as taken by the Queen) is sworn on the Bible while the Crown (and hence the country's sovereignty) is regarded as being in the gift of God. Just like those Old Testament kings, David and Solomon, our Queen had first to be acclaimed by the people while sitting on top of the Stone of Destiny. All this ceremonial was to reinforce the tradition: that Britain is indeed a new Israel.

Now, of course, these days Britain is a parliamentary democracy and the Queen's power is constrained by various constitutional acts to ensure that government fulfils the will of the people. Nevertheless, all elected MPs and Ministers have to swear their loyalty to the crown; likewise all acts of Parliament only come into force if they are signed by the Queen and stamped with her Great Seal. In theory (although she has been reluctant to use this power outside of her dominion of Australia), she also has the power to, at any time, dismiss Parliament and call for new elections. Not only that but the armed services of Britain are all subject to the crown as well. It is to the Queen and not to Parliament that officers and men swear their allegiance. Yet the Queen's power stems not from her birth but rather from her coronation. Uncrowned she would not be recognized as the ultimate authority in the land.

Now the Queen took her oath while sitting on Edward's chair with the Stone of Destiny secured firmly in its base. As we have seen, the archbishop of Canterbury, the most senior prelate in the Church of England, anointed her with oil, put the orb and scepters in her hands, and placed the Crown of St. Edward on her head. However, all was not quite as it seemed on the surface. For a start the so-called "Crown of St. Edward" is not the original that was worn by Edward the Confessor but a relatively modern replica. In 1649, following the execution of Charles I and the temporary abolition of the monarchy, Oliver Cromwell ordered that the regalia of royalty be treated as scrap. Consequently, all that remains now of the old Crown Jewels is a gold spoon (the one which is today used by the archbishop in the anointing ceremony). An entirely new set of Crown Jewels was created for the coronation of Charles II in 1661, and it is these which reside under close guard in the Tower of London.

Today's "Crown of St. Edward," which supposedly contains gold from the original crown of the Confessor, is the one made for Charles II. Its design, however, is modeled as exactly as possible on drawings and other representations of the original St. Edward's Crown which is also thought to have earlier belonged to Alfred the Great (r. 871–99). Likewise the orb and scepters are also re-creations with the added difference that the Scepter with the Cross was further remodeled (in 1910 for the coronation of George V) so that it could incorporate the Cullinan diamond. In addition to St. Edward's Crown there are a number of other crowns in the collection. These include the Small Diamond Crown of Queen Victoria, the Imperial State Crown of George VI (made in 1937), and possibly the most lavish of them all—the Imperial Crown of India. This was specially made for George V, who also bore the title of Emperor of India, to wear at the Delhi Durbar of 1911. It contains 6,170 cut diamonds as well as a number of choice sapphires, emeralds, and rubies. As she is not an Empress of India (the title was created for Queen Victoria in 1878 and relinquished by the British Royal Family in 1948), this crown has never been worn by Queen Elizabeth II.

So why does any of this matter and what does it have to do with the Stone of Destiny? Well, anybody watching video footage of the 1953 Coronation—the first ever to be televised with footage today viewable on YouTube—can be in little doubt that it was an extremely atmospheric occasion. In the film the Queen, then a young mother of twenty-seven, positively radiates an aura of regality; you can almost taste the atmosphere surrounding her. The fact that the crown, the orb, and the scepters that she wears or holds in the course of the coronation procedure were only about three-hundred years old is an irrelevance as far as the esoteric meaning of the ceremony is concerned. In reality these objects, albeit very expensive ones, were only props. The drama concerned human beings and the atmosphere or *ka* surrounding the event. The jewels, the robes, the presence of so many earls, viscounts, and dukes all dressed in their finest, the hymn singing, the trumpets playing, and of course, the venue itself, all added to the sense of occasion. However, when it comes down to it, all this frippery is just window dressing for what is actually very simple: a prospective ruler being acclaimed as undisputed Queen and then taking an oath to carry out certain responsibilities. In this sense a coronation resembles a marriage between sovereign and country. Indeed immediately after the anointing with oil and prior to her crowning, the archbishop gave the Queen a golden ring to symbolize her marriage to the country.

So where does this leave the Stone of Scone and why might it still be an important relic even if it is not, as tradition tells us, the self-same stone on which Jacob laid his head? What if, as critics of this tradition claim, it is really just a block of Perthshire sandstone that dates back only as far as our earliest written account of its use: the coronation of King Alexander III of Scotland in 1249? As an archaeological object it does, of course, makes a huge difference. If the Stone of Destiny is genuinely the very one that Jacob used as his pillow, then it is arguably an artifact of incalculable value. However, if we step back from the material world and consider it (as we do the modern Crown of Edward the Confessor) as the incarnation of an ancient symbol, then it really doesn't matter if it was made yesterday; what it embodies is an idea and that idea is both timeless and beyond materiality.

We can look at this by reference to other relics of extraordinary power. In an ideal world we would find the Holy Grail, the True Cross of

Christ, the Ark of the Covenant, and the Spear of Longinus. However, in the absence of these we are still free to make replicas and in rituals use these in their place. Thus every chalice used by every priest in every communion service is a simulacrum of the cup used by Jesus Christ at the Last Supper. The Holy Grail, long lost if it ever truly existed, is an archetype and as such is embodied in all these different chalices. Meanwhile the spear that Adolf Hitler stole from the Hofburg Museum is certainly not the same one as that purportedly used by the Roman centurion Longinus to pierce the side of Christ. We have only to look at it to see that it dates from a much later period than the first century AD and that it is nothing like the sort of spear used by the Romans.[14]

The fact that artifacts, such as the Hofburg Spear, are not genuinely as old as is claimed does not necessarily affect their potency as relics. For just as the ancient Egyptians believed that it was possible to endow a statue with *ka* or atmosphere, so too, used in the right way, a simulacrum of a sacred object can evoke the aura or presence of that which it represents. In this sense the Hofburg Spear is able, in the right circumstance, to manifest the *ka* of the Spear of Longinus.[15]

The Hofburg Spear may have been a Dark Ages forgery, but Hitler's intention to wield the power it symbolized and thereby recreate the old Holy Roman Empire or "Reich" of Charlemagne was not. This intention, coupled with the psychic power generated by centuries of ritual use, was enough to make it a seriously potent embodiment of the symbol. With hindsight we can see that having such a symbol fall into the wrong hands was extremely dangerous. The forces it is linked to drove Hitler mad (if he wasn't already) and gave him the false confidence that he could conquer the world. On September 1, 1939, Germany invaded Poland and started the Second World War. Two days later, as a direct result of this act, Britain, France, Australia, and New Zealand declared war on Germany (to be followed a week later by Canada).

At first Hitler was on a roll with German armies sweeping through Denmark, Norway, Belgium, Holland, and Luxembourg. By June 30, 1940, France was neutralized and forced to sign a peace treaty. To the east, the Soviet Union was at this time an ally of Germany. Indeed, Stalin used the opportunity of war between Germany and France to seize Eastern Poland and the Baltic States for the Soviet Union as well as to invade Finland. This left just Great Britain, her Empire, and Dominions (including the Anzac countries) as Hitler's only significant opponent still in the field. For the next year Britain went through her darkest hours as she sought to contain Hitler's spear-fueled ambitions. Germany did not invade the USSR until June 22, 1941, and the US did not enter the war against Germany until about six months later on December 11, 1941. Thus from the signature of the armistice between France and Germany on June 22, 1940 to the start of "Operation Barbarossa" (the German invasion of the USSR), the British Empire was the only major power opposing the Nazis.

Now if the Hofburg Spear of Destiny is linked by association with one occult power, then it is also the case that the Stone of Destiny is connected with another. In a sense this titanic struggle between Germany and Britain in the Second World War can be characterized as a fight between the Spear and the Stone: the irresistible thrust of a blitzkrieg lance against the immovable obstruction of unyielding Stone of Destiny. This conflict reached its climax in the Battle of Britain, which took place in the skies over southern England between July 10 and September 15, 1940. In this protracted struggle for air supremacy the Luftwaffe, which till then had swept all before it, was defeated by the much smaller RAF. It would not be an exaggeration to say that this was the crucial turning point of the Second World War. It was Hitler's inability to neutralize Britain in 1940 which meant that for the entire duration of the rest of the war there was always a western front that needed manning. It also meant that he could not focus all of Germany's energies on defeating the USSR; in due course Britain would act as the "unsinkable aircraft carrier" for the D–Day landings.

In a very real sense the Stone of Destiny was the symbol of British intransigence in the face of what looked to be overwhelming odds. This spirit of defiance was personified by the decision of the king, George VI, and his wife, Queen Elizabeth the Queen Mother, to remain in London at this critical time. He had been crowned, with the Stone as his witness, in 1933, and he believed in the tradition that the Royal Family is descended from King David of Israel. He also believed that the British as the "Lost Tribes of Israel" had inherited the covenant of Jacob that the Bible says was witnessed at Bethel by the stone the patriarch used as his pillow. This is a belief that was shared by many of the senior commanders of not just the British army, navy, and air force but also those of the Anzac dominions. According to this tradition, the Stone of Destiny was located in Britain for the very simple reason that this island was a new Promised Land and accordingly, London was to be a "New Jerusalem."[16] A further extension of this belief was (and in some quarters still is) that

the Stone of Destiny represents none other than that described symbolically in Chapter 2 of the Book of Daniel in the climax to his interpretation of King Nebuchadnezzar's dream:

> "You saw, O king, and behold, a great image. This image,
> mighty and of exceeding brightness, stood before you,
> and its appearance was frightening. The head of this im-
> age was of fine gold, its breast and arms of silver, its belly
> and thighs of bronze, its legs of iron, its feet partly of iron
> and partly of clay. As you looked a stone was cut out by
> no human hands, and it smote the image on its feet of
> iron and clay, and broke them in pieces; then the iron, the
> clay, the bronze, the silver, and the gold, all together were
> broken in pieces and became like the chaff of the summer
> threshing floors; and the wind carried them away, so that
> not a trace of them could be found. But the stone that
> struck the image became a great mountain and filled the
> whole earth." (Dan. 2: 31-35)

Daniel's interpretation of King Nebuchadnezzar's dream is that the
different parts of the statue represented successive world empires. The
head symbolized the king of Babylon's own empire that we today call
the "Neo-Babylonian." The breast and arms of silver symbolized the
Medo-Persian Empire that conquered Babylon in 539 BC. The belly and
thighs of bronze symbolized the Greek Empire of Alexander the Great.
He conquered the Persian Empire between 332 and 330 BC, and he died,
actually in Babylon itself, in 323 BC. The legs of iron symbolized the
Roman Empire, which reached its greatest extent under the Emperor
Trajan. In 116 AD he seized Ctesiphon (now called Baghdad) and
marched down the Tigris River, passing by the ruins of Babylon to the
Persian Gulf. He annexed this entire region to the Roman Empire as the
Province of Parthia although this territory was soon abandoned by his
successor Hadrian. The feet of iron mixed with clay symbolized the
successor kingdoms of the Roman Empire, most notably the Byzantine
Empire in the East and the Holy Roman Empire in the West but also
various other kingdoms (France, Spain, Austria, etc.) that grew out of
the remnants of the old Roman Empire.

The question then is: What does Daniel mean by the "stone cut by no
human hands?" Well, this is what Daniel himself has to say:

MAP 12: ROMAN EMPIRE

"And in the days of those kings [viz. rulers of the kingdoms symbolized by iron mixed with clay] the God of
Heaven will set up a kingdom which shall never be destroyed, nor shall its sovereignty be left to another people.
It shall break in pieces all these kingdoms and bring them
to an end, and it shall stand forever; just as you saw that
a stone was cut from a mountain by no human hand, and
that it broke in pieces the iron, the bronze, the clay, the
silver and the gold. A great God has made known to the
king what shall be hereafter. The dream is certain, and its
interpretation sure." (Dan. 2: 44-45)

Now the succession of world empires prophesied by Daniel is a matter of history. Many other prophecies by Daniel have also come true,
particularly those contained in Chapter 9 of his book.[17] Because of the
accuracy of the fulfilled prophecies it contains, it has been argued by
skeptics that Daniel's book is not authentic: that it was written after the
events described, probably during the period of the Maccabees (ca. 175
BC) rather than during the purported lifetime of Daniel (during the
Babylonian captivity, i.e., ca. 596–526 BC). The discovery of a copy of
Daniel among the Dead Sea Scrolls has undermined this argument.

These scrolls date from before 100 BC and predate the annexation of Judea to the Roman Empire (70 AD) or Trajan's annexation of Babylonia (116 AD).

On an esoteric level it is very easy to see that the Spear of Destiny personifies the power of the Holy Roman Empire, the chief of the successor states (iron mixed with clay) that succeeded the Western Roman Empire. In the East the Byzantine or Eastern Roman Empire was succeeded by the Ottoman. This empire, Islamic rather than Christian, took possession of both Babylon and Judea. The Ottoman Turks continued to rule over these territories right up until 1917. It was then that General Allenby, commander in chief of British Imperial Forces in the area, set about the conquest of the Holy Land.

Most people have heard of Lawrence of Arabia, who was sent by Allenby to stir the Arabs into revolting against the Ottomans, but his own accomplishments were equally significant, and they bear surprising links to other biblical prophecies. Before leaving England, Allenby was summoned to see Lord Fisher, who as First Sea Lord was the head of the navy. Unknown to Allenby, Fisher was an ardent believer in British–Israel, and now he made a strange prophecy. At the meeting Fisher told Allenby that it was his destiny to be God's instrument for the capture of Jerusalem and that to fulfill biblical prophecy, this must happen before Christmas 1917. In order for this campaign to be successful, he would need airplanes for thus it was prophesied in Isaiah 31:5, "As birds flying, so will the Lord of hosts defend Jerusalem; defending also he will deliver it; and passing over he will preserve it." Allenby was understandably stunned by what he was told. However, from his arrival in Egypt he set about reorganizing the forces at his command, including the introduction of aircraft. Then, in one of the most extraordinary campaigns of the entire First World War, he and his men succeeded in capturing Jerusalem. Allenby himself received the surrender of the city, entering through the Jaffa Gate on foot as he felt it improper to go mounted on a horse where Christ himself had had to walk.[18] Allenby went on to capture the rest of Palestine, as Israel was then known, fighting an important battle at Megiddo—the biblical "Armageddon." Afterwards, in recognition for his services to crown and country, he was given the title Viscount Allenby of Megiddo. Meanwhile, further to the east, British forces also drove the Turks out of Iraq. This meant that by the end of 1917, the British Empire was in possession of the whole of Mesopotamia: the province Trajan had called Parthia. To many in Brit-

ain this looked as though the stage was now set for the imminent return of Jesus Christ. With both Jerusalem and the Stone of Destiny in
British hands, there should be nothing to stop the messiah from taking
his seat on the later as King of the World and making the former his
capital city. History, however, has a habit of fooling us and destiny had
still a few tricks of its own to play.

11

Destiny's Revenge

*A*ccording to legend, the Stone of Destiny is a talisman of power. As long as a nation is in possession of it, it is invincible. Whether the notion is true or not, this legend has yet to be disproved. Edward I (himself a descendant of Scottish as well as Norman and Anglo–Saxon kings) removed the stone from Scotland in 1296. Since then, although attempts have been made to invade Britain, these have not succeeded—up until now, that is. Indeed, during this time Britain has built three empires: the first in France, the second in America, and the third (and by far the largest) worldwide. How much any of this was due to the presence of the Stone of Destiny, beneath the throne in Westminster, is anyone's guess. What cannot be doubted is that it was there and during this time only two monarchs were not crowned sitting on it. The first, Mary I, was hated by the English; her attempts at return-ing the country to Catholicism met with failure and she died childless.

The second was Edward VIII whose involvement with the American divorcee, Wallis Simpson, disqualified him from coronation and led to his exile in France. From the point of view of destiny, the abdication crisis was inevitable. Edward was a known Nazi sympathizer, and he would likely have betrayed his country to Adolf Hitler: the greatest enemy of the Jews since the time of the Romans. For him to have been crowned, while sitting on the Stone that many believe to be the token of Jacob/Israel's covenant with God would have been unthinkable.

In 1917, however, all this was yet to come. In many ways the surrender of Jerusalem to General Allenby (on December 11 of that year) marked the high water mark of the third and last British Empire. Yet even then there were cracks appearing in the edifice of British power. In Ireland, on the very fringes of Europe and as lands go, about as far away west from Jerusalem as you can go without first crossing the Atlantic, changes were afoot. The causes of these changes and the rights and wrongs of the politics involved are too complex to go into here. Suffice it to say that for the past eight hundred years or so—indeed ever since the Normans had taken possession of Ireland—Britain had had a difficult relationship with her near neighbor. In 1916 these simmering tensions erupted with tragic consequences. On Easter Sunday, an uprising in Dublin turned into street fighting. The rebels made no secret of the fact that they believed Britain's war with Germany was Ireland's opportunity to gain independence, and they were determined to make the best of it. However, a promised arms shipment from Germany was intercepted by the Royal Navy, and within a week the rebellion petered out. Nevertheless the "Easter uprising," as it is now known, had cost the lives of 106 British soldiers with a further 271 wounded. At a time when thousands of loyal Irish as well as English were dying in the trenches of Flanders, this "stab in the back" was regarded as outright treachery. Accordingly, fifteen of the rebels were hanged as traitors. This, however, just made them martyrs, and in 1918 the Dail, or national assembly, passed a resolution declaring Ireland's independence. A state of insurgency ensued which was relieved only when Ireland was granted full Dominion status. This was the same as Canada and Australia with one further difference: "The Irish Free State" abolished the monarchy and became a republic. Its territory, however, did not include the six counties making up the province of Ulster which remained (and still remains) under the sovereignty of the crown of Great Britain.

From the point of view of Britain's perceived destiny as a new "Israel," these developments in Ireland were not only unwelcome but a positive threat. Not only did the departure of Eire (as the Irish Republic came to be called) represent an economic loss, but Tara, where the Stone of Destiny is said to have resided prior to its being taken to Scotland, was now no longer under the jurisdiction of the king who had been crowned while sitting on it. This was not just a diminution of the sovereignty of the British crown but symbolic of an even greater religious conflict. Since 1530 Britain had been a Protestant country with the monarch as titular head of the established Church. Eire was Catholic and owed its allegiance to the Pope.[1] Thus a dividing line opened in the British Isles between those who looked to the throne of Britain as that of David (and hence of the expected Messiah) and those whose allegiance was to the throne of St. Peter in Rome.[2]

The Irish problem was not the only one to beset Britain during the interwar years. The First World War left the country in debt, and though she had come out of it victorious, the huge loss of life incurred in securing victory left the authority of the ruling class in tatters. The feeling that Britain had sent forth an army of lions led by donkeys undermined the authority of not just the aristocracy but the crown too. The vacuum thus created was eagerly filled by socialism, a new doctrine of equality that could point to the Soviet Union as the example of a country where the people had overthrown the tyranny of despots. The fact that both the late czar of Russia and also the now–deposed kaiser of Germany were his cousins was not lost on King George V. He knew that if he were to stay safely sitting on his throne that it was absolutely necessary for the Royal Family to modernize. The question was how?

By the 1920s the political split between the "upper" and the "working" classes was becoming ever more apparent. In 1926 a general strike broke out, the catalyst being conditions in the coal mining industry. The strike was by and large a failure but any euphoria the establishment may have felt over this was soon dashed. In 1929 the Great Wall Street Crash caused financial shock waves throughout the world, not least in Britain which was to endure an economic slump that was to last throughout the 1930s. Meanwhile the monarchy itself was racked with scandal. George V, who had been king since 1910, died on January 20, 1936. His eldest son, the Prince of Wales, had been groomed to inherit the throne, with the title King Edward VIII. He was a selfish, weak man with a shallow personality. When acclaimed king by the Privy Council, he was a forty–year–old bachelor. This status he was keen to change but in a way that would debar him from the throne. To the horror of the government he made clear his determination to marry his mistress, Mrs. Wallis Simpson. She was not only already married but a Catholic—both factors making it illegal for her to become queen.

At first the scandal of the king's relationship was kept secret from the public, but in October, after she obtained a divorce from her second husband, the story could not be contained. The Prime Minister gave Edward an ultimatum: if he married Mrs. Simpson, he would forfeit the throne. He chose Wallis in preference to coronation, abdicating on December 11 before he had ever been formerly crowned as king. As a result of the abdication crisis, it was Edward's younger brother "Bertie" who on May 12, 1937, sat on the Stone of Destiny as King George VI.

By this time, the clouds of war were already once more gathering. Nevertheless, the situation in Ireland notwithstanding, the British Empire was still a major power and a force to be reckoned with. Including perhaps a quarter to a third of the earth's population, it was still the largest empire the world has ever seen.

Hitler's invasion of Austria in March 1938, when he seized hold of the Spear of Destiny, was the prelude to a titanic struggle. At first he was able to wield his newfound power with almost supernatural effect. Poland, Denmark, Norway, and the Low Countries proved easy game, and even France, which had proved such a formidable opponent in the First World War, was defeated in just a few weeks. Now all that lay between the Nazis and their dreams of total domination of Europe was Britain and her Empire. During the summer of 1940 the blitzkrieging Spear of Destiny met its match and blunted itself against the immovable obstacle of the equally fateful Stone of Destiny. As the Messerschmitts of the Luftwaffe fought with the Spitfires and Hurricane's of the RAF, there was another battle taking place in unseen worlds. Both sides employed occultists with Churchill advised by people such as Dr. Walter Stein and Geoffrey Watkins[3] on what the stars indicated were likely to be Hitler's next moves. The defeat of the Luftwaffe in the Battle of Britain was not the end of the war, but it did prove to be the turning point. In fury Hitler hurled his armies and, symbolically the power of the Spear, eastwards into Russia.

Hitler's invasion of Russia, which was the largest military operation in world history, was called Operation Barbarossa.[4] The choice of this name was no accident. Barbarossa or "Red Beard" was the nickname of Frederick I, one of Germany's most famous Holy Roman Emperors and the creator of the Second Reich. In 1189, after a lifetime spent turning Germany into the strongest military power in Europe, he led the Third Crusade. The army that he took east was also one of the largest of its day, and thereafter he enjoyed mythic status as a sort of German "King Arthur" who would one day return to lead his country again.

The choice of Barbarossa for Hitler's drive to the east was, however, unfortunate. For though Frederick I had led a great army into what is now Turkey, it did not achieve its objective. He himself died on route in an accident at a river crossing, and it is said that at this moment the Spear of Destiny fell from his hand. After this omen of ill fortune, his followers lost heart, and most returned home empty handed. If Hitler had not been blinded by ego and filled with belief in his own invincibility, he would perhaps have realized that naming an invasion of the east "Barbarossa" was asking for trouble. As it was, he seems to have been completely oblivious of the risks involved, and as a result, the German armies became embroiled in a war of attrition that eventually was to lead to the complete destruction of the Third Reich and the emergence of Russia as a superpower.

Great Britain, meanwhile, found itself on the winning side: the only country in Western Europe to have withstood the might of the Third Reich. Any satisfaction this may have brought, however, was short-lived. On an esoteric level it was soon clear that Britain's was a Pyrrhic victory. The Spear of Destiny might have been blunted but not before it had dealt a devastating blow to the British Empire. Within just a few years, beginning with Indian independence in 1948, the Empire quickly disintegrated. In the same year and under pressure from the US, Britain's mandate over the Holy Land (in force since the First World War) was also brought to an end. In its place two new states were declared, a new Jewish "Israel" and an Arab state of Palestine. In the War that immediately followed this partition, Israel established itself as the new dominant force in the region. In the Six Day War of 1967 Israel was also to capture the Old City of Jerusalem itself, thereby calling into question the belief that one day, under Christian rule, the Stone of Destiny would be brought back to the Holy City and Jesus Christ would be crowned on it.

King George VI died in 1952, and, as we have seen, his eldest daughter, the Princess Elizabeth, was crowned in 1953. That is the most recent occasion on which the coronation seat has been called into action so it is not surprising that few people in Britain give the Stone of Destiny a second thought. Yet through all the turmoil of the Second World War, it, or rather its *ka*, stood as guardian over Britain. It symbolized that behind the bulldog spirit, epitomized by Churchill's stubbornness in the face of the seemingly overwhelming threat of invasion, there was something else entirely: a belief that God's promise of support to Jacob/Israel had been inherited by the British Empire.

That spirit has now all but evaporated, blown away by the same "winds of change" that blew away the autumn leaves of empire to leave the ancient oak of Albion a bare stump. During the course of the reign of Elizabeth II, London, the largest city in Europe and once the imperial capital of more nations than can easily be counted, has changed beyond recognition. No longer truly Christian or even British for the most part, in the space of a little more than a generation, it has moved from New Jerusalem to New Babylon. Under these circumstances it is hardly surprising that in 1996 John Major regarded the Stone of Destiny with such contempt that he was willing voluntarily to have it prized out of the ancient coronation chair where it had been kept safely for seven hundred years and sent back north as a political bribe. The question now is, does this matter?

Well, it is now fourteen years since the stone arrived in Edinburgh Castle and much has indeed changed, mainly for the worse. At the time of the 1997 General Election the British economy was looking extremely healthy: especially in relation to the rest of Europe. Today, after thirteen years of what historians will recognize as one of the worst periods of government in Britain's recent history, the country is all but bankrupt. Much worse than this and with long-term implications that no one can predict, in the space of a single decade the Labour Government allowed several million immigrants to settle in Britain. These came mostly from Third World countries, and they included a large number of criminals, terrorists, and other undesirables who seem actively hostile to the traditional British way of life. This situation is very much the, presumably unintended, result of another process that has been underway ever since the end of the Second World War: the unification of Europe.

In 1957, four years after the Stone of Destiny was put to use at the coronation of Queen Elizabeth II, a group of dignitaries from six countries: France, West Germany, Italy, the Netherlands, Belgium, and Luxembourg, found themselves gathered together in at the Palazzo dei Conservatori in Rome. This building is on the Capitol: the citadel at the very heart of ancient Rome. Used in the Middle Ages as a magistrates'

court, today it is a museum of art and sculpture. Among its most famous exhibits are a colossal head of Constantine the Great (the first
Christian Emperor of Rome) and the bronze she-wolf from the fifth
century that suckles the twin founders of Rome: Romulus and Remus.
The location was clearly carefully chosen for the representatives of the
six countries were there to sign the treaty that would bring into being a
Common Market. The larger (though unstated) plan was that in time it
would develop into a new "Holy Roman Empire" or United States of
Europe.

At first Britain stood outside of the loop where the Common Market
was concerned. However, the 1950s and 1960s were times of relative
decline in Britain as under investment, bad management, and poor la-
bor relations destroyed many of the industries that had once been world
leaders. The Common Market countries, by contrast, were seen to be
booming—their coordinated approach to industry, farming, mining, and
steelmaking were clearly paying big dividends. As a result, leading poli-
ticians in Britain had a change of heart and now actively sought to
bring the country into the EEC [European Economic Community]. At
first these overtures were rebuffed by President de Gaulle of France but
in 1973, under Prime Minister Edward Heath, Britain, along with Ireland
and Denmark, joined the EEC.

The 1970s were a time of oil shocks, hyperinflation, and industrial
unrest. For most Britons of that time, the EEC, with its high growth rates,
looked like an island of stability in a very uncertain world. Accordingly,
when a referendum on membership was held in 1975, the "Yes" camp
won a majority of the votes. This, however, was to turn out to be the
only time that they would be given a chance to express their opinion
on what has since then morphed from a trading association of independent nations to something that more and more resembles a federal
state. Since 1975 there has been a series of further treaties, the last being
the Lisbon Treaty of 2009. Under this treaty (really a constitution) the
European Union has taken most of the trappings of a state. It now has,
in addition to a flag and anthem, a full-time president and foreign affairs minister. The next ambition of the federalists is to gain powers to
raise taxes directly from European citizens without having to go through
national parliaments and to create an integrated, international police
force, army, navy, and air force that are under the jurisdiction of European bodies.

Now all of this is in direct conflict with the Constitution, statutes, and

indeed the royal oath that the Queen gave while sitting on the coronation seat and Stone of Destiny in 1953. In fact it can be said that by
signing these treaties, which give away the sovereignty of the people of
Great Britain to foreign control, the prime ministers who did so are
traitors. This is certainly the opinion of many people in Britain, the
majority of who regard it as a scandal that there has been no referendum on such issues. The argument that this is unnecessary cuts no ice,
because Parliament itself is elective and can take these decisions on
behalf of the people. All three major parties, Conservative, Labour, and
Liberal Democrat, are in favor of further EU [European Union] integra-
tion and because of the way elections are held, it is quite impossible for
smaller parties to gain power.

Now such political debates as these may seem irrelevant to the mysteries of the Stone of Destiny but really they aren't. The Stone itself,
whether or not it is original, represents something quite important. The
British Constitution is based on the Bible and the belief that the monarch is really a servant of God, charged with upholding his laws for the
good of the nation. EU sovereignty, on the other hand, looks back to
ancient Rome and is founded on the Code Napoleon. This is very different from British law which says that as long as something is not declared illegal, then it is legal. Under Napoleonic law, only that which has
been agreed as allowed is so. Not only that, unlike under British law
where a man is innocent till proven guilty, under European law, if a
person is charged with a crime, then it is down to him to prove his
innocence or he will be deemed guilty.

These are major changes in jurisprudence, and they stand in contradiction to one another. They symbolize a conflict that is highlighted in
the Bible where, in the Book of Revelation, there is a prophecy concerning a beast who rises out of the sea, i.e., emerges into consciousness:

> And I saw a beast rising out of the sea, with ten horns and
> seven heads, with ten diadems upon its horns and a blas-
> phemous name upon its heads. And the beast that I saw
> was like a leopard, its feet were like a bear's, and its mouth
> was like a lion's mouth. And to it the dragon gave his
> power and his throne and great authority. One of its heads
> seemed to have a mortal wound, but its mortal wound
> was healed, and the whole earth followed the beast with
> wonder. Men worshipped the dragon, for he had given his

authority to the beast, and they worshipped the beast,
saying, "Who is like the beast, and who can fight against
it?" (Rev. 13: 1-4)

Now there are many ways of interpreting this prophecy, which of
course relates to the end of days. The description of the "beast" indicates
that it represents the revived Roman Empire, which in the Book of
Daniel was described as: "terrible and dreadful and exceedingly strong"
and also as having ten horns. However, the statement that it was like a
leopard, i.e., a great cat that hunts by night, seems significant in view of
the way the EU has built its power–base by stealth. Also the "feet of a
bear" and "mouth of a lion," fits with it extending from Russia in the east
(symbolized always by a bear) to Britain in the west, which is often
identified with the royal lion. The EU began life with the Treaty of Rome
of 1957 and that this was signed in the middle of the ancient Capitol
close to the statue of the she–wolf feeding Romulus and Remus. Not
only that, a second council was held in Rome and in the same building
in December 1990. This meeting paved the way for two intergovern-
mental conferences: one on Economic and Monetary Union and the
other on Political Union. Under discussion were the frameworks on
which the EU was designed to morph from an association of trading
partners to a full-fledged Federal Union.

Ancillary to these moves but perhaps not as coincidental as it first
appears, something else happened during the previous year. On July 17,
1989, Austria made formal application to join the EU. Four months later
on November 9, the Berlin Wall collapsed signifying the end of the Cold
War and the start of a new era. Austria (along with Sweden and Finland)
actually joined the EU in 1995 while the reunification of Germany in
1990 meant that what had been the German Democratic Republic (East
Germany) was also brought into the EU. A subsequent "drive to the
east" means that today many other former Eastern Bloc countries are
also members of the EU. These include the Czech Republic, Slovakia,
Poland, Hungary, Romania, Bulgaria, and the Baltic States. In effect, the
EU now includes nearly all the countries occupied by Hitler's Third
Reich plus a few others (notably Britain, Ireland, Spain, Portugal, and
Sweden). Not only that, but with the accession of Austria into the EU,
the Spear of Destiny, though passively, is again at the center of European politics.

Now, while none of this may seem very important, it does have symbolic value in trying to understand prophecy. The displacement of the Stone of Destiny from the throne of Great Britain and the rebirth of a new Roman Empire appear to be linked events and to presage the period of three–and–a–half years tribulation that the Book of Revelation says have to be endured before the "Harvest of the World." We would appear to be living through the early part of that time. How it will all turn out is anyone's guess, but it is worthwhile keeping an eye on those two great talismans of power: the Stone and Spear of Destiny. Should either of them be removed and taken to some other place, then it could be a portent of further major changes.

Notes

Chapter 1

1. For more on the Reverend John McIndoe's speech at St. Giles' Cathedral, see http://www.aboutscotland.com/stone/destiny.html.

2. For more on Sir David Steel's statement about the return of the Stone of Destiny to Scotland see http:/www.publications.parliament.uk/pa/cm199596/cmhansrd/vo960703/debtext/60703-23.htm.

3. For more on John Maxton's statement about the return of the Stone of Destiny to Scotland see http:/www.publications.parliament.uk/pa/cm199596/cmhansrd/vo960703/debtext/60703-23.htm.

4. This is the title, equivalent to "Prime Minister," that is given to the chief minister of the Scottish Parliament.

5. Note: see articles in *The London Daily Telegraph* and *The London Times* dated Monday, June 16, 2008.

6. *Remember, Be Here Now* by Ram Dass (Richard Alpert) was published in 1971 and quickly achieved cult status as a textbook of eastern ideas on self-transformation made accessible to the western reader.

7. I have written more about this conversation in my earlier work *Signs in the Sky*.

8. I still have this Bible, now also heavily annotated. I am using it as a reference as I write this. *Holy Bible, Revised Standard Edition* (London: Collins' Clear-type Press, 1952).

9. Note: In the New Testament, Jesus preaches against anti-Samaritan prejudice. The antagonism between the Jews and Samaritans then was not so different from what exists today between the Israelis and Palestinians. There are still some Samaritans living in Israel to this day.

10. By the Babylonians rather than the Assyrians.

11. See Zech. 12:10, John: 31-37.

12. Trevor, Ravenscroft, *The Spear of Destiny* (London: Corgi, 1974), p. 20 with quotes presumably from the unpublished manuscript of Dr. Walter Stein which according Ravenscroft formed the research basis for his own book.

13. Prophecies given by the spirit of the late General Helmuth von Moltke, speaking through his mediumistic wife Eliza, shortly after his death in 1916. These are apparently contained in photostats of type-

scripts then circulating secretly in Germany among "Grail Groups." See Trevor, Ravenscroft, *The Spear of Destiny* (London: Corgi, 1974), p. 144.

14. Apparently written by Hitler as a gloss to a copy of Wolfram von Escenbach's *Parzifal* that Johannes Stein bought from a Viennese secondhand bookseller in 1912. Ibid. pp. 48–9.

15. Oliver Plunkett, Archbishop of Armagh, was martyred in 1681. He has the distinction of being the last Catholic to be hanged, drawn, and quartered in England. His head, still in remarkably good condition, is the most gruesome relic I have ever seen.

16. This was done at great cost to themselves. Between 1577 and 1680 over 160 of them were martyred.

17. The main chapel at St. Edmunds, designed by Augustus Welby Pugin, is one of the finest Victorian Gothic churches in England. The rude screen in particular is regarded as a major work of art and possibly the best of its kind in England. The stained glass windows, many of them depicting the life of St. Edmund, are also among the best examples of Victorian glass in the country.

18. Jan Huss was a Czech pastor and dissident who openly denounced church corruption. In 1414 he was arrested, tried, and burnt at the stake for his "heresy." For further details on his life and the Hussite movement he started, see my book *The New Jerusalem*. Adrian Gilbert, *The New Jerusalem* (London: Bantam Press, 2002).

19. The peerage comprises of all the titled nobility who at that time also had the right to sit in the House of Lords. This is no longer the case and most peers these days are of the "life" variety and cannot pass on their titles to their children.

20. Under British law the heirs to the throne takes the title of King or Queen immediately after the death of their predecessors. They do not have to wait until they have been actually crowned before they are called such. The importance of the coronation ceremony is that it is essentially a religious occasion. During it the monarch, like Jacob in the Book of Genesis, makes a formal contract with God.

21. The Queen takes a similar oath in respect to her duties as Queen to preserve the Presbyterian Church in Scotland.

22. One of the only pieces of the coronation regalia to survive the Commonwealth of Oliver Cromwell.

23. Original footage of the coronation can be seen today on YouTube.

Chapter 2

1. Llewellyn ap Gruffydd, the last native Prince of Wales, was killed in an ambush in 1283. His brother David was executed for treason soon after and the principality of Wales was fully annexed by Edward I.

2. Margaret and her husband were later buried there, to be followed by many other Scottish kings.

3. It was before this shrine in 1274 that Edward was crowned King of England and to its proximity that he later brought the Stone of Destiny.

4. "If fate is not in error, wherever this stone is found, the Scots will there take kingship." (author's translation).

5. Dean and Chapter of Westminster, *Westminster Abbey: Official Guide* (Norwich, UK: Jarrold Publishing, 1973), 98.

6. Ibid.

7. Ibid.

8. Prior to the building of a further extension to the east at the time of Henry VII (r.1485–1509), there would have been a small chapel dedicated to the Virgin Mary in the space now occupied by the staircase. This was the easternmost extension of the church.

9. This book was about the real history concerning King Arthur. Unlike Skene, who believed Arthur fought his battles in what is now Scotland, my co-authors and I placed him in Wales and England. Adrian Gilbert, Alan Wilson, and Baram Blackett, *The Holy Kingdom: The Quest for the Real King Arthur* (Lancaster, UK: Invisible Cities Press, 2002).

10. William F. Skene, *The Coronation Stone* (Edinburgh: Edmonston & Douglas, 1869) 10.

11. Ibid., 15–6.

12. Ibid., 16.

13. For Nennius, *Historia Brittonum*, see http://www.fordham.edu/halsall/basis/nennius-full.html, sec. 15.

14. For the text of the *Declaration of Arbroath 1320* see http://www.constitution.org/scot/arbroath.htm.

15. *Annals of Clonmacnoise*, (1896) 1993. trans. Conell Mageoghagan (Dublin: University Press). Reprint, Felinfach, Wales: Llanerch Publishers, 21–2.

16. Ibid., 26–7.

17. For the references to the *Annals of the Four Masters* see http://www.ucc.ie/celt/published/T100005A/index.html.

18. For the Irish version of Nennius' *Historia Brittonum*, see http://www.ucc.ie/celt/published/G100028/index.html.

19. The biblical story relates that God appeared to Jacob and made certain promises to him. Jacob subsequently consecrated the stone with oil and called it *Bethel* or "House of God".

Chapter 3

1. First published two years earlier in 1994. See Robert Bauval and Adrian Gilbert, *The Orion Mystery: Unlocking the Secrets of the Pyramids* (New York: Crown Publishing, 1994).

2. The English word "Pict" is derived from the Latin *pictum*, meaning "painted."

3. His most lasting achievement was an upgrade of Hadrian's original wall, which later historians now came to refer to erroneously as the wall of Severus.

4. *Columba* is Latin for "dove" and *Columkille* is Gaelic for "Dove of the church."

5. Hurling is a hockey–like game peculiar to Ireland that is played at great speed on a large pitch.

6. For the classic Donegal beauty think of Enya, formerly of the group *Clannad*, and also *the Corrs*, who, though from Dundalk on the east coast of Ireland, have family roots back in Donegal.

7. Vitruvius was a classical author who lived in the first century BC at the time of Augustus. He wrote the first textbook on architecture, which became in later centuries the bible of Classicism.

8. The highest of Edinburgh's volcanoes is the flat–topped table mountain known as "Arthur's Seat." It is 822 feet high.

9. *John of Fordun's Chronicle of the Scottish Nation*, Ed. by William F. Skene and trans. by Felix J.H. Skene (Edinburgh: Edmonston and Douglas, 1872).

10. Berwick–on–Tweed is a border town that has changed hands on numerous occasions. It is now in England, but at that time it was in Scotland.

11. The information is contained within this book: David Breeze, *The*

Stone of Destiny: Symbol of Nationhood (Edinburgh, Scotland: Historic Scotland, 1996).

12. Though Robert the Bruce was crowned at Scone, he did not sit on the Stone of Destiny, which by that time resided in Westminster.

13. A county south of Glasgow and in southwest Scotland.

14. The most popular legend of St. Patrick is that he came from Cowchurch in Glamorgan. He was taught at one of the Christian colleges there before being captured by Irish pirates and taken back to Ireland as a slave. Later he regained his freedom but went back to Ireland as a Christian missionary.

15. One of the reasons for St. Columba's success in this venture is that he is said to have banished the Loch Ness Monster: a water dragon said at that time to be terrifying the local people. Little did he know that in our times the story of the Loch Ness Monster would spawn a whole tourist industry and become the subject of endless speculation.

16. It was this Edwin who went on to conquer Lothian, the southeast of Scotland, giving his name to Ed(w)inburgh.

17. A rocky hill fort in Argyll that was regarded as the capital of the Dalriada Scots.

18. *John of Fordun's Chronicle of the Scottish Nation*, Ed. by William F. Skene and trans. by Felix J.H. Skene (Edinburgh: Edmonston and Douglas, 1872), p. clx.

19. The information is contained within this online file: *http://omacl.org/Anglo/part2.html*. Year 787.

20. Ibid., Year 793.

21. Jarrow is just to the south of Newcastle. It was the abbey where the Venerable Bede had lived and written his history of the English.

22. This castle guarded the entrance to Loch Etive, just to the north of the modern-day town of Oban. There is no real evidence, however, to indicate that the stone was ever kept there.

Chapter 4

1. This story is told in detail in the tenth century *Historia Brittonum* of Nennius and in Geoffrey of Monmouth's twelfth century *History of the Kings of Britain*. It is also recorded in many other sources such as genealogies. As I have written about this legend extensively in *The Holy King-*

dom and in *The New Jerusalem*, I won't say any more about it here.

2. The name *Fir Domnann* is so similar to the name of the pre-Roman, British county of *Dumnonia* (Devon) that some commentators think the legend of the *Fir Domnann* coming to Ireland is really a folk memory of a migration from Devon.

3. Clonmacnoise (pronounced "ClonMacneesh") is the name of an old ecclesiastical foundation on the River Shannon that was founded in 541 by St. Kieran. Several ancient books were compiled here. *The Book of Clonmacnoise* is possibly the most reliable of the ancient annals of Ireland and certainly the oldest.

4. The Giant's Causeway, on the coast of Antrim in Northern Ireland, is a remarkable geological feature and now a major tourist attraction. It consists of a "stairway" and "ramp" made out of huge, hexagonal crystals of basalt. Curiously, the same formation outcrops on the island of Staffa, off the coast of Scotland and just a few miles from Iona. Here "Fingal's (Finn macCool's) Cave", a cathedral sized cavern made of the same sort of hexagonal blocks, faces towards Iona Abbey. The mythical journey of Fingal, from Northern Ireland to Staffa, mirrors the very real one made by St. Columba to nearby Iona.

5. The Bible says an angel of the Lord struck down one hundred and eight-five thousand of the Assyrians camped outside Jerusalem.

6. G. Hawkins, *Stonehenge Decoded* (New York: Dorset Press for Doubleday, 1965 & 1987), 134–5.

7. This becomes Mount Killaraus in Geoffrey's version, for as usual he Latinizes the name by adding a –*us* ending. In a revealing note to the English translation of the *Brut Tysilio*, the editor adds a footnote stating that William Camden was an eminent English historian who lived from 1551–1623.

8. *The Chronicles of the Kings of Britain, translated from the Welsh copy attributed to Tysilio.* trans. Rev. Peter Roberts (London: E. Williams, 1811), 127–8.

9. "Menhir" is a Gaelic word that means "tall stone."

10. Huge numbers of animal bones have recently been found at a site two miles to the northeast of Stonehenge. They go back to the time when the monument was being built and indicate some sort of massive feast held at the winter solstice.

11. *Annals of Clonmacnoise*, (1896) 1993. trans. Conell Mageoghagan

(Dublin: University Press). Reprint, Felinfach, Wales: Llanerch Publishers, 26.

12. The name "Scotia" for the land of the Scots, was originally applied to northern Ireland. After the Scottish migration to northern Britain and more particularly the coronation of Aidan as King of the Dal Rhiada Scots (AD 574), the name Scotia was transferred from Ireland to their possessions in Britain.

13. *Annals of Clonmacnoise*, (1896) 1993. trans. Conell Mageoghagan (Dublin: University Press). Reprint, Felinfach, Wales: Llanerch Publishers, 21–2.

Chapter 5

1. See *Manetho: History of Egypt and Other Works* (Loeb Classical Library No. 350), trans. by W.G. Waddell (Cambridge, MA: Harvard University Press, 1940) to read a translation of Manetho's *Aegyptiaca*.

2. For a full discussion of this problem, please see *Centuries of Darkness* by Peter James et al. (London: Jonathan Cape, 1991) and *A Test of Time* by David Rohl (London: Random–Century, 1995).

3. The publication of *Worlds in Collision* led to a famous case where his publishers were threatened by a number of their most eminent, academic authors that if they carried on publishing his works, they would leave them. Caving in to the black–mail, the publishers dropped Velikovsky. Nevertheless his books were still published by other people and indeed some of them, such as *Worlds in Collision*, became bestsellers.

4. As Egyptologists generally insert e's between hieroglyphic consonants, this can be transliterated as "Peresett."

5. I. Velikovsky, *Peoples of the Sea* (London: Sidgwick & Jackson Ltd., 1977), 36.

6. Peter James et al., *Centuries of Darkness* (London: Jonathan Cape Ltd., 1991), xxi.

7. Ibid., xvii–xviii.

8. This is when the European La Tène culture, famous for its Celtic art, was at its height.

9. It is in this context that we have to understand the war against Troy, which contrary to received opinion, probably took place in the 9th century BC and therefore not long before the rise of the classical Greek

city-states of Athens, Sparta, Corinth, and so on. For details on how the chronology of the Trojan War needs to be reassessed, see Peter James, *Centuries of Darkness*.

10. The subsequent conquest of Egypt by Alexander in 332 BC occurred later than our period of interest.

11. The important pre–Socratic philosophers: Thales, Anaximander, and Anaximenes all came from Miletus.

12. This is the real context of the Trojan War, which probably took place during this period.

13. Caria and Lycia were non–Greek speaking states in the southwest of Turkey. Miletus itself was founded on what had been Carian territory.

14. Herodotus, *The Histories*, Oxford World's Classics, ed. Carolyn Dewald, trans. Robin Waterfield (New York: Oxford University Press, 1998), 2.152.

15. The name Naucratis means "Mastery of the Sea."

16. For details concerning the rise of Naucritis, see book 2 of Herodotus' *Histories*.

17. Herodotus, *The Histories*, 1.105.

18. Ibid., 1.106.

19. *Annals of Clonmacnoise, 22.*

20. Whether the wife of Heremon was the half–Egyptian daughter of a King of Jerusalem or the niece of Scota, we will probably never know. However, it is worth mentioning that "Ti" is a known Egyptian name.

Chapter 6

1. Haran, which is now an archaeological site in southeast Turkey, was then an important stopping off point on trade routes between east and west.

2. Literally "House of God."

3. This is thought by most scholars to have been located near to modern day Ramallah–an important Palestinian city in the West Bank.

4. J.B. Segal, *Edessa: 'The Blessed City'* (Oxford: Oxford at the Clarendon Press, 1970), 57.

5. Literally "pot–belly mound" in Turkish.

6. Today the stone is surrounded by a silver collar, but I have seen an earlier golden cover for the stone in the Topkapi Museum in Istanbul.

7. In the Greek myths Cronos, ruler of the universe, is warned that one day his position will be taken by a son. To avoid this eventuality, he swallows each of his children at birth. Tormented by the loss of her children, his wife Rhea can bear this no more, and when Zeus is born, in place of the baby god, she feeds Cronos a stone. The real Zeus grows up in hiding and eventually does overthrow his father, inducing him to vomit up the stone and all the other gods he has swallowed. Zeus, or Jupiter as he becomes in the Roman pantheon, takes over power as "Father of the Gods" and Cronos is deposed.

8. Marduk was the principle god of Babylon.

9. The "City" of London denotes the inner square mile, once surrounded by Roman walls, that is today the major banking center of Europe. The city enjoys certain privileges (such as having its own Lord Mayor) that are not extended to "Greater" London: the huge expanse of suburbs that surround the old city core.

10. Cade's claim to the throne was based on the presumption that he was descended from the extinct line of Roger Mortimer. This was, of course, a fabrication. See *Henry VI, Part 2*, Act 4, Scene 6.

Chapter 7

1. Herodotus, *The Histories*, 2: 73.

2. The Sirius or Sothic cycle is a period of 1461 Egyptian years of 365 days each or 1460 years of 365.25 days each. This is the period needed to re-harmonize the Sidereal and Tropical calendars so that the first appearance of Sirius at dawn occurs on the same calendrical day of the year.

3. According to Rundle Clark, the Egyptians saw the First Creation as mirroring the process whereby following its annual flood, the Nile River would retreat and muddy islands would appear. For them the Primeval Mound was the hill on which stood Heliopolis.

4. R.T. Rundle Clark, *Myth and Symbol in Ancient Egypt* (London: Thames and Hudson, 1978), 39.

5. The final "t" (normally a determinative of feminine gender) would have been absent because the *bennu* is male rather than female.

6. There is a Twelfth Dynasty obelisk still standing, but this is some distance from the subterranean pit that seems to have been the original Temple.

7. According to some translations, the name of the room is not "Repetition" but the "Hall of Revision." This would seem to fit better with the meaning of the story.

8. In Britain, especially in southern counties where other rock is scarce, flint has been used since Roman times, if not before, for the construction of churches and other buildings.

9. Julius Caesar, *The Conquest of Gaul*, trans. S. A. Halford (London: Book Club Associates, 1993), 110-1.

Chapter 8

1. These solar and lunar alignments were the subject of a famous book, *Stonehenge Decoded*, by astronomer Professor Gerald Hawkins of Boston University. In the early 1960s Hawkins used Boston University's IBM computer–there were no PCs in those days–to correlate the alignments of Stonehenge's trilithon archways against the extreme positions of sunrise, sunset, moonrise, and moonset. To the annoyance of the archaeological community, *Stonehenge Decoded* was a huge success, changing forever our perception of Neolithic man's scientific abilities.

2. See Geoffrey of Monmouth, *The History of the Kings of Britain*, trans. Lewis Spence (London: Penguin Classics, 1966), 165.

3. See John North, *Stonehenge, Neolithic Man and the Cosmos* (New York: Harper Collins Publishers, 1996), 349-50.

4. Caesar, *de Bello Gallico*, 6:14.

5. The Roman god Mercury, of course, equates with the Greek god Hermes and Egyptian god Thoth, to whom was dedicated the secret chamber, where the "flint box" was kept in the Temple of the Phoenix at Heliopolis.

6. *Barddas* (Vol.1), trans. and notes by Rev. J. Williams ab Ithel (London: Llandovery, Longman & Co., 1862), 17.

7. In Latin there is no letter "J" and "I" is used instead. Thus the father of the gods was *Iove* or *Iupiter*.

8. *Wen* is Welsh for "white" and the three lines of the arrow symbol or /|\ can be read together as a capital letter A. Thus God's first utterance is also white light meaning A.

9. Ibid., liii.

10. Ibid., 21.

11. *Iolo Manuscripts, A Selection of Ancient Welsh Manuscripts*, trans. Taliesin Williams (Liverpool: The Welsh MSS Society, 1888), 445–6.

12. W.M. Flinders Petrie, *Stonehenge: Plans, Description, and Theories* (London: Histories & Mysteries of Man Ltd., 1989), 23.

13. John Michell, *City of Revelation* (London: Garnstone Press, 1972), 53.

14. Ibid.

Chapter 9

1. It's a strange fact, but since Glaswegians are, in the main, descended from the ancient Britons (who spoke Welsh), Gallic signs would have been as foreign to their ancestors as they are to most Scots today.

2. James Boswell, *Boswell's Journal of a Tour to the Hebrides with Samuel Johnson, LL.D.* (New York: Viking Press, 1936), 341.

3. James Boswell, *Boswell's Journal of a Tour to the Hebrides with Samuel Johnson, LL.D.* (London: Routledge, Warne & Routledge, 1860), 265.

4. The Iona Community is an ecumenical Christian association with many of its members living on Iona full or part–time while others work in deprived areas of Glasgow and other cities. The Community, which takes its inspiration from St. Columba, has been responsible for the restoration of many of the monastery buildings on Iona.

5. This lasted until 1493 when it was brought to an end by James IV of Scotland. Since then the title "Lord of the Isles" has been held by the heir to the Scottish throne, who since 1603 (when the thrones of Scotland and England were merged) is the also the Prince of Wales. Today both titles are held by Prince Charles.

6. See Giorgio de Santillana and Hertha von Dechend, *Hamlet's Mill* (Jaffrey, NH: David R. Godine Publishers, Inc., 1977) and Adrian Gilbert, *Magi* (Montpelier, VT: Invisible Cities Press, 2002).

7. Again there is much about the connection between the Milky Way and the Way of the Dead in *Hamlet's Mill*.

Chapter 10

1. William Skene, *The Coronation Stone* (Edinburgh: Edmonston & Douglas, 1869), 8.

2. Ibid., 16.

3. Ibid., 26.

4. Ibid., 15.

5. One has only to visit Petra (which, incidentally means "rocks" in Greek) to see any number of tumbled sandstone blocks of roughly the same size and proportion as the Stone of Scone.

6. Ibid., 43.

7. At the time of writing this was available to read on the Internet at www.timesonline.co.uk/tol/news/uk/scotland/article567998.ece.

8. Ibid.

9. *Hermetica*, trans. Walter Scott (Shaftesbury: Solos Press, 1992), 133.

10. E.A. Wallis Budge, *The Mummy* (London: Collier Macmillan Publications, 1972), 159.

11. Mark Lehner, *The Complete Pyramids* (London: Thames and Hudson, 1997), 23.

12. This is very similar to the belief of certain tribespeople that having their photo taken steals a part of their soul.

13. Recently republished as a new edition by Covenant Publishing with the title *London: A New Jerusalem*.

14. Recent analysis by Dr Robert Feather, a metallurgist from the UK, indicates that the main body of the spear dates to only the seventh century AD. However, he also found that the nail enclosed within it (and said to be one of those used in the Crucifixion) was Roman and dated from the right period: first century AD.

15. This would also be true of other claimants to be the "genuine" Spear of Destiny. These include one kept in the Vatican and another in Poland.

16. See my earlier work *The New Jerusalem* for more details on this.

17. As this is a subject that goes well outside the present work, the interested reader is referred to other books on the subject, e.g., John F. Walvoord, *Every Prophecy in the Bible* (Colorado Springs, CO: David C. Cook, 1999).

18. Details of this extraordinary campaign can be read in the book: Andrew Adams, *As Birds Fly* (Colorado Springs, CO: David C. Cook, 2009).

Chapter 11
1. This excludes the period of the reign of Mary I (1553-8), eldest daughter of Henry VIII, when Catholicism was briefly restored in ngland.

2. Though, with the rise of secularism, a lot of the heat has now gone out of this religious conflict, it is still alive today and even now colors all debate about the future governance of the six counties of Ulster.

3. Geoffrey Watkins was the proprietor of the famous "Watkins Bookshop," still London's preeminent esoteric bookshop. The shop was started by his father, but he himself was an expert on Christian mysticism and the white occult.

4. The German expeditionary force that was sent into Russia comprised 4,500,000 men, 750,000 horses, and 600,000 motor vehicles. It was mounted across a front stretching from the Baltic in the north down to the Black Sea.

Bibliography

Adams, Andrew. *As Birds Fly*. Colorado Springs, CO: David C. Cook, 2009.

Anglo-Saxon Chronicle. The Online Medieval and Classical Library—Release #17. http://omacl.org/Anglo/part2.html.

Annals of Clonmacnoise. (1896) 1993. Translated by Conell Mageoghagan. Dublin: University Press. Reprint, Felinfach, Wales: Llanerch Publishers.

Barddas (Vol. 1). Translation and notes by Rev. J. Williams ab Ithel. London: Llandovery, Longman & Co., 1862.

Bauval, Robert, and Adrian Gilbert. *The Orion Mystery: Unlocking the Secrets of the Pyramids*. New York: Crown Publishing, 1994.

Boece, Hector. *The Bulk of the Cronicles of Scotland* (cited as *History of the Scottish People*). London: Longman, Brown, Green, Longmans, and Roberts, 1858.

Boswell, James. *Boswell's Journal of a Tour to the Hebrides with Samuel Johnson, LL.D.* London: Routledge, Warne & Routledge, 1860.

———. *Boswell's Journal of a Tour to the Hebrides with Samuel Johnson, LL.D.* New York: Viking Press, 1936.

Breeze, David. *The Stone of Destiny: Symbol of Nationhood*. Edinburgh, Scotland: Historic Scotland, 1996.

Budge, E.A. Wallis. *The Mummy*. London: Collier Macmillan Publications, 1972.

Byrne, Francis John. *Irish Kings and High Kings*. 2nd ed. London: B.T. Batsford Ltd., 1987.

Caesar, Julius. *The Conquest of Gaul*. Translated by S.A. Halford. London: Book Club Associates, 1993.

Clark, R.T. Rundle. *Myth and Symbol in Ancient Egypt*. London: Thames and Hudson, 1978.

Dass, Ram (aka Richard Alpert). *Remember, Be Here Now*. San Anselmo, CA: Hanuman Foundation, 1971.

de Santillana, Giorgio and Hertha von Dechend. *Hamlet's Mill*. Jaffrey,

NH: David R. Godine Publishers, Inc., 1977.

Dean and Chapter of Westminster. *Westminster Abbey: Official Guide*. Norwich, UK: Jarrold Publishing, 1973.

Geoffrey of Monmouth. *The History of the Kings of Britain*. Translated by Lewis Spence. London: Penguin Classics, 1966.

Gilbert, Adrian. *London: The New Jerusalem*, 2nd ed. Co Durham, England: Covenant Publishing Co, Ltd., 2010.

——. *Magi*. Montpelier, VT: Invisible Cities Press, 2002.

——. *The New Jerusalem*. London: Bantam Press, 2002.

——. *Signs in the Sky*. Virginia Beach, VA: A.R.E. Press, 2005.

Gilbert, Adrian, Alan Wilson, and Baram Blackett. *The Holy Kingdom: The Quest for the Real King Arthur*. Lancaster, UK: Invisible Cities Press, 2002.

Hawkins, Gerald S. and John B. White. *Stonehenge Decoded*. New York: Dell Publishing Co., 1965.

Hermetica. Translated by Walter Scott. Shaftesbury: Solos Press, 1992.

Herodotus. *The Histories*, Oxford World's Classics, Translated by Robin Waterfield and edited by Carolyn Dewald. New York: Oxford University Press, 1998.

Iolo Manuscripts, A Selection of Ancient Welsh Manuscripts. Translated by Taliesin Williams. Liverpool: The Welsh MSS Society, 1888.

James, Peter et al. *Centuries of Darkness*. London: Jonathan Cape, 1991.

Lehner, Mark. *The Complete Pyramids*. London: Thames and Hudson, 1997.

Lindsey, Hal. *The Late Great Planet Earth*. Grand Rapids, MI: Zondervan, 1970.

Manetho. *Manetho: History of Egypt and Other Works* (Loeb Classical Library No. 350). Translated by W.G. Waddell. Cambridge, MA: Harvard University Press, 1940.

Michell, John. *City of Revelation*. London: Garnstone Press, 1972.

North, John. *Stonehenge, Neolithic Man and the Cosmos*. New York: Harper Collins Publishers, 1996.

O'Flaherty, Roderic. *Ogygia*. Volume 2. Dublin: W. M' Kenzie, 1793.

Petrie, W.M. Flinders. *Stonehenge: Plans, Description, and Theories*. London: Histories & Mysteries of Man Ltd., 1989.

Ravenscroft, Trevor. *The Spear of Destiny*. London: Corgi, 1974.

Rishanger, William. *Opus Chronicum*. Edited by Henry Thomas Riley. London: Longman, Green, Longman, and Green, 1865.

Rohl, David. *A Test of Time*. London: Random–Century, 1995.

Sambhava, Padma. *The Tibetan Book of the Dead*. Translated by Robert Thurman. New York: Bantam Books, Inc., 1993.

Segal, J.B. *Edessa: 'The Blessed City'*. Oxford: Oxford at the Clarendon Press, 1970.

Shakespeare, William. *Henry VI, Part 2*. (Folger Shakespeare Library). Edited by Barbara Mowat and Paul Werstine. New York: Washington Square Press, 2008.

Skene, William F. *The Coronation Stone*. Edinburgh: Edmonston & Douglas, 1869.

The Chronicles of the Kings of Britain, translated from the Welsh copy attributed to Tysilio. Translated by Rev. Peter Roberts. London: E. Williams, 1811.

The Holy Bible Revised Standard Version. London: Collins' Clear–type Press, 1952.

Velikovsky, Immanuel. *Peoples of the Sea*. London: Sidgwick & Jackson Ltd., 1977.

Velikovsky, Immanuel. *Worlds in Collision*. New York: Doubleday & Company, Inc., 1950.

Walvoord, John F. *Every Prophecy in the Bible*. Colorado Springs, CO: David C. Cook, 1999.

Online Sources

Declaration of Arbroath 1320 see
http://www.constitution.org/scot/arbroath.htm.

John of Fordun's Chronicle of the Scottish Nation. Edited by William F. Skene
and translated by Felix J. H. Skene. Edinburgh: Edmonston and Douglas, 1872,
http://www.archive.org/details/johnoffordunschr00fordrich.

Nennius. *Historia Brittonum,* see *sec. 15*
http://www.fordham.edu/halsall/basis/nennius–full.html.

———— . *The Irish version of the Historia Britonum of Nennius,* see
http://www.ucc.ie/celt/published/G100028/index.html.

Index

A

Abraham 104, 105, 106, 107, 108, 110, 111, 112, 116, 125, 132, 162
Aegyptiaca 78, 203
Aeneas 60
Aidan 35, 43, 54, 165, 203
Alexander III, King 46, 47, 51, 179
Alexander the Great 10, 78, 85, 113, 182
Altars 31, 65, 67, 68, 72, 75, 115, 135, 136, 137
Amun 10, 112, 133
Anglo-Saxons 43
Annals of Clonmacnoise 32, 33, 62, 75, 83, 91, 93, 99
Antonine Wall 39, 43, 52
Apries 97, 101, 102
Archbishop of Canterbury 14, 18, 19, 54, 178
Ark of the Covenant 127, 128, 129, 133, 180
Arthur, King 17, 21, 69, 191, 199
Asclepius 173
Assyrians 7, 8, 66, 67, 85, 88, 109, 177, 202
Awen 141, 142

B

Babylon/Babylonia 8, 11, 82, 84, 85, 86, 89, 90, 95, 96, 97, 99, 100, 101, 114, 115, 116, 182, 183, 184, 192, 205
Babylonian Empire 11, 89, 115
Babylonians 67, 79, 84, 88, 94, 95, 97, 100, 101, 102
Baetylus 112, 113
Balliol, John (of) 26, 29, 47
Barbarossa, Operation 181, 190, 191
Barddas 140, 206
Bards 140, 141, 142, 143
Battle of Hastings 23
Benben 122, 123, 125
Bennu bird 121, 122
Bethel 26, 104, 105, 106, 110, 112, 113, 116, 167, 170, 171, 172, 177, 181, 200
Black Stone 114
Blair, Tony 3, 160
Book of Daniel 11, 182, 195
Boswell, James 155, 207
Brec, Simon 26, 30, 169
Bridei 43
Brut Tysilio 68, 202
Brutus 31, 60, 61, 118
Brutus Stone 118

C

Caesar, Augustus 11
Caesar, Julius 10, 11, 131, 139, 141, 206
Caledonians 38, 158
Cayce, Edgar 64, 67, 135, 137
Charlemagne 8, 12, 180
Charles II 28, 178
Chronicon Rythmicum 169, 177
Cleopatra 11, 78
Clube, Dr. Victor 123, 124
Columba, St. 35, 42, 45, 53, 55, 57, 151, 157, 160, 162, 163, 164, 165, 201, 202, 207
Coronation of Queen Elizabeth II 17, 27, 192
Cromlechs 72
Cromwell, Oliver 25, 178, 198
Crown Jewels 2, 17, 22, 45, 51, 178
Crown of St. Edward 178
Cullinan 20, 178
Cyaxares 91, 97, 98, 99

D

Dalriada 40, 43, 52, 55, 58
Dalriada Scots 35, 43, 47, 52, 54, 57, 58, 156, 157, 158, 163, 201
Danites 66, 74
Darius III 78
Daughters of Hezekiah 65, 67, 68, 73, 135
David, King 87, 177, 181
Declaration of Arbroath 31, 199, 215
Djedi 126, 131, 132, 167, 172
Donegal 41, 42, 200
Drogheda 14

E

Edinburgh Castle ix, 1, 4, 45, 50, 192
Edmund, St. 14, 15, 16, 198
Edward I 2, 4, 17, 21, 22, 23, 24, 26, 27, 29, 35, 47, 57, 168, 169, 187, 199
Edward the Confessor 17, 23, 24, 25, 45, 46, 50, 116, 178, 179
Edward VIII 188, 189
Edwin 45, 53, 54, 201
Elizabeth II, Queen 179, 192
Elizabeth II, Queen. See coronation. 17, 27, 192
Exodus 30, 79, 83, 84, 92, 127, 133

217

EDGAR CAYCE'S A.R.E.

What Is A.R.E.?

The Association for Research and Enlightenment, Inc., (A.R.E.®) was founded in 1931 to research and make available information on psychic development, dreams, holistic health, meditation, and life after death. As an open-membership research organization, the A.R.E. continues to study and publish such information, to initiate research, and to promote conferences, distance learning, and regional events. Edgar Cayce, the most documented psychic of our time, was the moving force in the establishment of A.R.E.

Who Was Edgar Cayce?

Edgar Cayce (1877-1945) was born on a farm near Hopkinsville, Ky. He was an average individual in most respects. Yet, throughout his life, he manifested one of the most remarkable psychic talents of all time. As a young man, he found that he was able to enter into a self-induced trance state, which enabled him to place his mind in contact with an unlimited source of information. While asleep, he could answer questions or give accurate discourses on any topic. These discourses, more than 14,000 in number, were transcribed as he spoke and are called "readings."

Given the name and location of an individual anywhere in the world, he could correctly describe a person's condition and outline a regimen of treatment. The consistent accuracy of his diagnoses and the effectiveness of the treatments he prescribed made him a medical phenomenon, and he came to be called the "father of holistic medicine."

Eventually, the scope of Cayce's readings expanded to include such subjects as world religions, philosophy, psychology, parapsychology, dreams, history, the missing years of Jesus, ancient civilizations, soul growth, psychic development, prophecy, and reincarnation.

A.R.E. Membership

People from all walks of life have discovered meaningful and life-transforming insights through membership in A.R.E. To learn more about Edgar Cayce's A.R.E. and how membership in the A.R.E. can enhance your life, visit our Web site at EdgarCayce.org, or call us toll-free at 800-333-4499.

Edgar Cayce's A.R.E.
215 67th Street
Virginia Beach, VA 23451-2061

EDGARCAYCE.ORG